# Heritage and Festivals in Europe

*Heritage and Festivals in Europe* critically investigates the purpose, reach and effects of heritage festivals. Providing a comprehensive and detailed analysis of comparatively selected aspects of intangible cultural heritage, the volume demonstrates how such heritage is mobilised within events that have specific agency, particularly in the production and consumption of intrinsic and instrumental benefits for tourists, local communities and performers.

Bringing together experts from a wide range of disciplines, the volume presents case studies from across Europe that consider many different varieties of heritage festivals. Focussing primarily on the popular and institutional practices of heritage making, the book addresses the gap between discourses of heritage at an official level and cultural practice at the local and regional level. Contributors to the volume also study the different factors influencing the sustainable development of tradition as part of intangible cultural heritage at the micro- and meso-levels and examine underlying structures that are common across different countries.

*Heritage and Festivals in Europe* takes a multidisciplinary approach and, as such, should be of interest to scholars and students in the fields of heritage studies, tourism, performing arts, cultural studies and identity studies. Policymakers and practitioners throughout Europe should also find much to interest them within the pages of this volume.

**Ullrich Kockel** is Professor of Cultural Ecology at the Intercultural Research Centre, Heriot-Watt University, UK.

**Cristina Clopot** is Postdoctoral Researcher in Heritage Diplomacy at the Wilberforce Institute for the Study of Slavery and Emancipation, University of Hull, UK.

**Baiba Tjarve** is Senior Researcher and Project Manager in the Research Centre at the Latvian Academy of Culture.

**Máiréad Nic Craith** is Professor of Cultural Heritage and Anthropology at the Intercultural Research Centre, Heriot-Watt University, UK.

**Critical Heritages of Europe**
**Series editors:** *Christopher Whitehead and Susannah Eckersley, both at the University of Newcastle, UK*

The Critical Heritages of Europe series seeks to explore the cultural and social politics of the European past in the present. Bridging theoretical and empirical research, the series accommodates broad understandings of Europe – a shifting and historically mutable entity, made both of internal tensions and exogenous encounters, re-imaginings and influences. 'Heritage' too is taken as an expansive paradigm, made in myriad practices where the past is valorised for the present, from folk traditions to museums and memorials, the management of historic sites and traditions, and everyday matters such as education, political discourse, home life, food consumption and people's relations with place. Consequently, the series spans a broad array of foci, disciplinary approaches and ways of investigating and questioning the diverse meanings of European heritages today.

**Classical Heritage and European Identities**
The Imagined Geographies of Danish Classicism
*Lærke Maria Andersen Funder, Troels Myrup Kristensen and Vinnie Nørskov*

**Heritage and Festivals in Europe**
Performing Identities
*Edited by Ullrich Kockel, Cristina Clopot, Baiba Tjarve and Máiréad Nic Craith*

**Dimensions of Heritage and Memory**
Multiple Europes and the Politics of Crisis
*Edited by Christopher Whitehead, Susannah Eckersley, Gönül Bozoğlu, and Mads Daugbjerg*

**European Heritage, Dialogue and Digital Practices**
*Edited by Areti Galani, Rhiannon Mason and Gabi Arrigoni*

https://www.routledge.com/Critical-Heritages-of-Europe/book-series/COHERE

# Heritage and Festivals in Europe

Performing Identities

Edited by Ullrich Kockel,
Cristina Clopot, Baiba Tjarve
and Máiréad Nic Craith

LONDON AND NEW YORK

First published 2020
by Routledge
2 Park Square, Milton Park, Abingdon, Oxon OX14 4RN

and by Routledge
52 Vanderbilt Avenue, New York, NY 10017

*Routledge is an imprint of the Taylor & Francis Group, an informa business*

© 2020 selection and editorial matter, Ullrich Kockel, Cristina Clopot, Baiba Tjarve and Máiréad Nic Craith; individual chapters, the contributors

The right of Ullrich Kockel, Cristina Clopot, Baiba Tjarve and Máiréad Nic Craith to be identified as the authors of the editorial material, and of the authors for their individual chapters, has been asserted in accordance with sections 77 and 78 of the Copyright, Designs and Patents Act 1988.

With the exception of Chapters 1, 2, 3, 10, 11 and 13, no part of this book may be reprinted or reproduced or utilised in any form or by any electronic, mechanical, or other means, now known or hereafter invented, including photocopying and recording, or in any information storage or retrieval system, without permission in writing from the publishers.

Chapters 1, 2, 3, 10, 11 and 13 of this book are available for free in PDF format as Open Access from the individual product page at www.routledge.com. It has been made available under a Creative Commons Attribution-Non Commercial-No Derivatives 4.0 license.

*Trademark notice*: Product or corporate names may be trademarks or registered trademarks and are used only for identification and explanation without intent to infringe.

*British Library Cataloguing-in-Publication Data*
A catalogue record for this book is available from the British Library

*Library of Congress Cataloging-in-Publication Data*
A catalog record has been requested for this book

ISBN: 978-0-367-18676-0 (hbk)
ISBN: 978-0-429-20296-4 (ebk)

Typeset in Bembo
by Newgen Publishing UK

# Contents

*List of figures* vii
*List of tables* ix
*List of contributors* x
*Foreword* xv
REGINA F. BENDIX
*Acknowledgements* xviii
*List of abbreviations* xix

1 Heritages, identities and Europe: exploring cultural forms and expressions 1
ULLRICH KOCKEL, MÁIRÉAD NIC CRAITH, CRISTINA CLOPOT AND BAIBA TJARVE

2 On the relationship between performance and intangible cultural heritage 18
SIMON McKERRELL AND KERSTIN PFEIFFER

3 Comparative aspects of the Song and Dance Celebration of the Baltic countries in the context of nation-branding processes 29
RŪTA MUKTUPĀVELA AND ANDA LAĶE

4 The construction of belonging and Otherness in heritage events 47
CRISTINA CLOPOT AND CATHERINE McCULLAGH

5 Nostalgic festivals: the case of Cappadox 63
BABAK TAHERI, MARTIN JOSEPH GANNON AND HOSSEIN OLYA

6 Events that want to become heritage: vernacularisation of ICH and the politics of culture and identity in European public rituals 79
ALESSANDRO TESTA

7   Performing identities and communicating ICH: from
    local to international strategies                                    95
    LAURENT SÉBASTIEN FOURNIER

8   Memory, pride and politics on parade: the Durham
    Miners' Gala                                                        110
    ANDREAS PANTAZATOS AND HELAINE SILVERMAN

9   Sound structure as political structure in the European
    folk festival orchestra *La Banda Europa*                           128
    SIMON McKERRELL

10  Performing Scots-European heritage, '*For A' That!*'                141
    MAIRI McFADYEN AND MÁIRÉAD NIC CRAITH

11  European Capitals of Culture: discourses of Europeanness
    in Valletta, Plovdiv and Galway                                     156
    CRISTINA CLOPOT AND KATERINA STRANI

12  Negotiating contested heritages through theatre
    and storytelling                                                    173
    KERSTIN PFEIFFER AND MAGDALENA WEIGLHOFER

13  Commemorating vanished 'homelands': displaced
    Germans and their *Heimat Europa*                                   188
    ULLRICH KOCKEL

14  Afterword: festival as heritage / heritage as festival              205
    VALDIMAR TR. HAFSTEIN

    *Index*                                                             211

# Figures

| | | |
|---|---|---:|
| 1.1 | Home and public identities | 6 |
| 4.1 | Proetnica Festival in Sighișoara, Romania | 49 |
| 4.2 | Lighting up ceremony, Lerwick *Up-Helly-Aa* | 51 |
| 7.1 | Processional Giants in Douai, France | 98 |
| 7.2 | A Breton Fest-Noz | 101 |
| 8.1 | The Gala, July 2018. Banner groups with their bands, accompanied by members of their pit villages, parade through Durham. All march past the Royal County on whose hotel balcony stand officials of the Durham Miners' Association and invited members of the Labour Party, greeting them. They are watched by tens of thousands of spectators | 112 |
| 8.2 | The iconography on the Chilton Lodge banner depicts miners marching with their aspirational banner and clearly affirms the fundamental role of banners in mining communities. Chilton's banner professes one dramatic sentiment in a single profound word: liberty | 114 |
| 8.3 | At the time of manufacture, the Harton and Westoe banner of South Shields stated this community's hopes, too soon dashed, that the 1947 nationalization of the coal industry would bring security to mining families. The banner's saying, 'Our Heritage', expresses the deep sense of identity of families with the industry that employed them | 115 |
| 8.4 | The banner of the Durham Colliery Mechanics Trust is post-industry as the trust was formed two years after the last mine was closed. It asserts six new goals in the post-mining era and iconographically argues for resolution of the displaced miners' demands through legal means. Of particular note is its heritage message. It cogently expresses in words the epistemic resistance of miners to the establishment's portrayal of them and how their incongruous heritage is deployed: 'The past we inherit. The future we build' | 116 |
| 8.5 | The banner of the Boldon lodge being paraded in the 2017 Gala. Note the pathos of its textual message, 'Sunset on an | |

viii  *List of figures*

|  | industry', and the image of miners departing their work shift for the last time. Soon that surface infrastructure would be demolished, leaving a landscape devoid of the evidence of a once thriving coal industry | 118 |
|---|---|---|
| 11.1 | Valletta 2018 programmes stand | 162 |
| 11.2 | Galway city centre | 163 |
| 12.1 | Theatre of Witness participants performing *I Once Knew A Girl…* | 176 |
| 12.2 | Performance planning for *SchwanenMostek* | 182 |
| 13.1 | Map of the Sudetenland regions within the Czech Republic (including 'linguistic islands') | 189 |

# Tables

3.1 Participation level of the residents of the Baltic countries in the Song and Dance Celebrations 39
4.1 Summary of themes discussed in the case studies 57

# List of contributors

**Regina F. Bendix** teaches cultural anthropology at the University of Göttingen, Germany. Her collection of articles on the intersection of culture, politics and the economy entitled 'Culture and value. Tourism, heritage, and property' appeared in 2018. She has co-edited a number of volumes on folklore and ethnology and currently also co-edits the journal *Narrative Culture*.

**Cristina Clopot** is a Research Associate at the Wilberforce Institute for the Study of Slavery and Emancipation (University of Hull, UK). She previously worked as a Research Associate for the CoHERE Horizon 2020 project at Heriot-Watt University (Edinburgh, UK). Cristina coordinates the Association of Critical Heritage Studies' Intangible Cultural Heritage Network and is a founding member of its Early Career Researchers Network.

**Laurent Sébastien Fournier** is Assistant Professor at Aix-Marseille University (France), member of the IDEMEC (Institute for Mediterranean, European and Comparative Ethnology), UMR 7307 CNRS-AMU. He is a specialist of traditional festivals, games and sports in Europe. He has worked as an expert for the Inventory of Intangible Cultural Heritage in France.

**Martin Joseph Gannon** is a Lecturer in Entrepreneurship at the Business School, Edinburgh Napier University, UK. He holds varied research interests in entrepreneurial philanthropy, family business governance and marketing, and consumer behaviour. His research is available in a number of leading publications, including the *Journal of Consumer Culture* and the *International Journal of Contemporary Hospitality Management*.

**Valdimar Tr. Hafstein** is Professor of Folklore, Ethnology, and Museum Studies at the University of Iceland. His latest book is *Making intangible heritage: El Condor Pasa and other stories from UNESCO* (Indiana University Press, 2018). His documentary film, *The flight of the condor: a letter, a song and the story of intangible cultural heritage* (2018, with Áslaug Einarsdóttir) is available online in Open Access.

List of contributors  xi

**Ullrich Kockel** is Professor of Cultural Ecology at Heriot-Watt University Edinburgh, Emeritus Professor of Ethnology at Ulster University and Visiting Professor of Social Anthropology at Vytautas Magnus University Kaunas. He is also a Fellow of the Academy of the Social Sciences and Member of the Royal Irish Academy.

**Anda Laķe (PhD in Sociology)** is Vice-Rector for science at the Latvian Academy of Culture. She is the Head and Senior Researcher in numerous local and international sociology of culture research projects. Her research interests are public policy evaluation and impact assessment, interdisciplinary cultural research, methodology of sociological studies, development of creative and cultural industries, participatory preservation practices and the sustainability of intangible cultural heritage.

**Catherine McCullagh BA, MSt Arch (Oxon), FSA Scot** is researching a SGSAH Studentship supported PhD: '*Curating heritage for sustainable communities in highly vulnerable environments*' at Heriot-Watt University. Formerly an independent and regional museum's curator, she also practices archaeology and ethnology. Her praxis is founded in her experiences in cross-community facilitation in Northern Ireland.

**Mairi McFadyen** is an Associate Member of the Intercultural Research Centre (Heriot-Watt University). Her PhD, undertaken at the University of Edinburgh, explored the aesthetics, poetics and transformative power of the traditional ballad and won the 2012 Michaelis-Jena Ratcliff Prize for ethnology and folklore. Outwith academia, Mairi has worked with various organisations, including Traditional Arts and Culture Scotland (TRACS) and ethnological community enterprise Local Voices.

**Simon McKerrell** is a Senior Lecturer in music at the International Centre for Music Studies at Newcastle University and has previously held positions at the Universities of Sheffield, Glasgow and the Royal Conservatoire of Scotland. He has published five books, numerous articles, is an expert performer of Highland-, Border- and Uilleann-pipes and has toured, taught and performed throughout the world and recorded twelve commercial albums.

**Rūta Muktupāvela** (PhD in Theory of Culture) is Rector of the Latvian Academy of Culture, Chairman of Latvian Rectors' Council, Representative of Latvia in UNESCO Intergovernmental Committee for the Protection and Promotion of the Diversity of Cultural Expressions and head of the Latvian National Council of Culture. Her research interests include interdisciplinary approaches and research methodologies in arts and humanities, intangible cultural heritage and performative practices.

**Máiréad Nic Craith** is Professor of Cultural Heritages and Anthropology at Heriot-Watt University in Edinburgh. A visiting scholar at Harvard University in 2018, she has held appointments in Ireland, the United

Kingdom, Germany and the United States. A Member of the Royal Irish Academy, her most recent monograph is *Narrative and nostalgia: the vanishing world of the Islandman* (Palgrave, 2019).

**Hossein Olya** is a Senior Lecturer in Consumer Behaviour at Sheffield University Management School, UK. He is one of the pioneers in the application of complexity theory and Qualitative Comparative Analysis within the domain of consumer behaviour research.

**Andreas Pantazatos** is Assistant Professor at the Philosophy Department and University College Research Fellow at Durham University. His interests are the ethics and politics of cultural heritage including the ethics of stewardship and trusteeship, epistemic injustice and museums, ethics of identity (immigration) and politics of the past (post-war heritage reconstruction) and ethics of post-industrial heritage.

**Kerstin Pfeiffer** is Assistant Professor of German and Intercultural Studies and a member of the Intercultural Research Centre at Heriot-Watt University. Her research interests centre on theatre and the role of performances of intangible cultural heritage in shaping, maintaining and challenging notions of identity and community.

**Helaine Silverman** is Professor of Anthropology at the University of Illinois and Director of the Collaborative for Cultural Heritage Management and Policy (CHAMP). She is especially interested in the social and political intersections of heritage production, heritage management, tourism and development. In addition to her own authored works, she is the editor/co-editor of nine volumes on cultural heritage issues.

**Katerina Strani** is Associate Professor and Head of Cultural Studies at the Department of Languages and Intercultural Studies, Heriot-Watt University. Her background is in Languages and Politics. Katerina's research is interdisciplinary, and she has published in the areas of race-related discourse, intercultural relations, communicative rationality and the public sphere.

**Babak Taheri** is an Associate Professor of Marketing at Heriot-Watt University, Edinburgh, UK. His research focusses on consumer behaviour and marketing management with interest in tourism, hospitality and heritage. Babak has over 100 academic publications and serves as Associate Editor for the *Service Industries Journal* and Senior Editor of *Tourism Management Perspectives*.

**Alessandro Testa** is a Marie Skłodowska-Curie/OPVVV Fellow at Charles University, Prague. In the last fifteen years he has studied, worked or undertaken ethnographic fieldwork for long periods in Italy, France, Estonia, Czech Republic, Germany, Austria, and Spain (Catalonia). His publications include three books and many articles in journals and chapters in volumes.

*List of contributors* xiii

**Baiba Tjarve** is a Researcher at the Research Centre of Latvian Academy of Culture, a lecturer, a cultural manager and a theatre scientist. She holds a PhD, and in 2013, she has defended a thesis focused on the institutional transformations in Latvian culture in the post-communist transition. Her main research interests relate to intangible cultural heritage and cultural policy.

**Magdalena Weiglhofer** completed her PhD dissertation at the Centre for Irish and European Ethnology at Ulster University. She is an Associate Member of the Intercultural Research Centre (Heriot-Watt University). Her research focusses on the processes, functions and risks of memory work and storytelling, especially in relation to memory of war and trauma that is told in public.

# Foreword

*Regina F. Bendix*

In 2025, it will once again be Germany's turn, alongside Slovenia, to present a 'European capital of culture'. Nine potential candidates already made an initial pledge to compete for the honour – a pledge that will cost each city millions in preparing for the potential nomination. Hanover is one of the brave candidates, and according to a news report in *Frankfurter Allgemeine Zeitung* from 21 June 2017, the leadership of Lower Saxony's capital felt confident. Wanting to become a European capital of culture is simply an urban development programme with culture as the motor, city representatives were quoted as saying. New projects were in the planning stages, but, as a city spokesperson opined, 'Our city commands a strong identity and has everything that a European cultural capital needs: tradition and cultural heritage, but also a great deal of modernity and activities that are directed toward the future'. The statement poignantly depicts the mixture of connotations that flow into what is considered an attractive and symbolically potent place – a city capable of making its inhabitants identify with it, and a city radiating beyond its boundaries to embrace a European spirit. Terms such as tradition, culture and heritage appear in such statements as if they were singular in connotation, available to be plugged into development opportunities ranging from the political to the economic and the social.

One of the tasks the present volume undertakes is to clarify that such terms are malleable, have a history and easily turn slippery. It does so in a manner that seeks co-operation between scholarship and the profusion of efforts to harness cultural resources to foster identification with territory and polities. The cultural capital of Europe programme as well as other heritage initiatives from the regional to the national and European level are key examples of how tradition and policy intersect. The contributors to the present volume address precisely these kinds of constellations that have emerged over the past decades. Their questions unfolded in the context of the Horizon 2020 project 'Critical heritages: performing and representing identities in Europe', suitably abbreviated into CoHERE. Gathering twelve institutions from nine countries into a consortium, CoHERE has been guided by an interest in and concern for Europe: who and what is Europe, and how do heritage festivals represent and contribute to the European imagination. For the present volume, scholars partnered from Newcastle University, Herriot-Watt University as well as the

Latvian Academy of Culture. With the goal to assess the potential of heritage festivals and associated initiatives, the authors offer an at once critical as well as productive examination of a diverse cases, ranging from events looking back at a long history to newer festivals invented with the aim to engender sociality and community. Largescale festivals are a global phenomenon, and in countries such as the United States, they have, for decades, been closely and overtly tied to city branding, with the hospitality and travel industry cooperating with television's travel channels. CoHERE focussed on efforts that may not neglect economic incentives, but whose sights are overtly set on identity building, including and especially within the European context.

The Cultural Capital programme is a fine example of the European Union's efforts to go beyond economic cohesion and build a web of significance to strengthen shared European identity. Festivity takes a core place in this endeavour and shows the inexorable interlinking of sociopolitical goals with economic needs and hopes. It is also a good example of a policy driven handling of culture much as are many of the efforts to garner a UNESCO nomination for a festive tradition. The latter was made possible by this international organisation's 2003 Convention for Safeguarding Intangible Cultural Heritage and has contributed to boost awareness of culture's resource nature. Festive frameworks have, of course, time and again been suggested as means to heighten social cohesion – one might recall Jean-Jacques Rousseau's draft submitted to the government of Poland from 1772. He urged that the effort to form a republic ought to be celebrated every ten years. The nineteenth-century Swiss novelist Gottfried Keller repeatedly depicted large scale festivities as opportunities for a people to overcome difference and find cohesion in joint, joyous activity for a limited, liminal time. Throughout the nineteenth and into the twentieth century, national holidays, too, were created to cement newly emerging democracies. For late modern actors entrusted with the well-being of Europe conceptualised as a polity, traditional expressions, now often synonymously referred to as heritage, have thus come to take a central place. Festive frameworks and ritual opportunities have been considered as viable vehicles for unlocking a European spirit. Studying a plethora of cases through a set of core terms is what this volume undertakes, allowing readers to evaluate the success of different festive modalities.

For scholars of culture, heritage festivals prove an important test of their documentary and analytic skills, particularly given the political and economic interest bestowed on them. Over the past decades, cultural expressions have grown to be an important resource; they are versatile but also frail, depending on the attachment and energies of a myriad of social actors involved in their performance. Accordingly, scholarship has to attend to these particulars and seek to communicate them beyond disciplinary confines also into arenas of policy and planning.

Festival and ritual have held a prominent place in research on culture since the nineteenth century. They were used as evidence pointing to cultural origins or historical change, as manifestations functioning as temporary safety valves or cures for societal stress, as enacted texts ready to be interpreted by the scholar, or as arenas negotiating or representing political domination. The most recent shifts in analytic attention focus ever more on actors and their motivations in creating, maintaining or transforming festivals; on institutions fostering as well as blocking festive activity; and on the role of political and economic concerns and potentials that flow into the shaping of cultural policy. The contributors of this volume are aligned with these most recent analytic interests and succeed admirably to at once assess the cultural labour flowing into heritage festivals and honour the intentions of the actors involved. In so doing, they deepen our understanding of festivals' fostering of a sense of coherence in our complicated twenty-first century.

# Acknowledgements

This book arose from a research project entitled *Critical heritages: performing and representing identities in Europe* (CoHERE), which received funding from the European Union's Horizon 2020 research and innovation programme under grant agreement No. 693289. We are thankful to have had this funding to develop our research, which allowed us to connect with researchers across Europe and involved case studies in locations across Europe, from Scotland to Romania, from the Baltic States to Turkey, and from Ireland to Malta.

We would like to thank each of the contributors, both from within the CoHERE project team and colleagues from outside who agreed to share their scholarship in this edited collection and promptly responded to tight deadlines. Moreover, we appreciate the input from CoHERE coordinators, Prof. Chris Whitehead and Dr Susannah Eckersley, whose support and guidance helped us throughout the research.

Thanks are due also to our academic colleagues who engaged in peer-reviewing of draft chapters and the anonymous reviewers who reviewed the book for Routledge. We are most grateful to the many stakeholders involved in our research, such as politicians, policymakers, artists, cultural entrepreneurs, traditional arts performers and representatives of cultural bodies from different countries and sectors, who gave freely of their time to support this project.

Our gratitude also goes to Dr Michael Richardson, who helped us in the last stages of the book to ensure the editorial style conditions are met.

Last, but not least, we want to thank Heidi Lowther and the Routledge editorial team, especially project manager Anitta Benice and copy editor Candice Roma, who helped us get the manuscript in the best shape.

*Ullrich Kockel, Cristina Clopot, Baiba Tjarve and Máiréad Nic Craith*
Edinburgh, February 2019

# Abbreviations

| | |
|---|---|
| AfD | Alternative für Deutschland |
| AHD | Authorised Heritage Discourse |
| BCD | Bretagne Culture Diversité |
| BEMIS | Black and Ethnic Minorities in Scotland |
| CD | Compact disc |
| CDA | Critical Discourse Analysis |
| CEO | Chief Executive Officer |
| CFPCI | Centre Français du Patrimoine Culturel Immatériel |
| CH | Cultural heritage |
| CHCfE Consortium | Cultural Heritage Counts for Europe Consortium |
| CND | Campaign for Nuclear Disarmament |
| CoE | Council of Europe |
| CoHERE | *Critical heritages: performing and representing identities in Europe* |
| CSU | Christian Social Union |
| DHA | Discourse Historical Approach |
| DJO | Deutsche Jugend in Europa (German Youth in Europe) |
| DMA | Durham Miners Association |
| EC | European Commission |
| ECoC | European Capitals of Culture |
| EFCO | European Folk Culture Organisation |
| EU | European Union |
| ICH | Intangible cultural heritage |
| IRA | Irish Republican Army |
| KGB | Komitet Gosudarstvennoy Bezopasnosti (Committee for State Security) |
| NGO | Non-governmental organisation |
| NUM | National Union of Mineworkers |
| SDC | Song and Dance Celebration |
| SdJ | Sudetendeutsche Jugend (Sudeten German Youth) |
| SdJ-JfM | Sudetendeutsche Jugend: Jugend für Mitteleuropa (Sudeten German Youth: Youth for Central Europe) |

| | |
|---|---|
| TMSA | Traditional Music and Song Association |
| ToW | Theatre of Witness |
| TRACS | Traditional Arts and Culture Scotland |
| UK | United Kingdom |
| UN | United Nations |
| UNESCO | United Nations Educational, Scientific and Cultural Organization |
| USSR | Union of Soviet Socialist Republics |
| V18 | Valletta 2018 Foundation |
| WoM | Word of Mouth |

# 1 Heritages, identities and Europe

Exploring cultural forms and expressions

*Ullrich Kockel, Máiréad Nic Craith,
Cristina Clopot and Baiba Tjarve*

Traditional arts practices and festivals have attracted increasing and diverse attention in the European context since policymakers discovered 'culture' as a resource in the 1980s (see, e.g., Kilday 1998). Their impact on their respective communities of practice, modes of production and exchange value in contemporary European society is under the spotlight from various angles within the newly emerged field of 'festival studies', which is deeply connected to policy issues (Frost 2016). However, much of this interest is instrumentally concerned with revenue potential, leaving key concepts, such as heritage, identity and indeed Europe, defined in rather vague and often contradictory terms (Kockel, Nic Craith and Frykman 2012; Logan, Kockel and Nic Craith 2015; Kølvraa 2016; Lähdesmäki 2016; Whitehead and Bozoğlu 2017). Moreover, the number and range of events labelled as 'festival' is growing (Frost 2016: 569), requiring a broader perspective on performances of heritage and identity.

The present volume arose from a research programme that set out to examine, from a critical heritage perspective, how the European project (Lähdesmäki 2011) has been manifesting itself in terms of policy, values, heritage, and performance of traditional arts. Empirically and theoretically concerned with both popular and institutionalised practices of heritage making, the programme has addressed especially the gap between discourses of heritage at official – including European – level and actual cultural practice, often informal or unofficial, at the local and regional level. Researchers have explored in particular heritage festivals – broadly defined – as sites for the reframing of collective memory and the reinterpretation of the notion of a common European heritage. With reference to the Olympic Games, MacAloon (1984: 1) claimed that festivals are 'occasions where as a culture or society we can reflect upon and define ourselves, dramatise our collective myths and history, present ourselves with alternatives and eventually changing ourselves in some ways while remaining the same in others'. And, as Fabiani (2005: 64) noted, '[f]estivals are always crowded with argumentative people, who disagree about many things but who hold at least one belief in common: that the festival is the archetype of public space, where physical closeness and a right to speak define the primary conditions of collective life'. In that sense, heritage festivals are opportunities for citizens to negotiate, articulate and transform their European identity (Fligstein et al. 2012; Kaina and Karolewski 2009) at local level. Given tourism's major and growing economic role, and its sociocultural as well as environmental impacts, several contributors to this volume consider heritage festivals as tourism events.

Cultural traditions, being part of cultural heritages, are significant factors that shape local, regional, national and European identities. From the late 1950s, Bausinger (1961) and others have turned the ethnological searchlight from the disappearing world of the European peasantry as the guardians of tradition and heritage towards contemporary and emerging cultural forms and expressions. Among other factors, demographic transformation through international migration and ageing established populations, the commercialisation and commodification of traditional lifestyle elements in the course of globalisation, and IT developments, including social media, have affected the continuity of traditions. The 'heritage boom' from the 1980s onwards has raised awareness of the importance of cultural resources in a broad sense, although much of this has shared the intuition of a 'salvage ethnology' concerned solely with the preservation of heritage items (Kockel 2002). Meanwhile in many European countries, cultural communities and cultural policymakers look for policy strategies and measures for how to develop cultural traditions, safeguard intangible cultural heritages (ICH) and ensure their sustainability for future generations (Nic Craith, Kockel and Lloyd 2019). Beyond this, there has been growing interest in the development of 'heritage futures' (Nic Craith and Kockel 2002; see also Holtorf and Högberg 2013), that is, new forms and expressions of tradition and heritage. The capacity of what the ethnologist Hamish Henderson called the 'carrying stream' (see Bort 2012) of tradition, to sustain and regenerate cultural heritages, arguably rests as much in its innovative power as it does in its potential for conservation (Kockel 2008). As ecological contexts (Frost 2016) for the making, unmaking and remaking of group identities, 'festivals can be seen as political formations open to multiple uses both from above and below' (Leal 2016: 594). The contributors to this book examine the different factors influencing the sustainable development of tradition as part of ICH at different levels and trace underlying common structures. Focussing on case studies of selected regions and cultural groups across Europe, they explore increasingly interconnected heritages and provide examples of heritage-making that simultaneously look backwards and forwards, at the same time addressing the complexities of heritage in contemporary Europe from different theoretical positions.

Most of the research presented here focusses on festivals and performances of different types and reflects the interdisciplinarity that has become somewhat of a hallmark of heritage research (Waterton and Watson 2015). The term 'performance' has acquired many possible meanings and applications in the arts, humanities and social sciences. A performance may be a specific event that involves presentation of rehearsed, often artistic, actions, such as a play or an opera, or it may refer to any kind of event involving a performer and a spectator, from a tennis match to a shamanic ritual. But performance is also a complex and contested concept that helps us to understand social and cultural processes. McKerrell and Pfeiffer (this volume), engaging with scholarship on performance from different disciplines, explore various scholarly approaches to performance and the cultural work performance does, from theatre and performance studies to ethnomusicology. They focus on performance as an embodied act of communication between performers and audiences that facilitates an affective exchange with effects that reverberate beyond the moment. Their analysis illustrates how performances as a means of meaning-making, in which meaning is co-created between performers and audiences, provide opportunities to explore questions about the social and cultural role of imaginative interpretations of ICH. In a sense, all chapters in this collection emphasise the performative aspects of festivals and of the issues and tensions arising from communities' efforts to transmit and transform practices, values and traditions through them. Performance and transformation of heritage are treated in the present collection as cultural forms and expressions of identity in general, and a European identity of sorts in particular. The key terms and underlying concepts directing and demarcating the research – heritage, identity, Europe – thus offer a useful way of framing the collection.

## 1.1 Heritage

Leal (2016: 594f.) analyses 'heritage making as group making'. Few discussions of heritage festivals can proceed without delimiting the scope of the slippery concept of heritage (see Logan, Kockel and Nic Craith 2015) and its limitations in current use, especially the increasingly contested separation between tangible and intangible heritage (Nic Craith and Kockel 2015). Moreover, institutionalised heritage-making practices (Harvey 2001) and grassroots efforts (Nic Craith 2012; McFadyen and Nic Craith, this volume) that might at times stand against such top-down approaches (Hafstein 2012; Taylor 2016), need to be problematised because '[t]he latter have become more salient under the current regime of "heritagisation" promoted by UNESCO's category of Immaterial Cultural Heritage' (Leal 2016: 594).

With its various conventions, the United Nations Educational, Scientific and Cultural Organisation (UNESCO 1954; 1970; 1972; 2001; 2003) has drawn attention to different dimensions of heritage. While much academic, policy and professional interest in heritage concentrates on material culture, and this therefore inevitably features throughout this book, our focus is on ICH. UNESCO's 2003 Convention for the Safeguarding of the Intangible Cultural Heritage suggests that ICH is particularly evident in the following domains:

- oral traditions and expressions, including language as a vehicle of the intangible cultural heritage;
- performing arts;
- social practices, rituals and festive events;
- knowledge and practices concerning nature and the universe;
- traditional craftsmanship.

While all of the above feature in case studies throughout the book, the notion of 'festivals' provides a focal point that brings together different aspects of ICH, with an emphasis on performance and on the issue of the European-ness of these heritages. Who owns the heritages that are celebrated at these festivals? How does one strike a balance between various local and translocal domains of ownership? How are the interests of tradition-bearers protected at the European level? Such tensions reflect the debate generated by the European Union's motto of 'unity in diversity', a term that can be interpreted in multiple ways. For example, a study of the European discourse of German expellee associations (Kockel, this volume) indicates the co-existence of conflicting versions – parallel versus integral – within the same historical heritage context. On the one hand, this might be regarded as an affirmation of diverse expressions of ICH, which ultimately remain at the local level. On the other hand, where policy supports one or other of these versions, it might be regarded as appropriation of expressions of identity by the centre for its own ends; this may wrest ownership of ICH from the local level just as much as commodification can (Kockel 2007).

A key case study in the research programme from which this book arose is the Song and Dance Celebration tradition in the Baltic States, designated by UNESCO as a masterpiece of the oral and intangible heritage of humanity in 2003. The research covered several aspects of this festival: cultural, economic, social and governance. Muktupāvela and Laķe (this volume) develop a quantitative analysis of the potential of festivals for national branding. Two forms of how international recognition may be developed are outlined: special strategies created either by experts more or less spontaneously and national identity brands stemming from traditional cultural symbols that are important for people on the ground. At the beginning of the twenty-first century, the Baltic States have attempted via purposeful, state-financed policies to 'brand' their nations. During this process, the use of informal symbols, such as the 'singing nations', so characteristic for the Baltic region, was deliberately avoided. Nevertheless, this symbol, which is rooted in the Song and Dance Celebration, has remained an important and influential agent from cultural, social, ideological and economic points of view.

Driven in part by an increased awareness of tourism benefits, the appeal of heritage festivals has increased exponentially across Europe (Testa 2017). It is now widely accepted that festivals represent occasions for identity-building (Frost 2016) and that they can foster belonging (Kuutma 1998). Reflecting on identity as a binary process, with self-identification involving the drawing of boundaries in relation to 'others' (Barth 1969), Clopot and McCullagh (this volume) examine identity processes of performers and participants at heritage festivals. Drawing on ethnographic fieldwork in two distinct locations, they analyse these processes by taking a comparative view of two festivals celebrating migrant heritage. A Scottish fire festival related to Viking heritage, *Up-Helly-Aa* in Shetland, is contrasted with the multicultural Romanian festival *Proetnica*. Whereas in the former, 'othering' appears set across gender divisions, the latter illustrates the difficulties of negotiating majority/minority relations even in the context of a festival designed to promote pluralism and diversity.

Heritage is often associated with nostalgia, an issue that 'in many ways [has] been a persistent and even notorious issue within the field of heritage studies from its very inception' (Campbell, Smith and Wetherell 2017: 609). Regarded as inaccurate and sentimental, it has been shunned as a research topic and considered inappropriate for framing heritage interpretation. Drawing on data collected at the Cappadox festival in Turkey, research by Taheri, Gannon and Olya (this volume) offers a different perspective on heritage and nostalgia. Grounding their study in a perspective of interactive sociality, they reflect on the instrumentalisation of nostalgia (Clopot 2017) for enhancing belonging. While it is acknowledged that festivals and cultural events are powerful, interactive venues that have the potential to stimulate feelings of nostalgia, they serve as key sites and moments for individuals to engage in 'sense making', 'self-exploration', 'self-discovery' and 'yearning for a past' through interactive sociality. Taheri, Gannon and Olya draw attention to the 'transformative' and 'nostalgic' nature of festivals and events as 'part of the varied embodied semiotics produced when dealing with "the past"' (Campbell, Smith and Wetherell 2017: 609).

The promotion of local and regional 'heritage' as a resource especially for tourism has been linked to the rise of neo-liberalism, which sees local culture and identity as assets if they can be harnessed to provide foundations for social and economic growth in the face of a decline in manufacturing (Kockel 2007). With sustainability of the resource base seen as a growing issue, the utilisation of heritage is supposed to boost rather than deplete the cultural resource base. This, however, provokes questions concerning the character of heritage as a 'product' and its relation to 'tradition' as a creative process, pointing to the individual as a cultural actor and to issues of authenticity and identity. 'How can an individual, or even a small group, pretend to express collective feelings?', asks Fabiani (2005: 54), putting his finger on a key issue of sociocultural agency. While expressed as a challenge to a purely aesthetic representation of the world, his question points directly to the dark heart of populism as much as to struggles for reconciliation through revisioning of heritages and identities (for examples of the latter, see Pfeiffer and Weiglhofer; also Kockel, this volume).

## 1.2 Identity

The link between heritage and identity has become a commonplace topic (Smith 2006). In anthropological literature, explorations of festivals and identities in general tend to mirror the Durkheimian concern with 'the relationship between festivals and social cohesion (social cohesion being rephrased as collective identity)' (Leal 2016: 586). Festivals, in this analysis, are events engendering what Durkheim would have called 'collective effervescence', which generates a unified group identity based on social organisation and relationships. However, the specific festival form of the Carnival tends to be analysed as 'disruptive – or anti-structural ... – events that challenge hegemonic social categories' (Leal 2016: 586).

Developing an interdisciplinary approach, the authors in this volume share an anthropological understanding of identity as processual (Hall 1999). Most see heritage, with Bortolotto (2007), in similar terms, although its processual character may differ from that of tradition (Kockel 2007). Identity has many facets (Bauman 2001; Triandafyllidou 2014). Kockel (2010: 125f.) has distinguished two types of identity: 'home identities' and 'public identities'. All identities are relational, defined vis-à-vis an 'other', but their orientation may differ. In this model (Figure 1.1), 'home identities' are directed 'inward', defining individuals and groups for themselves, and can be described as 'autological' and 'xenological', depending on whether they are primarily targeting the 'self' or the 'other'. 'Public identities' are directed 'outward', projecting these actors to a wider public, and may be categorised in terms of a 'performance' versus a 'heritage' aspect. Arguably, these distinctions might equally be expressed in terms of 'essentialist' and 'constructivist' identities, but the present distinctions avoid some of the discursive traps associated with those terms.

'Autological' (A) and 'xenological' (X) identification conveys, respectively, insights into one's Self and one's Other(s). 'Performance' (P) identities are expressive, whereas 'heritage' (H) identities are referential. Performing, for example, a commitment to European heritage(s) autologically affirms one's identity for oneself while at the same time referring to a particular heritage

|  |  | Public Identities ||
|  |  | Performance (P) | Heritage (H) |
| --- | --- | --- | --- |
| Home Identities | Self-Identification Autological Identities (A) | AP => "I"<br><br>Identity construed solely with reference to the **Self** ('mirror view')<br><br>**Others excluded** as irrelevant for **performance** of own identity | AH => "**We**"<br><br>Identity construed with clear reference to (certain) Others<br><br>**Inclusion of Others** necessary to determine one's own **heritage** via the group identity |
|  | Other-Identification Xenological Identities (X) | XP => "You"<br><br>Identity construed for target audience<br><br>**Inclusion of Others** necessary for **performance** of identity => audience with certain interest | XH => "**They**"<br><br>Identity construed in clear segregation from (certain) **Others**<br><br>**Others excluded** from a certain **heritage** |

*Figure 1.1* Home and public identities (Adapted from Kockel 2010: 126)

perceived as shared with Others. The same performance xenologically involves an audience who may not share the same heritage(s) but appreciate the significance to the actor(s), while it excludes all those deemed alien to the particular heritage(s) invoked.

In promoting culture and identity in terms of heritage, with a view to furthering inclusion and cohesion, the EU aims at the socioculturally inclusive fields marked AH and XP. Public policy is understandably focussed on 'public' identities. Whether or not identity-related policy and politics works is decided from the 'home' angle, where we often encounter the opposite pattern, AP and XH, with a focus on exclusion, as the Brexit vote in 2016 and the global rise of populism have demonstrated. Yet such an AP-XH constellation need not be confrontational but may merely express neo-liberalism's prevalent spirit of individualism, stressing particularity over similarity and being more concerned with what separates an individual from others.

A note of caution before we proceed: While the concept of 'performance' has been fashionable across humanities and social science disciplines for some time, it needs to be applied with care in a heritage context. The concept implies a certain virtuality that challenges the authenticity of its subject quasi by definition. As Kockel (2010: 126) has highlighted, 'in a performance of Macbeth, we do not see the Scottish king and political reformer, but someone who is pretending to be him, playing out a rather propagandistic horror story'. In considering identity in terms of a performance, are we assigning it a comparable 'as if' quality, marking identity as something we are just play-acting rather than having one? That depends not least on how we think about heritage and tradition as patterns and processes.

The process of creating cultural heritage out of more or less formalised collective ritual practices and 'traditions' has been the object of a certain scholarly curiosity of late. This is due in part to the rather interesting and complex set of sociocultural phenomena and dynamics that are involved, such as top-down and bottom-up policies, construction of meaning, symbolic negotiation and circulation, the emergence of economic and/or political motivation and so on. Testa (this volume) explores the ways certain festivals can be (or aspire to be) considered part of cultural heritage by different social agents or groups in Europe today and tries to explain why such a transformation (or aspiration towards change) is happening. His observations and analysis are based on empirical evidence gathered from ethnographic fieldwork undertaken in Italy, the Czech Republic and Catalonia, augmented by case studies drawn from the literature. The contribution highlights common, indeed pan-European patterns in the politics of European festive culture and 'immaterial' heritagisation processes, thus advancing some key themes of our research programme, such as how tension between the local and European level pans out in different parts of Europe.

Fournier (this volume) also approaches the performance of different identities in the process of communicating ICH through festivals from the perspective of anthropology, drawing on two examples of festivals appearing on the

8   Ullrich Kockel et al.

UNESCO representative list of the ICH of humanity. With the 'Processional Giants and Dragons in Belgium and France', he profiles a multinational candidature including several local town festivals. Comparing and contrasting this with a regional festive practice in France, the 'Fest-Noz festive gathering based on the collective practice of international dances of Brittany', Fournier sheds light on the different strategies used to perform and to communicate ICH.

Focussing on the mining heritage of County Durham in England, Pantazatos and Silverman (this volume) interrogate how the Durham Miners' Gala was created and perpetuated, seeking to explain why the Miners' Gala is growing even though the last pit in the area was closed in 1993. They explore the relationship between local mining communities and Durham Cathedral as manifested in the blessing that the mining communities' banners receive during a special service within that building, which is at the core of Durham's World Heritage Site. The success of the Gala is shown to be due to several interacting factors, especially the discursive flexibility of the Gala, whose organisers have been able to generate messages relevant and responsive to particular moments. At the same time, the very iconography of the banners – which form the visual and ideological heart of the Gala – maintain consistency, each one depicting the history, people or legacy of mining, or the deepest identity of the community carrying it. The current success of the Gala is thus entangled with the safe space it provides for epistemic resistance.

Parades are one of the chief means of identity performance, whether as the controversial annual Orange Order parades down the Garvaghy Road in Northern Ireland in the mid-1990s (Kockel 2010) or the rather more subtle ceremonial entry of different banner-bearing groups during the main rally at the annual festival of Sudeten German heritage (Kockel, this volume). Requiring a degree of organisation, they tend to be a feature of institutionalised autological identification, whereas marches and other collective expressions may arise more spontaneously. Autocratic governments, extreme exponents of the AP identity field, tend to use mainly military parades as a regular element of their ritual calendar. In terms of projecting a European identity of any kind, parades are not a common part, although they may feature on occasion, for example, at sporting events or during a European Capital of Culture programme.

## 1.3   Europe

A geopolitical entity whose boundaries and meanings have been subject to protracted debate (see, e.g., Delanty 2017; Kockel, Nic Craith and Frykman 2012; Nic Craith 2006; 2008; 2009), 'Europe' is used as a shorthand for different entities and thus difficult to define precisely (Kockel, Nic Craith and Frykman 2012: 2):

> 'Europe' as a sociocultural construct has increasingly come under the magnifying glass and one cannot help the impression that the keener the gaze, the deeper the subject recedes into a haze. Part of the problem with

the definition of […] Europe is that its frontiers to the south and east are rather fuzzy. Is Russia part of Europe, or where does Europe's eastern boundary run? Both Turkey and Israel regularly compete in the Eurovision Song Contest, as do various former Soviet Republics whose geographical Europeanness depends rather on where one draws an arbitrary line on the map … And yet, in much of western and northern Europe, 'Europe' is considered to be somewhere else.

For the purpose of this book, it is not so much 'Europe' as a geographical entity that interests the contributors as the concept of European-ness and whether and how that can be defined. Throughout, we will deal with notions such as 'European landscape', 'European Capitals of Culture', 'European heritage festivals' and 'European languages' – concepts that we use with a certain unease, given our awareness of the 'fuzziness' of such descriptions and the diverse usage across the regions of Europe (see Kockel 1999). What could be Europe's 'imagined communalities' (*geglaubte Gemeinsamkeiten*; Max Weber); what is the imagined space this generates? The empirical research presented in this book confirms analytical observations (e.g., Delanty 2017; Stock 2017; Chopin 2018) that concepts of Europe differ widely, depending on social as well as geographical location – even when these are not very far apart physically. In the context of Brexit, for example (see Delanty 2017), the concept of 'Europe' triggers different reactions in Scotland compared to England (see Kockel 2015).

Music has long been seen as a key element of European heritage and identity, although that tends to be in the context of 'high culture'. European folk musical expressions, by contrast, are diverse and have been strongly tied to national and regional politics for at least two centuries. Attempts to construct pan-European musical identities, in this context, rely on bringing forward new, original compositions based on these diverse musical identities and often occur in the context of festival commissions. As part of the research programme that gave rise to this book, team members developed and performed a folk oratorio, *Rivers of our Being*, composed by the Latvian ethnomusicologist Valdis Muktupāvels, drawing on European folk musical traditions. Inspired by 'the rivers of Europe that cross different countries, bringing together diverse cultures across the continent' (CoHERE 2018), the oratorio's official premiere took place on St Andrew's Day, 30 November 2018, symbolising a shared European heritage. It concluded a month-long festival of heritage-related musical and poetic performances, workshops and public lectures. At the time the idea for this kind of European heritage event was initially aired, the organisers could not have foreseen that it would take place in a United Kingdom rocked by that most seismic of European identity performances – the 2016 Brexit vote and its political fallout. The oratorio is at the core of a research-by-practice project, an ongoing endeavour to examine heritage festivals 'from within', which has included the impromptu addition of a coda on the night that referenced Scotland's place in Europe. We will continue to analyse the creative and performance process in all its aspects, as well as the aftermath of the oratorio premiere and its festival context.

Drawing on ethnomusicological theories of sound structure and social structure, McKerrell (this volume) examines the ways in which concepts of the 'new' and pan-European belonging surface in a festival folk-orchestra designed, like the oratorio, specifically to express it, while simultaneously drawing upon the sonic affordances of long established, traditional musical heritage from across Europe. His focus is on *La Banda Europa*, an ensemble formed in 2007/8 specifically to perform complex, new folk-orchestral compositions while drawing on some of the most well-established European folk musical traditions, including the Scottish bagpipes, Swedish *nyckelharpa*, French hurdy gurdy, Austrian accordion, Galician *gaita* and Armenian *duduk*.

Instrumental music as an important element of ICH is complemented by song, and the oratorio therefore comprised both forms of performing heritage and identity; it also incorporated spoken word recitals of both prose and poetry, highlighting the significance of language in this context. Language – both verbal and pragmatic – is a key element in any performance. Similarly, every speech act is itself a communicative performance. It is therefore important to examine language practices in both official communications and everyday usage and to explore how language(s) is/are used to express, preserve, negotiate and transform identities. Language has the capacity to draw, redraw, extend and transcend boundaries of identity. McFadyen and Nic Craith (this volume) draw attention to these issues by focussing on a contested language, Scots. Drawing parallels with other contested European languages, they examine the significance of linguistic boundaries for identity and a sense of belonging at transnational level. Asking how imaginative and creative forms of performance can accentuate key concepts that are at the core of Europe's cultural heritage, they investigate how heritage practices in a contested language can express uniqueness at a local level, while also promoting social cohesion within a European ideal of 'unity in diversity'.

Building extensively on musical and linguistic heritages as well as on the notion of culture as a resource for economic development, the European Capitals of Culture (ECoC) programme is one of the most expansive initiatives to develop a sense of shared European space, heritage and identity. Clopot and Strani (this volume) reflect on Europeanisation and the attempts to expand and mobilise the concept of a European shared heritage through this programme, focussing on recent and upcoming designations – Valletta (Malta, 2018), Plovdiv (Bulgaria, 2019) and Galway (Ireland, 2020). For more than three decades this programme, described by some researchers (e.g., Immler and Sakkers 2014) as large-scale bottom-up cultural programming, has made cities across Europe compete for the accolade of ECoC. Given this history, the topic has attracted significant research effort, with themes such as identity-building through ECoC (Sassatelli 2002), its empowering agency for regeneration (Meekes, Buda and De Roo 2017), and the reframing of heritage narratives (Hudson et al. 2017; Lähdesmäki 2014). With new guidelines in place for the period past 2019, the analysis of the present case study is timely, as it illustrates how one of the main programmes for strengthening European heritage and identity falls short of its mission.

Although the European 'project' has been mythologised to have had a long prehistory, as a vision of peaceful coexistence it was born out of the carnage of two World Wars (see, e.g., Delanty 2017). That this vision appeared until recently to have been achieved may account for some of the apparent contemporary disenchantment with 'Europe' (Kølvraa 2016). In these circumstances, it comes perhaps as no surprise that a 'European spirit' remains most detectable in regions and among groups that have had to grapple with difficult and contested heritages. In this context, Pfeiffer and Weiglhofer (this volume) explore notions of contested places, coping with trauma and long-lasting effects of conflicts. Theatre and storytelling are both means of exploring narratives of self, place and community. Exposing real or fictionalised personal narratives through storytelling and drama has been applied in processes of peace building and reconciliation in contested places because it is an accessible means of dealing with one's own experiences, as well as those of others, in a facilitated space. When stories of life – especially of life within a contested space – are portrayed on a public platform, such as a theatre stage, the meaning of stories is multiplied. Pfeiffer and Weiglhofer explore the use of storytelling and theatre for negotiating reconciliation through two case studies from regions facing historical conflicts of different types. One of these is Northern Ireland, where friction between Protestant and Catholic communities continues today and has increased since the Brexit vote. This is compared and contrasted with frictions in the cross-border region between German Bavaria and Czech Bohemia. The authors reflect on the potential of theatre projects in these regions to not only appease past conflict but also shape identities for the future.

Because Prague was once the capital of the Holy Roman Empire, Bohemia is often described as 'the heart of Europe', not only by the Sudeten Germans. It is one of the three 'heartlands' of *Mitteleuropa* (Central Europe), a vision invoked in the 1920s and again after the fall of the Iron Curtain (Kockel 1999). The annual festival of Sudeten Germans provides the main case study for Kockel's (this volume) analysis of discourses of displacement and replacement (see Kockel 2012), supplemented by a close look at the multiregional German Youth of the East – since 1974 multinationalised as German Youth in Europe. Kockel considers performances of lost heritage and reconnection with a former homeland, examining how 'vanished homelands' of expellees are performed both in terms of physical spectacle and rhetoric, and in the material and non-material representations of heritage. Placing his investigation in the wider context of post-War reconstruction and European integration, he asks to what extent and how expellee associations have indeed been exponents of a 'European spirit', as they are often nowadays portrayed by their leadership and in their literature, and what, if anything, we might be able to learn from their experience.

## 1.4 Heritage policy for Europe

How do we translate the findings of research programmes such as ours into policy and/or practice? Strictly speaking, there are no binding legal instruments for culture at a European level, so the answer has to be: by persuasion and example – hence our attempt to create, with the oratorio, a possible vehicle and route for this purpose. Culture falls under the responsibility of each European Union (EU) member state, possibly following the German federal model of *Kulturhoheit* (cultural sovereignty). Although two other influential supranational institutions, UNESCO and the Council of Europe (CoE), have produced legislation for heritage, these are for the most part 'soft' legal instruments. UNESCO, the leading international standard-setting organisation in the field of cultural heritage, operates through five legally binding Conventions (UNESCO 1954; 1970; 1972; 2001; 2003). However, these conventions also respect national sovereignty. They are signed and ratified at the level of national government, and their terms must be translated into national laws.

The CoE, with its 47 European member states, has issued several conventions regarding cultural heritage, establishing standards for European co-operation and coordination of architectural conservation policies, broadening understanding of cultural heritage to audio-visual heritage and highlighting the social and economic role of ICH (Council of Europe 1985; 1992; 2001; 2005.

The concept of cultural heritage is also at the very heart of the EU constitutional basis, as the Treaty of Lisbon states that the EU shall 'ensure that Europe's cultural heritage is safeguarded and enhanced' (European Union 2007: Article 3.3.).

Although we have described the international conventions above as examples of 'soft' power (Nye 1990), we can nevertheless witness the strong influence of the transnational institutions that issued them on conceptual developments in the cultural heritage field, at both the European and the national levels. Conventions such as those listed above give profile to different aspects of ICH and raise issues of shared knowledge and expertise at a European level, which can generate a substantial body of knowledge, mutual understanding and significant developments in the field of cultural heritage. In the context of this book, there are a number of areas that we would like to draw attention to.

Firstly, many of these conventions raise issues regarding the notion of a 'common European heritage' and the extent to which such an idea can genuinely provide a meaningful framework of shared identity, values and history for people across Europe. European conventions on heritage raise the question of whether a common heritage concept can provide 'enduring points of reference for the present' (Delanty 2017: 2). There is also the issue of whether shared past values are still relevant for, and inclusive of, all European traditions, which include those of minorities we have covered in this book.

As time passes, policy developments with regard to cultural heritage are blurring what were previously regarded as separate and distinct categories. Conceptual links between policies for the preservation of natural heritage and the safeguarding of cultural heritage are increasingly debated (Lenzerini and Vrdoljak 2014), as is the distinction between tangible and intangible heritage (Kockel and Nic Craith 2015). The focus in this book is on festivals and other performative activities. While the chapters draw extensively on traditions and intangible cultural heritage, they are all situated in specific places, located in particular built and/or natural environments. For this reason, place-making is a key theme throughout the book.

Heritage festivals provide opportunities to develop this thinking further in that their activities impact far beyond a narrow heritage base. As some chapters in this volume illustrate, heritage festivals, and cultural heritage policies more generally, do not constitute a narrowly defined sector. Increasingly important is their capacity to interact with, and serve, other policy areas. The CoE's 2005 Faro Convention, for example, highlighted the social and economic benefits of preserving cultural heritage as a prerequisite for achieving sustainable development; this is an area of research that deserves considerable further attention. The recent establishment of a Heritage Task Group by Learning for Sustainability Scotland, a United Nations University–recognised Regional Centre of Expertise in this field, is a case in point.

The economic potential of cultural heritage at a transnational level has been recognised by the European Commission (see European Commission 2015; also CHCfE Consortium 2015). In its resolution on new challenges and concepts for the promotion of tourism in Europe, the European Parliament highlighted new opportunities for developing sustainable tourism based on cultural and industrial heritage sites and local traditions (European Parliament 2015). The theme of cultural heritage contributes to the *Europe 2020 Strategy* for smart, sustainable and inclusive growth. In addition, EU presidencies over the years have highlighted different roles cultural heritage can play, for example, in economic growth or promotion of cultural diversity.

A further trend, also highlighted in our analysis of cultural heritage festivals, involves new developments in the governance of cultural heritage. People and human values are much more central to the concept of cultural heritage than they used to be, and a participatory approach in governance is coming to the fore. In relation to ICH in particular, the UNESCO 2003 Convention for the Safeguarding of the Intangible Cultural Heritage emphasised the central role of communities themselves in safeguarding their heritage. At European level, participatory governance is outlined in the Council of the European Union conclusions on participatory governance of cultural heritage (Council of the European Union 2014). The idea that the user or participant him- or herself can modify the meaning of heritage has indeed come through consistently in our exploration of cultural heritage festivals. Although rooted in traditional knowledge, symbolic meanings are an important feature of ICH that can be adapted and reshaped according to the needs of local communities, in accordance with the process of tradition (Kockel 2007). This reshaping can occur through performance or through contemporary cultural or artistic productions. That flexibility of ICH can ensure the continued meaningfulness and validity of cultural forms and expressions for future generations. Finding ways to encourage it that take due account of issues around authenticity and ownership is a key challenge for heritage policy at the global, European, national and local level.

## Acknowledgement

This publication is a result of the European Union-funded Horizon 2020 research project: CoHERE (Critical Heritages: performing and representing identities in Europe). CoHERE received funding from the European Union's Horizon 2020 research and innovation programme under grant agreement No. 693289

## References

Barth, F. (1969), 'Introduction', in F. Barth (ed.), *Ethnic groups and boundaries: the social organisation of culture difference* (London: Allen & Unwin), 9–38.

Bauman, Z. (2001), 'Identity in the globalizing world', *Social Anthropology* 9(2): 121–129.

Bausinger, H. (1961), *Volkskultur in der technischen Welt* (Stuttgart: Kohlhammer).

Bort, E. ed. (2012), *Borne on the carrying stream: the legacy of Hamish Henderson* (Edinburgh: Grace Note).

Bortolotto, C. (2007), 'From objects to processes: UNESCO's "Intangible Cultural Heritage"', *Journal of Museum Ethnography* 19: 21–33.

Campbell, G., L. Smith and M. Wetherell (2017), 'Nostalgia and heritage: potentials, mobilisations and effects', *International Journal of Heritage Studies* 23(7): 609–611.

CHCfE Consortium (2015), Culture heritage counts for Europe. Available at: www.encatc.org/culturalheritagecountsforeurope (accessed 14 October 2018).

Chopin, T. (2018), 'Europe and the identity challenge: who are "we"?', *European Issues* 466, 19 March 2018. Available at: www.robert-schuman.eu/en/doc/questions-d-europe/qe-466-en.pdf (accessed 12 January 2019).

Clopot, C. (2017), 'Ambiguous attachments and industrious nostalgias', *Anthropological Journal of European Cultures* 26(2): 31–51.

CoHERE (2018), *Rivers of our Being*. Programme leaflet for the premiere of the CoHERE folk oratorio, 30 November 2018.

Council of Europe (2005), 'Council of Europe framework convention on the value of cultural heritage for society'. Available at: www.coe.int/en/web/conventions/full-list/-/conventions/treaty/199 (accessed 11 January 2019).

Council of Europe (2001), 'European convention for the protection of the audiovisual heritage'. Available at: www.coe.int/en/web/conventions/full-list/-/conventions/treaty/183 (accessed 11 January 2019).

Council of Europe (1992), 'European convention on the protection of the archaeological heritage (Revised)'. Available at: www.coe.int/en/web/conventions/full-list/-/conventions/treaty/143 (accessed 11 January 2019).

Council of Europe (1985), 'Convention for the protection of the architectural heritage of Europe'. Available at: www.coe.int/en/web/conventions/full-list/-/conventions/treaty/121 (accessed 11 January 2019).

Council of the European Union (2014), 'Council conclusions on participatory governance of cultural heritage (2014/C 463/01)'. Available at https://eur-lex.europa.eu/legal-content/EN/TXT/?uri=CELEX%3A52014XG1223%2801%29 (accessed 11 January 2019).

Delanty, G. (2017), *The European heritage: a critical re-interpretation* (London: Routledge).
European Commission (2015), *Getting cultural heritage to work for Europe: report of the Horizon 2020 Expert Group on Cultural Heritage.* (Luxembourg: Publications Office of the European Union).
European Parliament (2015), 'European Parliament resolution of 29 October 2015 on new challenges and concepts for the promotion of tourism in Europe (2014/2241(INI))'. Available at: www.europarl.europa.eu/sides/getDoc.do?pubRef=-//EP//TEXT+TA+P8-TA-2015-0391+0+DOC+XML+V0//EN (accessed 11 January 2019).
European Union (2007), 'Treaty of Lisbon amending the Treaty on European Union and the Treaty establishing the European Community, signed at Lisbon, 13 December 2007'. Available at: https://eur-lex.europa.eu/legal-content/EN/TXT/?uri=celex%3A12007L%2FTXT (accessed 11 January 2019).
Fabiani, J.-L. (2005), 'Should the sociological analysis of art festivals be neo-Durkheimian?', *Durkheimian Studies* 11: 49–66.
Fligstein, N., A. Polyakova and W. Sandholtz (2012), 'European Integration, Nationalism and European Identity', *Journal of Common Market Studies* 50(S1): 106–122.
Frost, N. (2016), 'Anthropology and festivals: festival ecologies', *Ethnos* 81(4): 569–583.
Hafstein, V. (2012), 'Cultural Heritage', in: R. Bendix and G. Hasan-Rokem (eds), *A companion to folklore* (Malden, MA: Wiley), 500–519.
Hall, S. (1999), 'Whose heritage? Un-settling "The Heritage", re-imagining the post-nation', *Third Text* 13(49): 3–13.
Harvey, D. (2001), 'Heritage pasts and heritage presents: temporality, meaning and the scope of heritage studies', *International Journal of Heritage Studies* 7(4): 319–338.
Holtorf, C. and A. Högberg (2013), 'Heritage Futures and the Future of Heritage', in: S. Bergerbrant and S. (eds), *Counterpoint: essays in archaeology and heritage studies in honour of Professor Kristian Kristiansen* (Oxford: Archaeopress), 739–746.
Hudson, C., L. Sandberg and U. Schmauch (2017), 'The co-creation (of) culture? The case of Umeå, European Capital of Culture 2014', *European Planning Studies* 25(9): 1538–1555.
Immler, N. and H. Sakkers (2014), '(Re)Programming Europe: European Capitals of Culture: rethinking the role of culture', *Journal of European Studies* 44(1): 3–29.
Kaina, V. and I. Karolewski (2009), 'EU governance and European identity', *Living Reviews in European Governance* 4(2). Available at: http://europeangovernance-livingreviews.org/Articles/lreg-2009-2 (accessed 27 August 2018).
Kilday, A. ed. (1998), *Culture and Economic Development in the Regions of Europe* (Llangollen: ECTARC).
Kockel, U. (2015), '"Aye'll be back!": The quest for Scotland's independence, *Anthropology Today* 31(1): 1–2.
Kockel, U. (2012), 'Toward an ethnoecology of place and displacement', in: U. Kockel, M. Nic Craith and J. Frykman (eds), *A companion to the anthropology of Europe* (Oxford: Blackwell), 551–571.
Kockel, U. (2010), *Re-Visioning Europe: frontiers, place identities and journeys in debatable lands* (Basingstoke: Palgrave).
Kockel, U. (2008), 'Putting the folk in their place: tradition, ecology, and the public role of ethnology', *Anthropological Journal of European Cultures* 17(1): 5–23.
Kockel, U. (2007), 'Reflexive traditions and heritage production', in: M. Nic Craith and U. Kockel (eds), *Cultural heritages as reflexive traditions* (Basingstoke: Palgrave), 19–33.
Kockel, U. (2002), *Regional culture and economic development. explorations in European ethnology* (Aldershot: Ashgate).
Kockel, U. (1999), *Borderline cases: the ethnic frontiers of European integration* (Liverpool: Liverpool University Press).

Kockel, U., M. Nic Craith and J. Frykman eds (2012), *A companion to the anthropology of Europe* (Oxford: Blackwell).

Kølvraa, C. (2016), 'European fantasies: on the EU's political myths and the affective potential of utopian imaginaries for European identity', *Journal of Common Market Studies* 54(1): 169–184.

Kuutma, K. (1998), 'Festival as communicative performance and celebration of ethnicity', *Folklore: Electronic Journal of Folklore* 7: 79–86.

Lähdesmäki, T. (2016), 'Politics of tangibility, intangibility, and place in the making of a European cultural heritage in EU heritage policy', *International Journal of Heritage Studies* 22(10): 766–780.

Lähdesmäki, T. (2014), 'European Capital of Culture designation as an initiator of urban transformation in the post-socialist countries', *European Planning Studies* 22(3): 481–497.

Lähdesmäki, T. (2011), 'Rhetoric of unity and cultural diversity in the making of European cultural identity', *International Journal of Cultural Policy* 18(1): 59–75.

Leal, J. (2016), 'Festivals, group making, remaking and unmaking', *Ethnos* 81(4): 584–599.

Lenzerini, F. and A. Vrdoljak eds. (2014), *International law for common goods: normative perspectives on human rights, culture and nature* (Oxford: Hart).

Logan, W., U. Kockel and M. Nic Craith (2015), 'The new heritage studies: origins and evolution, problems and prospects', in: W. Logan, M. Nic Craith and U. Kockel (eds), *A companion to heritage studies* (Malden, MA: Wiley), 1–25.

MacAloon, J. (1984), 'Olympic Games and the Theory of Spectacle in Modern Societies', in: J. MacAloon (ed.), *Rite, drama, festival, spectacle: rehearsals toward a theory of cultural performance* (Philadelphia, PA: ISHI), 241–280.

Meekes, J., D. Buda and G. de Roo (2017), 'Leeuwarden 2018: complexity of leisure-led regional development in a European capital of culture', *Tijdschrift voor Economische en Sociale Geografie* 108(1): 129–136.

Nic Craith, M. (2012), 'Europe's (un)common heritage(s)', *Traditiones* 41(2): 11–28.

Nic Craith, M. (2009), 'Writing Europe: a dialogue of "liminal Europeans"', *Social Anthropology* 17(2): 198–208.

Nic Craith, M. (2008), 'Intangible cultural heritages: the challenges for Europe', *Anthropological Journal of European Cultures* 17(1): 54–73.

Nic Craith, M. (2006), *Europe and the politics of language: citizens, migrants and outsiders* (Basingstoke: Palgrave).

Nic Craith, M. and U. Kockel (2015), '(Re-)building heritage: integrating tangible and intangible', in: W. Logan, M. Nic Craith and U. Kockel (eds), *A companion to heritage studies* (Malden, MA: Wiley), 426–442.

Nic Craith, M. and U. Kockel (2002), 'Culture and economy: towards an agenda for future research', in: U. Kockel (ed.), *Culture and economy: contemporary perspectives* (Aldershot: Ashgate), 231–240.

Nic Craith, M., U. Kockel and K. Lloyd (2019), 'The Convention for the Safeguarding of the Intangible Cultural Heritage: absentees, objections and assertions', in: N. Akagawa and L. Smith (eds), *Safeguarding Intangible Heritage: practices and politics* (London: Routledge), 118–132.

Nye, J. S. (1990), 'Soft power', *Foreign Policy* 80: 153–171.

Sassatelli, M. (2002), 'Imagined Europe: the shaping of a European cultural identity through EU cultural policy', *European Journal of Social Theory* 5(4): 435–451.

Smith, L. (2006), *Uses of heritage* (London: Routledge).

Stock, P. (2017), 'What is Europe? Place, idea, action', in: A. Amin and P. Lewis (eds), *European Union and disunion: reflections on European identity* (London: British Academy), 23–28.

Taylor, D. (2016), 'Saving the "Live"? Re-performance and Intangible Cultural Heritage', *Études Anglaises* 69(2): 149–161.

Testa, A. (2017), '"Fertility" and the carnival 1: symbolic effectiveness, emic beliefs, and the re-enchantment of Europe', *Folklore* 128(1): 16–36.

Triandafyllidou, A. (2014), 'National identity and diversity: towards plural nationalism', in: J. Dobbernack and T. Modood (eds), *Tolerance, intolerance and respect: hard to accept?* (Basingstoke: Palgrave), 159–185.

UNESCO (2003), 'Convention for the Safeguarding of the Intangible Cultural Heritage 2003'. Available at: http://portal.unesco.org/en/ev.php-URL_ID=17716&URL_DO=DO_TOPIC&URL_SECTION=201.html (accessed 11 January 2019).

UNESCO (2001), 'Convention on the protection of the underwater cultural heritage 2001'. Available at: http://portal.unesco.org/en/ev.php-URL_ID=13520&URL_DO=DO_TOPIC&URL_SECTION=201.html (accessed 11 January 2019).

UNESCO (1972), 'Convention concerning the Protection of the world cultural and natural heritage 1972'. Available at: http://portal.unesco.org/en/ev.php-URL_ID=13055&URL_DO=DO_TOPIC&URL_SECTION=201.html (accessed 11 January 2019).

UNESCO (1970), 'Convention on the means of prohibiting and preventing the illicit import, export and transfer of ownership of cultural property 1970'. Available at: http://portal.unesco.org/en/ev.php-URL_ID=13039&URL_DO=DO_TOPIC&URL_SECTION=201.html (accessed 11 January 2019).

UNESCO (1954), 'Convention for the protection of cultural property in the event of armed conflict with regulations for the execution of the convention 1954'. Available at: http://portal.unesco.org/en/ev.php-URL_ID=13637&URL_DO=DO_TOPIC&URL_SECTION=201.html (accessed 11 January 2019).

Waterton, E. and S. Watson (2015), 'Heritage as a focus of research: past, present and new directions', in: E. Waterton and S. Watson (eds), *The Palgrave handbook of contemporary heritage research* (London: Springer), 1–17.

Whitehead, C and G. Bozoğlu (2017), 'Heritage and memory in Europe: a review of key concepts and frameworks', *CoHERE Critical Archive*. Available at: http://cohere-ca.ncl.ac.uk/#/grid/319 (accessed 2 October 2018).

# 2 On the relationship between performance and intangible cultural heritage

*Simon McKerrell and Kerstin Pfeiffer*

'Performance' is one of those terms that defy easy definition. It has become a particularly elastic term in English, where it has a wider range of meanings and applications than in French or German, for instance.[1] The term has a continuum of meanings that range from the utilitarian statement, such as, 'The car performs well', through to the affective when discussing the rich and plural meanings of aesthetic arts. A Shakespearean play, a football match, a shamanic ritual or even the way someone dresses can all be considered under the heading of 'performance'. However, there is a crucial difference between looking at something *as* performance and saying that this action or event *is* performance (Schechner 2013: 38–40; see also Carlson 2018: 4–5). Looking at human behaviour *as* performance can serve as a way of studying the world around us, from everyday interactions to sociocultural, political and economic processes (Schechner 2013; Kirshenblatt-Gimblett 1998; McKenzie 2001). Yet any singular definition of what performance *is* posits a challenge because it involves cautiously tiptoeing through an epistemological minefield of disciplinary understandings of the term (Carlson 2018; Lehmann 2006: 134–138; McKenzie 2001).

This chapter deliberately ranges across disciplines because we wish to move towards a better understanding of the notion of performance in relation to ICH, where both terms are inherently transdisciplinary. We first examine the concept of performance as it is understood in Theatre and Performance Studies, focussing on those aspects which are pertinent to ICH – embodiment, liminality and efficacy. Second, we turn to Heritage Studies and outline how ideas of and about performance shape our understanding of heritage and its sociocultural dimensions. Thirdly, and finally, we investigate aspects of the tension between the performance of and the research on ICH through the lens of ethnomusicology, a discipline that is shaped by the tensions between the wealth of tacit cultural knowledge acquired by learning to perform works of ICH and the need to communicate such knowledge in research outputs.

## 2.1 Understandings of performance

There are three elements that mark out, frame and heighten some events so they stand apart from examples of everyday life in action and become aesthetic or social performances. The first is location, as a performance invariably takes place in a specific space. This can be a building, the wider or civic environment or, as Fischer-Lichte and Schechner have pointed out, sometimes between people (Fischer-Lichte 2008; Schechner 2013: 30, 2003: 14–19). The location of performance influences the second constituent aspect: the relationship between those who create and those who view, hear or experience. The roles of performer and spectator or audience member may be fluid, yet the performance emerges from their bodily co-presence and involves a cycle of interaction. This sort of interaction sometimes produces outwardly perceptible responses (e.g., laughter, snoring) which in turn trigger a response in the performer. Interaction between performers and audience(s) during performance is often highlighted as one of the key attractions of live performance, resting upon a shared, collective experience. Yet spectators or audiences also respond to one another. Fischer-Lichte uses the term 'autopoietic feedback loop' to describe this interdependence of performers and spectators from which performance emerges (2008: 179). Thirdly, there needs to be some action or thing that is presented, shown, heard or experienced. This can involve the (public) demonstration of a particular skill (Carlson 2018: 3) or 'restored' or 'twice-behaved behaviour' (Schechner 2003: 163): actions and behaviours that are rehearsed or practiced and which constitute a recognised, culturally coded pattern of behaviour.

In any case, performances always have an aim or overlapping aims: 'to entertain, to create beauty, to mark or change identity, to make or foster community, to heal, to teach or to persuade, to deal with the sacred and the demonic' (Schechner 2013: 46). Richard Bauman defines performance as a self-conscious process of demonstrating communicative competence to an audience and stresses that we should think about what is 'conventionally performed' and also 'what range of speech activity is considered susceptible to performance, and what range is conventionally performed' (Bauman 1975: 290–311). We suggest, that performance can usefully be thought of as the communication or display of consciously aesthetic behaviour.

As Thompson and Schechner observe, 'performance [in general] can transform the practitioners, the participants, and the public's existing knowledge and experience' (2004: 13) because the experience they undergo in the course of a performance is considered to be a liminal one – one which opens up possibilities. The notion of liminality and the idea that performance itself is a liminal or liminoid activity, which does not merely involve a transition but a transformation of its participants, is based on Turner's theory of liminality derived from his study of tribal cultures (Turner 1969, 1974; Schechner 2003).[2] Liminality, McKenzie posits, is the 'spatial, temporal and symbolic "in betweenness" [of performance that] allows social norms to be suspended, challenged, played with, and perhaps even transformed' (2001: 50). The notion of liminality and an understanding of aesthetic performances as liminoid activities has therefore come to be seen as one of the most important attributes of performative efficacy, as the definition with which Carlson closes his section entitled 'Conclusion: what is performance?' exemplifies:

> [Performance] is a specific event with its liminoid nature foregrounded, almost invariably separated from the rest of life, presented by performers and attended by audiences both of whom regard the experience as made up of material to be interpreted, to be reflected upon, to be engaged in – emotionally, mentally, and perhaps even physically.
>
> [Carlson 2018: 253]

While Schechner (2003: 159–160) and McKenzie (2001) locate the transformative power of performance in its position between theatre and ritual, the German theatre scholar Erika Fischer-Lichte emphasises the importance of the encounter between performers and spectators: '[L]iminality emerges out of the event character inherent in autopoiesis' (2008: 179). In other words, collapsing the binary opposition between artist and audience, between body and mind, between art and life produces a potentially transformative experience of liminality. Studies in musical performance similarly emphasise the transgressive nature of musical experience in altering our conception of time and the Self. As Fischer-Lichte observes, this 'can provide a torturous or lustful experience for the spectator' (2008: 179).

Whether the experience of a performance has an effect beyond the moment (or can alter our somatic perceptions of the moment itself), and what this effect might be, is a matter for debate across the arts. For Carlson, theatrical performance is 'one of the most powerful and efficacious procedures that human society has developed for the endlessly fascinating process of cultural and personal self-reflexion, experimentation, and understanding' (2018: 253). Kershaw (1999) and Dolan (2005) are similarly optimistic about the power of live performances, especially those that fall into the category of applied theatre. Dolan argues in *Utopia in Performance* that live performances provide 'a place where people come together, embodied and passionate, to share experiences of meaning making and imagination that can describe or capture fleeting intimations of a better world' (2005: 2).

In musicology, there are different flavours of what constitutes performance study. As Simon Frith notes, in the musicology of art music, the notion of performance studies has, since it re-emerged in the noughties, largely been confined to forensic comparative analysis of live or recorded performances of classical music. This is an attempt to give even greater understanding of the musical work. And he goes on to observe correctly, that in popular and traditional music, the visual and other modes of communication are usually critical to the construction of a performance (Frith 2015). What is clear is that in any musical performance, from an aunt singing at a family gathering to a stadium rock concert, there are numerous elements of a performance that usually include a musical text, musical co-texts, a performance context and structural, sonic, visual, gestural, somatic and cultural intertextuality with what has gone before (music almost always involves more than one mode of communication–sound, text, image, gesture etc). Key to all of these constituent elements of a musical performance is a social reading of their significance, that is to say, the social semiotics of a performance. Every audience (or analyst) of a performance floods their interpretative understanding with social signs and frames that help us to make sense and meaning out of what is heard, seen and felt. And all these different modes of communication have many varied possible social meanings: volume can be understood in terms of social distance of intimacy and publicness; pitch in terms of gender, age or social energy; instrumentation almost always signals aspects of authenticity and belonging; and the social understanding of melody and harmony can lead to interpretations of class, sexuality, race, ethnicity, indeed, almost any of the key social categories by which humans seek to belong and divide themselves.

Performance, then, provides a site of negotiation, of exploration and of (potentially) social and cultural resistance because it lets people imagine a different, putatively better future whether collectively or for oneself. Yet while a performance brings about a temporary community of performers and spectators who co-create the event, any such community can break down. As Snyder-Young cautions: '[W]hen the audience leaves, so does the moment' in which communication and a feeling of community is possible (2013: 139; see also Thompson 2009). Nevertheless, performances do significant cultural work as all societies use performance as a means to cultural ends.

## 2.2 Performing intangible cultural heritage

The idea of performance permeates discussion of heritage and its possibilities in a variety of contexts, not least because it sits well with conceptions of intangible heritage as a set of practices or processes rather than a set of tangible things and because both heritage and performance are profoundly bound up with questions of identity (Smith 2006; Haldrup and Bærenholdt 2015; Nic Craith and Kockel 2015). There is an increasing interest in performative heritage practices such as re-enactments, living history events, festivals, musical styles or craft traditions (Barrio, Devesa and Herrero 2012; Howard 2012; Pfeiffer 2019), but also in engagement with heritage sites and museums as a performative bodily practice (Smith 2006, 2011). As Haldrup and Bærenholdt (2015) argue, we can broadly distinguish between performances *of* heritage, which revive the past in the present, people's performances *at* heritage sites, which shape the experiences produced at these sites, and, lastly, people's performances *with* heritage which draw on pre-existing scripts provided by the media and wider society. All of these can occur within authorised heritage discourses (Smith 2006) but can also provide examples of creative ways in which people make use of their heritage and give voice to a multiplicity of narratives and experiences that can challenge official heritage discourses. We would like to focus here on two aspects of performance that are particularly pertinent to the preoccupations of this book: firstly, the fact that performance *of* or *with* ICH is always an embodied practice and an act of communication and, secondly, that this embodied practice has a function in the present. Not just *performing* the past in the present but *experiencing* it also.

Theorists have frequently emphasised the liveness and ephemerality of performance (Schechner 2003; Kirshenblatt-Gimblett 1998; Phelan 1993). Peggy Phelan's famous privileging of performance's disappearance is one of the most frequently cited *dicta* to this effect:

> Performance's only life is in the present. Performance cannot be saved, recorded, documented, or otherwise participate in the circulation of representations: once it does, it becomes something other than performance. […] Performance's being […] becomes itself through disappearance.
> [Phelan 1993: 146]

Yet as Auslander (2008) has pointed out, the stark binary between performance and reproduction that Phelan draws up is challenged by the development of mass media. Moreover, this understanding of performance as 'that which does not remain' is based on what Schneider calls 'the logic of the archive' (2001: 100), that is, the predominantly Western impulse to collect materials. For Schneider (2001), Kershaw (2011), Thompson (2009) and Taylor (2003, 2016) among others, a past performance event is not necessarily gone for good because it involves, impacts on and leaves traces in the living body.

In musical heritage performances, too, our bodies are crucially embedded in our responses to musical (and any) performances, and our only access to shared understanding is always temporally distant and rendered in talk and text. Hence, the key emphasis in ethnomusicology of understanding music from inside the culture (emically), so as not to drain musical sounds of their cultural meaning. But, importantly in recent years, scholars have begun to more fruitfully know and theorise the somatic, both through individual musical reflections, and more importantly, through others' descriptions of musical sound. It is astonishing how deeply embedded our bodies are in both the generative and aesthetic perception of musical sound, and how this emerges in language. People routinely talk about music in terms of the body: 'I just felt uplifted when the strings come in there', 'it's a punchy chorus', 'she has a wonderfully smooth voice', 'the fiddle sounds a bit scratchy to me'. Wittgenstein had it right when he suggested that:

> Music, with its few notes & rhythms, seems to some people a primitive art. But only its surface is simple, while the body which makes possible the interpretation of this manifest content has all the infinite complexity that is suggested in the external forms of other arts & which music conceals. In a certain sense it is the most sophisticated art of all.
> [Ludwig Wittgenstein in Shusterman 2012: 50]

Performance can thus be understood as a means of storing and transmitting knowledge because it involves a repertoire of embodied memory, conveyed in movement, gesture, words, dance and song. As Kershaw asserts, 'performance can foster the sustainable durability of live events from the past' (2011: 141), as made manifest in the continued success of tribute bands or in the deliberate performance of strict sonic authenticity in early or folk music performances. Yet whether or not an artistic performance of historic traditions becomes meaningful to its audiences and spectators in the present depends somewhat on whether it is motivated by the desire for historical accuracy or social and cultural memory (Taylor 2016). The former carries the risk of fossilising the very practice it seeks to preserve. Reconstructing or 'reviving' medieval biblical plays, for example, can serve as a kind of archaeology of practice because it tells us a lot about the practicalities of staging such as the use of space and props. However, whether such biblical plays are meaningful to a modern audience does not depend on the accuracy or perceived authenticity of a performance but on the immediacy of the exchange between participants in live performance. Contemporary adaptations and re-imaginations of medieval plays, in other words plays that take place in the present tense rather than the past tense, can thus sometimes have more resonance with modern audiences (Tyler 2010).

We should remind ourselves here that performance is a communicative process: it is always *by* someone *for* someone. Consequently, any embodied heritage performance can only make a cultural intervention if the audience plays along. As Susan Bennett notes: 'A performance can activate a diversity of responses, but it is the audience which finally ascribes meaning and usefulness to any cultural product' (1997: 156), often brutally proxied in the commercial logic of the new song streaming services such as Spotify or YouTube. The participants in a performance, that is performers and spectators, co-create new or different meanings with each performance. In other words, any performance is an event, whose meaning, effects and outcomes are unstable, because each component of the performance (e.g., performers, spectators, materiality etc) has the potential to influence how the others unfold. This holds true for the theatre as much as for the battle re-enactment, the music session or the street festival.

When considering performance in the context of national or local heritage, there are numerous angles of study to better understand what we see, hear and feel in the performance of ICH such as a concert, play, festival, song or informal pub session. Simply put, the core problem for scholars interested in how performance relates to and enacts people's heritage is to understand how performance constructs and embodies belonging and identity in the communication and the relational understanding of symbolic historicism. Here we take 'symbolic historicism' to be the agent of performative heritage, that sense in which we share with other people in a sense of belonging or affect that is grounded in collective understanding of the past. The 'symbolic' nature of this simply refers to the powerful agency of shared narratives and could be as simple as the recognition of a particular language or dialect or cultural phrase constructions such as 'Her blood red hands' or 'down by the greenwoodside' (Scottish ballad tradition) or as complex as a shared sense of elation and belonging expressed in the recognition of a religious origins story such as the Israelites exodus from Egypt through the parting of the Red Sea (Hebrew: '*keriat yam suf*'). In the remainder of this chapter, we will turn our focus to the question of how performance of ICH can perform this symbolic agency.

One of the key problems of theorising the performative agency of ICH across different cultures is its lack of an internationally shared canon of repertoire and the strong sense of locality and regional or national specificity. What sounds like an authentic fishing song sung in Irish on the West Coast of Ireland is unlikely to be even understood by others elsewhere. This lack of a central shared canon of performance (such as found in the Western classical music canon, through religious narratives or in Anglo-American Christmas traditions, for instance) means that understanding the agency and symbolic historicism of performances of heritage, including authorised heritage discourses, usually means more than a passing familiarity with the cultural history and practices of a particular town, region or nation. In the case of musical sound as opposed to theatrical performance there are additional complex issues surrounding the semantic ambiguity of music set against the specificity of things like written words, pictures, pottery, buildings or films. Objects and language have a materiality and semantic intertextuality that affords analytical specificity (one can trace the history of a phrase such as 'blood red hand' or the historical authenticity of a costume or building). Musical sound was not recorded until the 1870s, and moreover, even early twentieth-century recordings are subject to numerous mediations of technology, commerce and representation, which often makes the scholarship of provenance a meaningless task.

There are therefore very few means for cross-cultural analysis that do not elide the local and specific situatedness of ICH performances. One of these however is understanding the embodied and somatic agency of these practices through ethnographic interview and close participant observation. This sort of research allows an understanding of the sense of shared symbolic historicism that emerges in performance and can be produced in widely different performances of different artistic or narrative traditions from around the world, founded as it is on the one true universal–our bodies. And in so doing we can understand how re-enactments, living history events, festivals, musical styles or craft traditions actually perform a sense of symbolic power and belonging.

This sense of the affective and the symbolic is at the heart of why people continue to perform old stories, plays, tunes and songs and to prepare meals or partake in ritualised festivals that celebrate their shared history. The task then of the analyst is to understand and to *feel* how this emerges in performance and to be able to translate or to explain these phenomena across cultural boundaries, and thus help us to understand our others and our selves through the way in which ICH is performed. This involves translating and understanding the sense of liminality, location (or 'place'), interaction and coded behaviour from the inside. It is with this in mind then that the research on ICH can serve the ideal of better understanding each other's own heritage, and of appreciating that local nuances are critical in that they communicate and describe the tacit or embodied knowledge and skills that lie at the heart of performance. However, this is no easy task, and as we know, our disciplines tend to privilege the textual over the tacit, the objective over the embodied, and the challenge of performance in research is to access and translate for those beyond the tradition just what it is that makes a play, song or reconstruction so powerful for those taking part and for their audiences.

The emphasis in ethnomusicology has been on reflexive ethnographic understanding, as embodied in its methods that include thick description, interviews, participant observation, field notes, desk research and, ultimately, peer-reviewed publication. Essentially, the temptation has always been to place easily knowable and communicable facts or observations above the more slippery, aesthetic, performative and tacit knowledge, so critical to the performance of traditional music: why comment in an academic publication on the aesthetic importance of a narrow, nasal vocal timbre critical to the production of authenticity when the words of the song and performance context enable one to comment upon the importance of that social group and oral transmission to the wider national sense of Self (as in, for example, the case of the Scottish traveller singers). This privileging of textual knowledge is deep seated and is one of the key challenges of understanding performance in and through research. As Lucy Durán has noted elsewhere, she can have a far greater impact with a sensitively produced and detailed CD with liner notes than she can have with a peer-reviewed article published within the field (Durán 2011: 245).

Similarly, Larry Witzleben acknowledges this and insists that as part of the broader academy of scholars, ethnomusicologists, '…seem to be increasingly hesitant to acknowledge the profound differentness of music' (2010: 151). Witzleben, relying on Charles Seeger and Kofi Agawu, takes musical performance and argues for a special ontological compartmentalisation from other forms of 'performance-like phenomena' which he bases on the shifting sense of temporal reality experienced in musical performance events. He argues for music space-time to be different to our general experience of the world and time passing. In this, he is on well-trodden ground: intellectuals as far back as Immanuel Kant (the Godfather of positivism) have been arguing the case for a link between temporality and music. Kant (1793: 225) suggested that music's real aesthetic value lay in its ability to 'play in sensations (of time)'. As a traditional musician, one can control the internal rhythmical nuances and stress within musical performance which communicates a lot of the really significant aesthetics to a knowledgeable audience. Playing with rhythm can demonstrate the difference in performance between a Donegal and a Clare fiddle tune and also has the power to communicate just what makes the individual performer unique and special in a highly stylised performance of tightly controlled traditional music. In other words, the temporal play, in both metre and rhythm and internal stress patterns is very much the stuff of musical performance that we have ignored in favour of more easily knowable understandings of music's significance. The same can be said of dramatic, narrative and other traditions; we have focused on the easily knowable at the expense of the very stuff that matters to people taking part or spectating.

Importantly this does not mean that conscious performance of ICH cannot be a space for the production, dissemination and understanding of new knowledge – it absolutely can. In fact, performance itself can, and should be, an object of study. However, there is an absolutely irrevocable ontological challenge that intangible traditional knowledge is simply not knowable in the same semantic way as textual knowledge, so that if we want something to be research rather than professional practice, then we must be able to communicate its symbolic agency through text. This always involves an act of translation and is very much the responsibility of heritage scholars. We would not expect to be able to understand the performative, affective or, for that matter, cultural or social significance of a new and innovative twenty-first-century ritual Navajo dance or Turkish maqam simply by witnessing its performance as an outsider. What is important however is that the previously underacknowledged, tacit, affective and downright emotionally powerful aspects of intangible heritage performance that have remained locked into performance and its reception without making the transition to the page emerge as the object of our research. The use of practice in research about ICH can then quite rightly be configured as an act of translational scholarship; exposing and translating insider artistic and aesthetic knowledge to a global audience, and potentially serving to stimulate understanding of others and potentially leading to new forms of performative expression.

## 2.3 Conclusion

The performance of ICH is an act of communication that can support the construction and reconstruction of identity, place and a sense of belonging. Whether it is a fishing song or a performance of *Galoshins*,[3] the live performance constructs embodied knowledge through and for the participants offering powerful affective experiences of the past within our lived experience. To be able to understand the performance of ICH or to benefit from the performative turn therefore means that we have to be able to demonstrably share knowledge across social and cultural boundaries, which is one of the key reasons why disciplines such as ethnomusicology, theatre studies, heritage studies, literature and linguistics and ethnology are well placed to lead in understanding performance and its symbolic agency. The relativism at the heart of these disciplines challenges us to explain and translate the tacit knowledge acquired in highly specialised ICH contexts for our colleagues and publics elsewhere. We should be able to discuss the embodied understanding of place or location, liminality, interaction and coded behaviours that function at the heart of performance. This is an epistemological challenge across disciplines interested in ICH. What is required is an understanding not just of the contextual and the local but also the ability to put into words the embodied knowledge that emerges from re-enactments, living history events, festivals, musical styles or craft traditions and their significance. Only in so doing will we be able to have a deeper discussion about how it *feels* to perform the past in the present.

## Acknowledgement

This publication is a result of the European Union-funded Horizon 2020 research project: CoHERE (Critical Heritages: performing and representing identities in Europe). CoHERE received funding from the European Union's Horizon 2020 research and innovation programme under grant agreement No. 693289.

## Notes

1 The German equivalent, *Performanz*, is used almost exclusively in the contexts of theatre studies and linguistics, where it refers to the act of performing (e.g., a play or the linguistic performance of an individual respectively). The performance event itself is usually referred to as an *Aufführung* (the performance of a play, an opera, a concert etc) or a *Vorführung* (show), *Darstellung* (the performance of a part) or *Darbietung* (e.g., of a musical piece), while performance in the sense of effectiveness is covered by the term *Leistung*, and performance as the execution of an act can be translated by a whole range of terms from *Ausübung* to *Erfüllung*. The French word *performance* is primarily used in the context of discussing results or data, indicating the capacity of someone or something to achieve a certain measurable standard, for example, a car's fuel consumption or an athlete's sporting performance. It is also used in the same linguistic sense as in German.
2 Turner distinguishes between liminal and liminoid activities and phenomena based on the notion of choice, using the difference between a tribal ritual and carnival to illustrate his point: participation in a tribal ritual is usually compulsory, but we can choose to watch or avoid or even to participate in a street-performance festival (1974: 74). Liminoid activities *resemble* liminal ones in that they, too, allow their participants to cross a sociocultural threshold. Yet while a social or religious rite, for example, results in a change of status for the participant, taking part in the carnival or watching a performance can – but does not necessarily have to – provide a transformative experience because participation is optional and because the liminoid, unlike the liminal, is a form of leisure rather than an integral part of the social process.
3 *Galoshins* is an old Scottish folk play with a tradition going back to the thirteenth century. It was regularly performed in the Borders and the Central Belt by young guisers (mummers) during Halloween and Hogmanay up until the twentieth century and is being revived in many places now.

## References

Auslander, P. (2008), *Liveness: performance in a mediatiatized culture*, 2nd ed. (London: Routledge).
Barrio, M., M. Devesa and L. Herrero (2012), 'Evaluating intangible cultural heritage: the case of cultural festivals', *City, Culture and Society: The Societal Function of Cultural Heritage* 3(4): 235–44.
Bauman, R. (1975), 'Verbal art as performance', *American Anthropologist* 77(2): 290–311.
Bennett, S. (1997), *Theatre audiences: a theory of production and reception*, 2nd ed. (London: Routledge).
Carlson, M. (2018), *Performance. A critical introduction* (London: Routledge).
Dolan, J. (2005), *Utopia in performance: finding hope at the theater* (Ann Arbor: University of Michigan Press).
Durán, L. (2011), 'Music production as a tool of research, and impact', *Ethnomusicology Forum* 20: 245–253.
Fischer-Lichte, E. (2008), *The transformative power of performance: a new aesthetics* (London: Routledge).

Frith, S. (2015), 'What you see is what you get: notes on performance'. Available at livemusicexchange.org/blog/what-you-see-is-what-you-get-notes-on-performance-professor-simon-frith/ (accessed 12 September 2016).

Haldrup, M. and J. Bærenholdt (2015), 'Heritage as performance', in E. Waterton and S. Watson (eds), *The Palgrave handbook of contemporary heritage research* (Basingstoke: Palgrave Macmillan), 52–68.

Howard, K. (2012), *Music as intangible cultural heritage: policy, ideology, and practice in the preservation of East Asian traditions* (Farnham: Ashgate).

Kant, I. (1793), Critique of Judgement 2nd ed. (Berlin: Königlich Preußische Akademie der Wissenschaften).

Kershaw, B. (2011), 'Nostalgia for the future of the past: technological environments and the ecologies of heritage performance' in A. Jackson and J. Kidd (eds), *Performing heritage* (Manchester: Manchester University Press), 123–143.

Kershaw B. (1999), *The radical in performance: between Brecht and Baudrillard* (London: Routledge).

Kirshenblatt-Gimblett, B. (1998), *Destination culture: tourisms, museums, and heritage* (Berkley: University of California Press).

Lehmann, H.-T. (2006), *Postdramatic theatre* (London: Routledge).

McKenzie, J. (2001), *Perform or else* (London: Routledge).

Nic Craith, M. and U. Kockel (2015), '(Re-)building heritage: integrating tangible and intangible', in W. Logan, M. Nic Craith and U. Kockel (eds), *A companion to heritage studies* (Malden, MA: Wiley), 426–442.

Pfeiffer, K. (forthcoming 2019), 'Rewriting the script: updating the Massacre of the Innocents for the 21st century', *Skenè: Journal of Theatre and Drama Studies* 5(1), 113–127.

Phelan, P. (1993), *Unmarked: the politics of performance* (London: Routledge).

Schechner, R. (2013), *Performance studies: an introduction*, 3rd ed. (London: Routledge).

Schechner, R. (2003), *Performance theory* (London: Routledge).

Schneider, R. (2001), 'Performance remains', *Performance Research* 6(2): 100–108.

Shusterman, R. (2012), *Thinking through the body, essays in somaesthetics* (Cambridge: Cambridge University Press).

Smith, L. (2006), *The uses of heritage* (London: Routledge).

Smith, L. (2011), 'The "doing" of heritage: heritage as performance', in A. Jackson and J. Kidd (eds), *Performing heritage* (Manchester: Manchester University Press), 69–81.

Snyder-Young, D. (2013), *Theatre of good intentions: challenges and hopes for theatre and social change* (Basingstoke: Palgrave Macmillan).

Taylor, D. (2016), 'Saving the "live"? re-performance and intangible cultural heritage', *Études Anglaises* 69(2): 149–161.

Taylor, D. (2003), *The archive and the repertoire: performing cultural memory in the Americas* (Durham, NC: Duke University Press).

Thompson, J. (2009), *Affects: applied theatre and the end of effect* (Basingstoke: Palgrave Macmillan).

Thompson, J. and R. Schechner (2004), 'Why "social theatre"?', *TDR* 48(3): 11–16.

Turner, V. (1969), *The ritual process* (Chicago, IL: Aldine).

Turner, V. (1974), 'Liminal to liminoid in play, flow, and ritual: an essay in comparative symbology', *Rice University Studies* 60(3): 53–92.

Tyler, M. (2010), 'Revived, remixed, retold, upgraded? the heritage of the York cycle of mystery plays', *International Journal of Heritage Studies* 16(4–5): 322–336.

Witzleben, J. (2010), 'Performing in the shadows: learning and making music as ethnomusicological practice and theory', *Yearbook for Traditional Music* 42: 135–166.

# 3 Comparative aspects of the Song and Dance Celebration of the Baltic countries in the context of nation-branding processes

*Rūta Muktupāvela and Anda Laķe*

Traditions rooted in cultural heritage are a key element behind the well-known motto of the European Union, 'Unity in Diversity'. The year 2018 was designated as the European Year of Cultural Heritage, with the aim to raise awareness about the uniqueness and richness of national, regional and local heritage, while stressing its significance in overcoming modern global challenges such as demographic and climate changes, natural or man-made disasters, community isolationism and serious violations of the values of freedom, tolerance and democracy on which European societies are based. The European Cultural Heritage Strategy for the twenty-first century stresses that it is 'a key factor for the refocusing of our societies on the basis of dialogue between cultures, respect for identities and diversity, and a feeling of belonging to a community of values' (Council of Europe 2017). Both tangible and intangible forms of cultural heritage are considered as equally important in this Strategy. The forms of intangible cultural heritage (ICH) include several elements, among them the oral traditions, performing arts, social practices, rituals and festive events. In this chapter, festival events are presented as one of the most popular and accessible formats of cultural performative practices. Not only do they serve the purpose of constructing national identity and presenting the peculiarities of culture but they also perform the function of the so-called soft power (Nye 2004: x), often referred to as one of the most powerful tools of cultural diplomacy, based on values and positive experiences, rather than military force and fears, as well as based on things that are often the products of people, cultural institutions and brands rather than governments (Dubber 2015). Cultural festivals as a powerful ICH transmission channel are important in a nation's branding process not only because of their aesthetic and entertainment aspects but also as powerful agent of social and political influence (Jovićević 2017: 140).

Among the various values constructing European identity, one of the most spectacular and noticeable traditions and performative practices, characteristic of all the three Baltic countries – Estonia, Latvia and Lithuania – is the Song and Dance Celebration (SDC). This chapter focusses on an analysis of the SDC in the context of the development of nation-branding. Two ways of developing international recognition can be outlined: special strategies created by experts and spontaneous, endogenous branding, stemming from traditional cultural symbols important to people. At the beginning of the twenty-first century, the Baltic countries were involved in a purposeful state-financed policy to create their nation brands. During this process, the use of the informal symbol of 'singing nations', typical of the Baltic countries, was consciously avoided because of the recommendations of nation-branding professionals. Nevertheless, this symbol, expressed in the form of the SDC, is an important and influential agent from the cultural, social, ideological and economic point of view, as well as in contexts of international communication.

The SDC is a cultural tradition that best characterises and unites the Baltic countries. It is the only location in Europe where this tradition has not only survived but evolved into a distinctive manifestation of the heritage and culture of the Baltic countries, often perceived by researchers and the general public as a symbol of pan-national identity. On 7 November 2003, the tradition and symbolism of the SDCs in Estonia, Latvia and Lithuania were included in the UNESCO list of the Masterpieces of the Oral and Intangible Heritage of Humanity (UNESCO Latvijas Nacionālā komisija, n.d.).

Although there is a set of features common to the manifestations of the tradition in all the three countries, each country has specific strategies for transmitting the tradition and different performative practices that influence the use of the SDC phenomenon in nation-branding. The experience of Estonia, Latvia and Lithuania gained in nurturing the SDC tradition reveals not only various scenarios for safeguarding the ICH but also different approaches to integrating certain cultural symbols into nation brands. The objectives of this chapter are to (1) explore whether and in what ways the SDC as an element of ICH is used in Estonian, Latvian and Lithuanian nation-branding practices, (2) comparatively analyse elements of the tradition that allow it to constitute itself as an endogenous nation brand, and (3) determine whether or not the tradition is used in the new nation brands created by experts in the twenty-first century.

In order to achieve this objective, this chapter contains a brief description of the SDC as an element of the ICH and its historical genesis, analyses the theoretical aspects of the nation brand and the strategic nation-branding process in the Baltic countries, describes cultural heritage as a resource in nation brand management, as well as selects and compares those aspects of the SDC tradition that form a link with the nation-branding practice. The empirical comparative analysis of the SDC traditions is based on quantitative methodology, with data from a survey of the residents of Estonia, Latvia and Lithuania (Survey 2017).

## 3.1 The SDC tradition as an essential element of cultural heritage

Despite the obvious triumph of globalisation in the twenty-first century, everyday experience bears evidence to the opposite trend – the revival of the local and traditional forms of culture and the actualisation of various aspects of local identity in social relations and cultural practices, which manifest themselves in different types of festivals and collective performances in Europe.

Cultural performances not only represent but also constitute various typical elements of national and local identity, such as traditional local lore and crafts, folklore, culinary heritage and other manifestations, which are considered as part of cultural heritage.

Cultural heritage, especially in its intangible form, has become the basis for self-determination of European nation states 'when nineteenth-century elites constructed readings of the past that were intended to generate a collective consciousness of a national historical destiny' (Nic Craith 2008: 63), at the same time continuing the search for answers to the problematics of what factors legitimate the power of definition concerning the aspects of belonging to a cultural heritage.

Cultural heritage is considered to be one of the basic driving forces that cultivates a sense of local belonging, enhances cultural and creative space and contributes to the development of the society in general: '[Cultural] Heritage is seen as something that unites us. A solution to social problems. But it can be an engine of division, as people call on the past to make it their own, and to make futures of exclusion' (Whitehead, Kockel and Nic Craith 2018). Researching practices of cultural heritage, it becomes possible 'to identify means of sustaining and transmitting European heritages that may help foster more inclusive identities, and counteract division within European space' (Whitehead, Kockel and Nic Craith 2018).

The most massive phenomenon of cultural heritage, which is of greatest significance to national identity and invariably surfaces in all the discussions of the collective performative culture of the Baltic countries, is the festival known in English as the Nationwide Song and Dance Celebration. In Lithuania it is called *Lietuvos dainų šventė*, in Latvia *Vispārējie latviešu Dziesmu un deju svētki*, in Estonia *Eesti laulu- ja tantsupidu*. It should be mentioned that this festival played a crucial part in the formation of the statehood of the three Baltic nations, resistance to the Soviet occupation and the so-called Singing Revolution that led to their liberation from the Soviet regime (Šmidchens 2014). Also nowadays when the Baltic countries are celebrating their centenary, the SDC is positioned as the central event of the whole festive cycle. At present the SDC tradition in the Baltic countries is supported both at the national level, through institutional and normative acts, and at the international level, through its inclusion into the UNESCO list of the intangible heritage where the Celebration is described as a 'vital tool in nation-building in all three countries, while evolving into the most massive and inclusive communal event to celebrate Estonian, Latvian or Lithuanian cultural identity' (UNESCO 2003).

The SDC is a traditional mass performance of amateur choirs and dance groups, every five or four years taking place in the capitals of the Baltic Countries. The main features of the SDC are:

- continuity of the process, which includes the intermediate preparatory period (i.e., preparation and acquiring of the repertoire, public shows, competitions, craft exhibitions, local regional festivals etc);

- high artistic quality, provided by professional composers, professional conductors, regular courses and workshops for participants and elaborated selection process; and
- multidisciplinary cultural events of different kinds of amateur arts and crafts.

Song festivals are considered a stable tradition, and their origins are to be found in the mid- and late nineteenth century, when Europe saw a surge of ideas related to national statehood (Lajosi and Stynen 2015). On the eastern coast of the Baltic Sea, as elsewhere in Europe, collective singing and choral movement became one of the most effective vehicles for disseminating the ideas of nationhood. Social singing became a symbol which, according to Habermas, helped nationals transcend their inherited loyalties to village and clan, landscape and dynasty and construct a new form of collective identity generating an imaginary unity and making them aware of a collective belonging that, until then, had been merely abstract and legal, and only this symbolic construction makes the modern state into a nation state (Habermas 2001: 85). It was social collective singing that became the transnational phenomenon capturing nineteenth-century Europe and mobilising people to form nation states (Leerssen 2015; Habermas 2001; Brüggemann and Kasekamp 2014).

## 3.2 Historical aspects of song celebrations

The nation states of Lithuania, Latvia and Estonia were founded in 1918, while the tradition to organise song festivals and celebrations in these territories is half-a-century older. It is based on the Swiss and German choral singing movement that was spread in the territories of Estonia and Latvia by a distinctive ethno-social group, the so-called Baltic Germans, who linguistically identified themselves with the German-language space but saw themselves as culturally belonging to the eastern coast of the Baltic Sea. Having adopted the Germanic structure of the song festivals, the leaders of the national awakening movements did not hesitate to fill it with original content derived from the local, ethnic culture – Latvian and Estonian composers arranged folk songs for choirs and created original compositions for instrumental groups and orchestras. In the late nineteenth century, this choral movement in the Baltic provinces of the Russian Empire started to consolidate, and as a result, the First Estonian Song Celebration took place in Tartu (Dorpat) in 1869 (Kasekamp 2010: 79; Leerssen 2015: 31); the First Nationwide Latvian Song Celebration took place in Riga in 1873 (Grauzdiņa and Poruks 1990: 4–5; Grauzdiņa 2004: 34; Bērzkalns 1965: 45); and the first Lithuanian song celebration took place in Kaunas in 1924 (Zubrickas 1999: 731).

The tradition of song celebrations in the Baltic countries is unique due to its vitality and ability to adapt to various historical circumstances without losing its spirit of freedom even in the darkest years of the Soviet occupation. The Soviet regime introduced into the Song Celebrations a repertoire that lauded militarism, the Communist Party, Lenin, Stalin and other red dictators in the hope that the popular appeal of the celebration would make it a powerful instrument for eliminating the unique cultural identity and creating a species of faceless *Homo sovieticus* obedient to authoritarianism.

However, according to the Latvian musicologist Arnolds Klotiņš, the plans of the USSR ideologues did not really come true, because

> the most far-sighted part of conductors and choir singers upheld singing and the great celebration as virtually the only legal opportunity to experience and manifest national and universal values together with such a large section of society. Tribute to the alien ideology and tastelessness had to be duly paid; the repertoire always had to accommodate a number of compulsory Soviet propaganda songs. However, people often sang these unloved lyrics just not to lose the opportunity to sing, come together and express their national identity and patriotic feelings by their stance alone, as folk songs and part of the traditional repertoire were allowed.
> [Klotiņš 1998: 34]

As an idiosyncratic and spontaneous form of resistance and protest against the dominant communist ideology, there sprang up in Latvia the phenomenon of informal communal singing, involving both the participants of the SDC and the audience. After the closing concert, they went home and on their way to the public transport stops and in trams sang together songs popular at that time, including songs the Soviet regime considered unwanted or had banned: 'In difference from the concerts of the Song Celebration, on these occasions there were no conductors and division into choir singers and listeners. Everybody sang, possibly even the ever-present KGB agents and informers to disguise their black duty' (Muktupāvels 2012: 314). After the Baltic countries regained their independence in 1991, the SDC also shed the fetters of the Soviet ideology. It is still considered one of the most essential elements of the national cultures of the Baltic countries and functions as a symbol and brand of 'the singing nations' being a relevant and influential agent from the cultural, social, ideological and economic point of view while apprehending identity, as well as in contexts of international communication or branding.

## 3.3 Interpretation of the nation brand and its role in promoting international visibility

In the age of globalisation, the dominance of mass culture and consumerism heightens the value of originality and authenticity; therefore, the brand is gaining ever greater relevance not only at the individual but also the collective level. In the broad sense, the brand is an image, word, symbol or a combination of all these elements directed at marking or constructing identity with the aim to differ from others through demonstration of one's abilities, views and values in the competitive space of individual and cross-cultural communication. In the contemporary consumerist socio-economic system, the greatest value is an unceasing growth of the consumption/supply of goods and services, and purchasing power is the main indicator of the welfare of an individual and the whole society. Under circumstances when, in almost all the spheres, values are confused with price (Mazzucato 2018), market terminology is increasingly more often found also in the discourse of national identity. In the twenty-first century, several countries of the world are literally obsessed with promoting their visibility and forming a positive image in the name of 'selling itself' wisely. If the idiom 'to sell one's country' used to be a euphemism for treason, then at present 'to sell one's country' wisely (Saffron Brand Consultants 2009) as if it were 'a tin of beans or a box of soap powder' (Anholt 2011: 8) is a necessity prescribed by globalisation. At present the nation brand helps to improve the country's image, attract investments and gain economic benefits. In the present chapter, preference is given to the definition of the nation brand offered by the local branding expert Keith Dinnie, who describes the nation brand as 'the unique, multidimensional blend of elements that provide the nation with culturally grounded differentiation and relevance for all of its target audiences' (Dinnie 2016: 5).

The nation brand in principle is the quintessence of the country's image created for cross-cultural communication and has a dual nature – it is based on the past and the present, yet functionally it is oriented towards development and the future. It is both reactive and proactive and tends to emphasise the opportunities the country offers to the international community (Jordan 2014: 22–23, 45). Positive news about the nation and the country helps to attract investments and increase export, to involve foreign talents and highly qualified labour or strengthen international partnership (Dinnie 2016: 17). Needless to say that nation branding is especially topical for small and relatively poor countries that wish to swiftly and effectively announce themselves as competitive players on the world stage. The nation brand usually consists of several traditional elements topical for international communication, such as language, culture, nature, history and culinary heritage; however, also contemporary globally recognisable commercial national brands, national iconic personalities, etc. can be used (Fan 2006: 12). Notionally, the branding process involves two ways of promoting international visibility, that is, strategic branding specifically created by professionals and internal or endogenous branding based on highlighting the symbolic aspects important for the given nation.

## 3.4 Strategic nation-branding process in the Baltic countries in the twenty-first century

The strategic nation-branding process in the Baltics became especially active at the beginning of the twenty-first century when the governments initiated a purposeful, state-financed work on the brands that would help to highlight the individual nature of each country after the incorporation of the region in the European Union. It coincided with the state of affairs of that time, which in line with the EU integration policy has manifested itself in a motto 'United in diversity' (Lähdesmäki 2016) with the aim 'to work for peace and prosperity, while at the same time being enriched by the continent's many different cultures, traditions and languages' (European Union 2018).

At the time one of the suggestions made by foreign brand management experts was to avoid the seemingly self-evident idea of the commonality of the Baltic countries rooted in the twenieth-century history, since it might be an obstacle to their individual visibility (Saffron Brand Consultants 2009: 88), which is a precondition for creating the so-called brand value or capital (Lee et al. 2015: 41).

Thus Estonia, for example, after its victory in the Eurovision Song Contest 2001, created the brand 'Positively transforming', stressing Estonia's readiness for positive changes. In 2009 it was changed to 'Positively surprising', sending the world a message about Estonia as 'a small but proud nation that integrates extremes – old and new, established and innovative, cold and warm' (Mändmets 2010: 76). At the moment, Estonia presents itself as a country of advanced information technologies, wittingly modifying the name of the country as 'e-Estonia' (e-Estonia, n.d.).

In 2008, Lithuanian society was introduced to a specially created brand 'Lithuania the Brave Country', which communicated the concepts of innovation and cultural diversity combined with a unique nature, warm-hearted people and a progressive approach to science (Lietuvos prekės ženklas n.d.). However, the communication of this brand was discontinued as early as in 2009 due to interior disagreements and financial insecurity (Puidokas and Kinzytė 2014: 50–64). In October 2016, the Lithuanian State Department of Tourism presented a new brand, 'Real is Beautiful', representing the nature and cultural heritage of Lithuania (Valstybinis turizmo departamentas 2016).

In 2003, at the invitation of the Latvian Institute, a team of specialists from Oxford University led by Wally Olins created the pilot project 'A Brand for the Nation of Latvia' and advised positing Latvia as 'The Keystone of the Baltics' (Frasher et al. 2003: 41–47). At the time Latvia was presenting itself with the brand 'The Land that Sings', selected at a nationwide competition as the best representation of self-identity, incorporating notions about nature, culture, business and people characteristic of Latvia (Frasher et al. 2003: 26). However, the foreign experts considered this brand 'peasantlike' and consequently insufficiently effective for communicating the idea of a modern, developing country (Frasher et al. 2003: 45). Despite the recommendations of the experts, the brand of 'The Land that Sings' remained in place for some time and only in 2010 was replaced with 'Latvia – Best Enjoyed Slowly', offering pleasant leisure time in a sauna (Your friend in Riga 2010).

## 3.5 Cultural heritage and crowd symbols as a resource in nation-branding

It must be admitted that the contemporary formal cross-cultural communication is dominated by strategic nation brands created by professional business companies; however, the reputation and image of a nation are influenced also by other factors independent of the experts' opinions and recommendations such as nature, state policy, economic situation, national stereotypes and especially culture. During the nation-branding process, culture arguably manifests itself in three aspects – landscape, art and cultural heritage (Dinnie 2016: 139). Nowadays precisely the tangible and intangible cultural heritage not only is becoming a source of inspiration for creativity and new aesthetic forms but also a relevant soft power and nation-branding tool for all countries, regardless of their geopolitical impact in a global perspective (Schreiber 2017: 52). Cultural heritage, as it is featured in UNESCO's definition of ICH, is closely related to such elements of national identity as language and folklore, traditional crafts, culinary heritage etc. With regard to cross-cultural communication, it plays a special role in promoting visibility, upholding dialogue and encouraging tolerance and inclusiveness (UNESCO 2018).

Cultural heritage manifests itself in symbols and collective practices that serve each nation not only to represent its values but also to confirm its idiosyncratic and unique nature to itself and others. This self-understanding rooted in culture and expressed through symbols becomes the basis for the interior or endogenous nation brands which in a way resonate with 'national crowd symbols'. 'National crowd symbols' is a concept coined by the Nobel Prize winner writer Elias Canetti and designates the notions and emotions people usually associate with their nation. According to Canetti, crowd symbols may represent natural phenomena, such as the seas, forests and mountains appearing as symbols in myths, dreams, tales and songs. They can be also mythic or historical events and artefacts, which have played a significant role in the self-definition process of a nation (Canetti 1978: 170).

The crowd symbol for the countries on the eastern coast of the Baltic Sea is singing and the song, which, according to Johann Gottfried Herder, 'loves the masses, it loves to take shape from the common voice of the multitude: song commands the ear of the listener and the chorus of voices and souls'. (Herder and Bohlman 2017: 50). Singing, as it was mentioned above, is embodied in the idea of the statehood of all the three Baltic countries and their independence would be hardly imaginable without the collective singing, reaching its highest point in the national crowd symbol we call the Song and Dance Celebration. The SDC is not only collective performances and concerts. An equally important aspect of the celebration is the nurturing of local identity and creativity in the interim periods when choirs and dance groups practice intensively in the regions and traditional costumes, jewellery and symbolic objects are made, which leads to interpreting the SDC as a social movement, whose function is to confirm the cultural identity and to promote social self-initiative, self-organisation and inclusiveness. The Baltic SDC tradition as the quintessence of traditional collective performative practices has become one of the most relevant endogenous, not exogenous (from outside), strategically created nation brands, which despite the recommendations of branding experts serves as a symbol uniting the Baltic region.

The SDC is a performance of traditional collective culture, the greatest celebration of communicating ethnicity/nationality rooted in the traditions of the three Baltic countries (Kuutma 1998). As this celebration has regularity, stability of the form, clearly predictable diachronic structure, rich symbolism and emotionality, it recalls and consolidates in the social memory the narrative about the late nineteenth-century cultural movement, which grew into a sociopolitical force and crystallised the will, ability and power of the Baltic peoples to become independent nations. The symbolic meaning of the SDC is so great that it is sacralised and likened to a ritual at various levels of communication not only in daily publications but also in academic discourse (Brüggemann and Kasekamp 2014: 259–276; Lauristin and Vihalemm 2013: 46; Veidemann 2015: 49; Rubavičius 2015: 16–29; Repšienė 2015; Bula 2000: 95; etc.).

## 3.6 Current branding practices of the Baltic countries and the SDC

The sacralising attitude of the public and academic discourse consolidates the positions of the SDC as a nation brand. At the same time, observations of strategic branding lead to the conclusion that the dominant trend in this sphere still marginalises the symbol of the singing nations. Thus Estonia continues to develop its brand highlighting the kinship of its environment and temperament with the Nordic countries, especially Finland (Jordan 2015: 228). The Lithuanian nation brand is still based on the events, images and figures from medieval history (Eidintas and et al. 2013), and Latvia brands its nation using other aspects of its rich cultural heritage, its unique art and language followed by the concepts of a 'green' country, innovative technology and the regional visibility of Riga (Latvijas Institūts 2018).

Nevertheless, the SDC tradition maintaining the images of 'the singing nations' still exerts a very strong influence on the discourse of national culture and identity in the Baltic countries, which makes it possible to describe this tradition as a sustainable endogenous brand. The sustainability of this tradition and the complex artefact in the cultural environment depends on several factors, such as:

- the involvement of the state and public sectors through legislation and financing,
- culture infrastructure,
- system of cultural education,
- models for transmitting the tradition in families,
- interaction between amateur arts and professional arts within the framework of the tradition,
- principles of drawing up artistic programmes etc.

However, the three most relevant aspects in the context of nation-branding are participation of the population, local belonging/identity and emotions.

In order to do a comparative analysis of the relevance of the three abovementioned factors in the development of the Estonian, Latvian and Lithuanian endogenous brands, a cross-sectional research strategy was used to obtain representative quantitative data about the participatory experience, attitude and opinions on issues related to the SDC of the residents of the Baltics. The methodology and instruments of the research were developed by the staff of the Research Centre of the Latvian Academy of Culture within the framework of the project CoHERE of the programme Horizon 2020 financed by the European Commission. The fieldwork of the survey was carried out simultaneously in all three Baltic countries in August 2017 (the fieldwork was carried out by the research, information and consulting agency Kantar TNS Latvia). The target group of the survey were the residents of Latvia, Lithuania and Estonia in the fifteen to seventy-four year age bracket. Considering the ethnic composition of the populations of the Baltic countries, the method for obtaining data was a specialised survey using as an instrument a questionnaire in Estonian, Latvian, Lithuanian and also in Russian. The population of the survey was: in Latvia, 1,611,326; in Lithuania, 2,150,968; and in Estonia, 980,821 residents. For the purpose of the survey, socio-demographic parameters of the target group, such as gender, nationality, age and region, were monitored. The sample size was 3,030 (1,010 in each country). The data obtained can be generally referred to all the residents of the Baltic countries; their interpretation is based on the obtained qualitative data, analysis of political documents and other sources.

## 3.7 Participation of the population

One of the most essential indicators of the Baltic SDC as an endogenous brand is the high degree of participation of the population both in the events of the Celebration week and the SDC movement in the interim period. The extensive participation largely depends on the fact that in practice there exist different forms of participation in the nurturing of the tradition. The research identified three levels of participation: active participation, passive direct participation and passive indirect participation. In measuring active participation several indicators were used:

1) being a participant of the SDC (members of choirs or folk dance groups, conductors, dance group leaders etc);
2) working as a paid professional with the arts groups participating in the SDC (répétiteurs, accompanists etc);
3) organising the celebration (also as a volunteer or an assistant/ a coordinator appointed by the organisers);
4) supporting the celebration (rendering financial support/providing accommodations/sewing the costumes, etc.);
5) informing about the celebration (journalist, researcher etc); and
6) rendering services during the celebration (catering, trading, providing technical support etc).

Passive participation was measured using the following parameters (see Table 3.1):

1) went to some events of the celebration;
2) went to see the procession of the participants;
3) followed the events of the SDC week through the mass media;
4) followed the events through the social networks; and
5) watched the events of the SDC on TV and/or listened to the radio broadcasts.

Passive forms of participation require less time and fewer financial resources, consequently a higher percentage of the population has the opportunity to be involved. At the same time, the great number of passive participants in the tradition attests to the size of the community supporting transmission of the celebration and makes it possible to discuss the wish of this group of the population for emotional involvement and solidarity with the active participants and the support for the values and symbols of cultural heritage manifested during the celebrations. The passive forms of participation are of considerable social significance because they demonstrate that the tradition creates the frame for multiform expressions of cultural participation and not only this. The segment of passive participants may introduce new interpretations of the symbolic meanings of the elements of the tradition, encouraging dynamic transformations of the tradition corresponding to the modern cultural, social, economic and technological context and contributing to the development and interpretation of the SDC tradition as a part of the ICH. If we compare the dispersion of various forms of participation in the Baltic countries (see Table 3.1), the data indicate different strategies of participation and tradition transmission, which largely determines the different practices of the natural constitution of the tradition as a brand.

*Table 3.1* Participation level of the residents of the Baltic countries in the Song and Dance Celebrations (Survey 2017)

| Participation Level in the Song and Dance Celebrations | | | | |
|---|---|---|---|---|
| LATVIA | Non-participants | **13%** | | |
| | Participants | **87%** | Passive indirect participation | 74% |
| | | | Passive direct participation | 45% |
| | | | Active participation | 38% |
| ESTONIA | Non-participants | **5%** | | |
| | Participants | **95%** | Passive indirect participation | 82% |
| | | | Passive direct participation | 65% |
| | | | Active participation | 37% |
| LITHUANIA | Non-participants | **16%** | | |
| | Participants | **84%** | Passive indirect participation | 63% |
| | | | Passive direct participation | 51% |
| | | | Active participation | 31% |

The analysis of the forms of participation of the residents of Estonia, Latvia and Lithuania in the Song and Dance Celebrations indicates different branding strategies in relation to this element of intangible cultural heritage both within one country and across the countries. In the case of Estonia the tradition represents a distinctive national symbol, which is evident from the support of Estonian society rooted in democratic participation. The residents of Estonia 'position' the SDC tradition as a national and ethnic brand, which is expressed in the emotionally heightened attitude to this phenomenon and the experience of ethnic unity created by this celebration.

Furthermore, in the context of the celebration associations with ethnic belonging dominate over associations with belonging to a nation or a state. In Latvia the artistic quality and management of the celebration are guaranteed by the financial and administrative support of the state and local authorities indicating that the SDC is strategically and purposefully used as a nation brand. State intervention in the brand maintenance is supported by a large sector of society (almost 45%) that at some point in their lives has practised one of the forms of active participation, and there is also a considerable community of passive participants. In Lithuania, the SDC is rather perceived as the brand of the community of the tradition bearers (members of the arts groups, artistic directors and chief conductors). The data cast doubt on the assumption that the residents of Lithuania predominantly perceive the SDC tradition as a symbol of national or ethnic belonging and a nation brand. It implies that in Lithuania participation in the SDCs associates rather with the opportunity to increase one's social capital than to strengthen one's sense of identity and national belonging, which lessens the effectiveness of the celebration as an endogenous nation brand.

## 3.8 Branding local belonging/identity through the SDC

The SDC is a part of the cultural process in the Baltic countries allowing the constitution of various levels of identity and belonging such as the local place of residence, the country and the European Union. According to the data, there exists a certain correlation between the forms of participation in the SDCs and the assessment of the sense of belonging to the place of residence, region, country and the European Union. Those residents of the Baltic countries who are not involved in the SDCs have a weaker sense of belonging to the place, region, country, the Baltics and Europe (Survey 2017: 43–44). The data indicate that the SDC as a cultural practice on the national scale is closely related to branding local identities on a higher (national) level, which makes it possible 'to show your district through song and dance' (Jaunzems 2018). The representation of the residents of the country and town territories in the celebrations has left an impact on the symbolism of the celebration and the development of the tradition. According to sociologist Tālis Tisenkopfs, '[a]lthough the Song Celebrations take place in a city, they are not a city celebration. They are a celebration in a city made special by the singers and dancers from the regions' (Tisenkopfs 2002: 78). According to the survey of the participants of the SDC in 2013, 40% of the active participants came from the countryside, 30% from towns and cities and 17% from the capital Riga (Laķe 2014). The data of the 2017 survey also attest that regional representation is prominent in all three Baltic countries. In Latvia, rural residents constitute 36% of the active participants of the SDC, while urban residents and the residents of Riga constitute 34% and 30% of the active participants, respectively. Similarly, in Estonia the rural segment also constitutes 36% of the respondents actively involved in the celebration, with the urban residents and the residents of Tallinn constituting 29% and 34% of the active participants, respectively. In Lithuania, rural respondents represent 36% of the actively involved respondents, while urban locations and Vilnius account for 29% and 18% of the actively involved respondents, respectively.

One of the most powerful manifestations of local identity during the SDCs is the procession of the participants; one of its major goals is to represent various municipalities as it embraces practically all the regions and districts, demonstrates the banners of arts groups, regional folk costumes and other symbols typical of the local communities of ICH. The procession is broadcast on television and social networks; there are interviews with the participants, comments on the individual traits of each district etc. According to the survey, the procession is listed among the most important events. For example, 51% of the residents of Estonia, 62% of the residents of Lithuania and 34% of the residents of Latvia have at some point in their lives attended the procession of the celebration (Survey 2017: 18). We can conclude that the SDC is a sustainable and useful platform for manifesting the specific traits of various territorial cultures and exchanging local values. The participation of amateur arts groups from various districts augments and enriches the symbolism of the celebration strengthening its position of an endogenous nation brand.

### 3.9 Emotional aspects of the Song and Dance Celebration

As it was mentioned before, the most significant events of Baltic cultural history, including the so-called periods of national awakening, are closely related to collective singing. It has accompanied the social restructuration processes inspired by social conflict. Collective singing as aesthetical, performative practice permits to effectively initiate, accumulate and translate both symbolic meanings, both strong emotions, characteristic for the situation of unclear social identity (Turner 1991). Similarly, Tisenkopfs also considers the possibility to treat the Song and Dance Celebration as a transition from one cultural situation to another, from one symbolic extreme to another: individual–society, past–future, life–death. They are saturated with a special emotionality and cancellation of usual social norms (Tisenkopfs 1987: 21).

The emotions experienced during the SDCs enhance the sustainability and vitality of the celebration as an endogenous nation brand. 'Feeling moved', 'elated' and 'inspired' are keywords used to characterise the SDC phenomenon (Survey 2017: 35). The results of the survey demonstrate that participation in the SDCs is explained by the argument that it creates strong feelings not to be experienced anywhere else. Some 40% of the residents of Latvia and 61% of the residents of Estonia agree with this statement. In Lithuania, 22% of the residents consider the emotional aspect the main benefit of participating in the SDCs.

It is important to view the emotional aspect of SDC in the context of regularity and tradition. The data show that for the most part adults participate in the tradition of celebration because they have been involved in it already in their childhood or school years and have a positive experience, often connected to bright, inimitable emotions, which humans wish to experience again. This is a motivation to participate in the celebration also in later periods of life. The biggest part of the population have been involved in different informal, out-of-school activities (for example, in singing, dancing, instrumental music-making etc) already during the school years, as they have a need to express themselves creatively. In the case of Baltic countries, these processes are stimulated by a special school youth song and dance celebration, which is organised on a regular basis. The survey of school students carried out within the framework of the project CoHERE also attests that 74% of the respondents consider emotions the main benefit of participation in the SDCs (Survey 2018).

The strong emotions experienced through participation in the SDCs are probably related not only to patriotism and aesthetic experience but also to the large scale of the events in combination with the synchronicity instantly recognised and accepted by the community of the participants of the SDC (Turner 1982: 48; Lewis 2008: 41) manifesting itself in various activities: communal singing, dance patterns, the procession etc, which strengthens the solidarity of the community of participants and offers an answer to the question significant to the whole nation 'who we are?' using a cultural performance as a meaningful system of symbols, which gives value and significance to the existence of nations and states (Gīrcs 1998: 238). The range of unique emotions experienced and demonstrated during the SDCs is both a powerful motivation for participation in the celebration and an instrument for communication of the acquired artistic experience. Thus emotions become an essential element in maintaining the SDC as an endogenous nation brand.

## 3.10 Conclusion

The Baltic countries currently have different practices of strategic brand management; at the same time, many common parameters presuppose the development of the SDC as an endogenous brand indicating, for example, the performative expressions of tradition, or the celebration as a platform for the interaction between local and national identities. Of special significance for the development of the SDC as an endogenous nation brand are the high degree of involvement among the population and the genesis of various forms of participation, the dynamics of constituting local identity and the presence of strong emotions in the manifestations of the tradition. However, there are also several factors, such as the uneven structure of participation in the celebration in Estonia, Latvia and especially Lithuania, and differences in the intensity of emotional involvement among the residents of the Baltic countries. It should be also noted that the scenarios of the development of the SDC tradition, and the image of 'the singing nation' as endogenous brand, have the potential to make a significant impact on strategic brand management practices. The strong emotional attachment of the active heritage community encourages the transference of this tradition as an endogenous brand to the strategic brand management practices.

Although the SDC and the brand of 'the singing nation' may be oriented towards the past and 'peasant-like', they are imbued not only with strong symbolic and emotional significance but also with political, social and economic contents. There are several indications that, despite the variety of expressions and attitudes, these endogenous brands will continue to exist and unite the Baltic region in the future, resisting the pressures of globalisation, technological development and contrary recommendations of branding experts. Returning to the concept of the crowd symbol, it may be added that a nation's consciousness of itself is characterised by persistence and stability and changes only along with its symbols, which 'are not as changeable as it may seem' (Canetti 1978: 171).

The study of the experience of the inhabitants of the Baltic states shows the importance of mass participation and emotional uplifting in maintaining sustainability and vitality of the endogenous and exogenous national brand associated with ICH and performative practices. While our analysis of participatory and emotional aspects in maintaining ICH practice was established by quantitative and qualitative data collected on the Baltic SDC, more generalised conclusions need further comparative research rooted in different cultural environments (both in Europe and other regions of the world), considering diverse performative practices and nation branding experiences and focussing on sources of participation and emotions and their importance in preserving cultural heritage and maintaining traditional performative practices. Interesting case studies in this regard include the Mòd tradition in Scotland or the Eisteddfod in Wales, both high-profile festivals linking ICH with nation-branding efforts. Comparative analysis of sources of participation and flow of emotions in the context of diverse cultural heritage practices could help to (1) identify effective local heritage conservation tools, (2) develop cultural 'soft power' tools for intercultural and international heritage communication and (3) clarify scenarios linking inheritance practices with endogenous and exogenous nation brands.

## Acknowledgement

This publication is a result of the European Union-funded Horizon 2020 research project: CoHERE (Critical Heritages: performing and representing identities in Europe). CoHERE received funding from the European Union's Horizon 2020 research and innovation programme under grant agreement No. 693289.

## References

Anholt, S. (2011), 'Beyond the nation brand: the role of image and identity in international relations', *Exchange: The Journal of Public Diplomacy* 2(1): 6–12.
Bērzkalns, V. (1965), *Latviešu dziesmu svētku vēsture: 1864–1940* (Bruklina: Grāmatu draugs).
Brüggemann, K., and A. Kasekamp (2014), '"Singing oneself into a nation". Estonian song festivals as rituals of political mobilisation', *Nations and Nationalism* 20(2): 259–276.
Bula, D. (2000), *Dziedātājtauta. Folklora un nacionālā ideoloģija* (Rīga: Zinātne).
Canetti, E. (1978), *Crowds and power* (New York: Seabury).
Council of Europe (2017), *Recommendation of the Committee of Ministers to member states on the European Cultural Heritage Strategy for the 21st century*. Available at: www.coe.int/en/web/culture-and-heritage/strategy-21 (accessed 15 May 2018).
Dinnie, K. (2016), *Nation branding: concepts, issues, practice*, 2nd ed. (London: Routledge).
Dubber, J. (2015), 'How soft power can help meet international challenges'. Available at: www.britishcouncil.org/organisation/policy-insight-research/insight/how-soft-power-can-help-meet-international-challenges (accessed 10 September 2018).
e-Estonia (n.d.), 'We have built a digital society and so can you'. Available at: e-Estonia.com (accessed 05 May 2017).
Eidintas, A., A. Bumblauskas, A. Kulakauskas and M. Tamošaitis (2013), *The history of Lithuania* (Vilnius: Eugrimas).
European Union (2018), 'The EU motto'. Available at: https://europa.eu/european-union/about-eu/symbols/motto_en (accessed 03 December 2018).
Fan, Y. (2006), 'Branding the nation: what is being branded?', *Journal of Vacation Marketing* 12(1): 5–14.
Frasher, S., M. Hall, J. Hildreth and M. Sorgi (2003), *A brand for the nation of Latvia* (Oxford: Said Business School).
Gīrcs, K. (1998), *Kultūru interpretācija* (Rīga: AGB).
Grauzdiņa, I. (2004), *Dziesmu svētku mazā enciklopēdija* (Rīga: Musica Baltica).
Grauzdiņa, I. and A. Poruks (1990), *Dziesmu svētku garā gaita* (Rīga: E. Melngaiļa Tautas mākslas centrs).
Habermas, J. (2001), *The postnational constellation. Political essays* (Cambridge, MA: MIT Press).
Herder, J. and P. Bohlman (2017), *Song loves the masses: herder on music and nationalism* (Oakland, CA: University of California Press).
Jaunzems, U. (2018), 'Bija emocijas, nolija asaras…'. Available at: https://skaties.lv/zinas/latvija/sabiedriba/bija-emocijas-nolija-asaras-dziesmu-un-deju-svetki-caur-gulbeniesu-piedzivojumiem/ (accessed 10 July 2018).
Jordan, P. (2015), 'Walking in singing: brand Estonia, the Eurovision song contest and Estonia's self-proclaimed return to Europe, 2001–2002', in L. Clerc, N. Glover and P. Jordan (eds), *Histories of public diplomacy and nation branding in the Nordic and Baltic countries* (Leiden: Brill Nijhoff), 217–236.
Jordan, P. ed. (2014), *The modern fairy tale: nation branding, national identity and the Eurovision song contest in Estonia* (Tartu: University of Tartu Press).
Jovićević, A. (2017), 'Festivals as social dramas and metaphors: between popular and subversive', in Dragićević Šešić, M. (ed.), *Cultural diplomacy: arts, festivals and geopolitics* (Belgrad: Creative Europe Desk Serbia).
Kasekamp, A. (2010), *A history of the Baltic states* (London: Palgrave Macmillan).
Klotiņš, A. (1998), *Latviešu koru fenomens* (Rīga: Jumava).
Kuutma, K. (7 May 1998), 'Festival as communicative performance and celebration of ethnicity', *Folklore*. Available at: www.folklore.ee/folklore/vol7/festiva.htm (accessed 22 April 2017).

Lähdesmäki, T. (2016), 'Politics of tangibility, intangibility, and place in the making of a European cultural heritage in EU heritage policy', *International Journal of Heritage Studies* 22(10): 766–780.
Lajosi, K. and A. Stynen (2015), *Choral societies and nationalism in Europe* (Leiden: Brill).
Laķe, A. (2014), 'Dziesmu un deju svētku saglabāšana un attīstība 2014–2018. gads'. Available at: https://culturelablv.files.wordpress.com/2009/04/dziesmu_un_deju_svetku_saglabasana_un_attistiba_2014.pdf (accessed 15 May 2018).
Latvijas Institūts (2018), 'Zīmolvedība'. Available at: www.li.lv/lv/latvijas-instituts/zimolvediba-456 (accessed 15 May 2018).
Lauristin, M. and P.Vihalemm (2013), *Minu laulu- ja tantsupidu: Sotsioloogilise uuringu aruanne* (Tartu: Eesti Laulu- ja Tantsupeo Sihtasutus).
Lee, A., J.Yang, R. Mizerski and C. Lambert (2015), *The strategy of global branding and brand equity* (London: Routledge).
Leerssen, J. (2015), 'German Influences. Choirs, repertoires, nationalities', in K. Lajosi and A. Stynen (eds), *Choral societies and nationalism in Europe* (Leiden: Brill) 14–32.
Lewis, L. (2008), 'Toward a unified theory of cultural performance', in G. St. John (ed), *Victor Turner and contemporary cultural performance* (New York: Berghahn), 41–58.
Lietuvos prekės ženklas (n.d.), 'Logotipo naudojimo aprašas'. Available at: http://beta.tourism.dev12.kryptis.lt/uploads/documents/LT-prekes-zenklas/LT-naudojimo-aprasas.pdf (accessed 20 April 2017).
Mändmets, L. (2010), 'The story of creating Brand Estonia. Estonian Ministry of Foreign Affairs Yearbook'. Available at: http://vm.ee/sites/default/files/content-editors/Leitti_Mandmets_0.pdf (accessed 15 May 2018).
Mazzucato, M. (2018), *The value of everything. Making and taking in the global economy* (Harmondsworth: Penguin).
Muktupāvels, V. (2012),'Vai tā pati dziedātājtauta? No "Dziesmu rotas" līdz "Latvieša dziesmu kladei"', in J. Kursīte (ed), *Inkluzīvi* (Rīga: LU Akadēmiskais apgāds), 308–321.
Nic Craith, M. (2008),'Intangible cultural heritages: The challenge for Europe', *Anthropological Journal of European Cultures* 17(1): 54–73.
Nye, J. (2004), *Soft power: the means to success in world politics* (New York: Public Affairs).
Puidokas, M. and J. Kinzytė (2014), 'Šiuolaikinių mažųjų valstybių įvaizdžio formavimas taikant viešosios diplomatijos principus ir plėtojant nacionalinį prekės ženklą. Lietuvos atvejo analizė', *Viešoji politika ir administravimas* 13(1): 50–64.
Repšienė, R. (2015), 'Apie kultūros vertybes, prioritetus ir naujus iššūkius: Dainų šventė', in: R. Repšienė (ed.), *Dainų šventė. Tapatybės savastis ir modernybės trajektorijos* (Vilnius: Lietuvos kultūros tyrimų institutas), 54–74.
Rubavičius, V. (2015), 'Dainų šventė – lietuvybei tvirtinti ir palaikyti', in R. Repšienė (ed.), *Dainų šventė. Tapatybės savastis ir modernybės trajektorijos* (Vilnius: Lietuvos kultūros tyrimų institutas), 16–29.
Saffron Brand Consultants (2009), *Selling Lithuania smartly. A guide to the creative-strategic development of an economic image for the country*. Available at: http://static1.1.sqspcdn.com/static/f/274066/2783606/1238531821587/Lithuania_AW_Spreads.pdf?token=18ZCGiLZkecLkuqhUzwXFWiTUGo%3D (accessed 06 April 2017).
Schreiber, H. (2017),'Intangible cultural heritage and soft power – exploring the relationship', *International Journal of Intangible Heritage* 12: 44–57.
Šmidchens, G. (2014), *The power of song. Nonviolent national culture in the Baltic Singing Revolution* (Seattle: University of Washington Press).
Survey (2018), *Leisure time, extracurricular activities and cultural heritage of young people* (Rīga: Research Centre of the Latvian Academy of Culture).

Survey (2017), *Survey of the residents of the Baltic countries on the SDCs 2017*. Available at: https://static.lka.edu.lv/media/cms_page_media/2018/6/28/Iedzivotaju_aptauja_Dziesmu_svetki_2017%20(1).pdf (accessed 15 May 2018).
Tisenkopfs, T. (2002), *Dziesmu svētki mainīgā sociālā vidē. Valsts pārvaldes institūcijas pasūtītais pētījums* (Rīga: Baltijas studiju centrs).
Tisenkopfs,T. (1987), *Mākslas svētki un estētiskā audzināšana: (metodiska izstrādne)* (Rīga: Latvijas PSR Zinību biedrība).
Turner, V. (1991), *The ritual process. Structure and anti-structure* (New York: Cornell University Press).
Turner, V. (1982), *From ritual to theatre: the human seriousness of play* (New York: PAJ).
UNESCO (2018), 'What is intangible cultural heritage?'. Available at: https://ich.unesco.org/en/what-is-intangible-heritage-00003 (accessed 15 May 2018).
UNESCO (2003), 'Tradition and symbolism of the Song and Dance Celebration process in Estonia, Latvia and Lithuania'. Available at: www.unesco.lv/files/Tradition_and_Symbolism_of_the_Song_and_Dance_Celebration_Process_in_Estonia_Latvia_and_Lithuania_e9aa0010.pdf (accessed 15 April 2017).
UNESCO Latvijas Nacionālā komisija (n.d.), 'Dziesmu un deju svētku tradīcija'. Available at: www.unesco.lv/lv/kultura/nematerialais-kulturas-mantojums-6/dziesmu-un-deju-svetku-tradicija-2/dziesmu-un-deju-svetku-tradicija-1/, (accessed 1 October 2018).
Valstybinis turizmo departamentas (2016), 'Lietuvos pažadas turistams: gražu tai, kas tikra'. Available at: www.tourism.lt/lt/naujienos/lietuvos-pazadas-turistams-grazu-tai-kas-tikra (accessed 20 April 2017).
Veidemann, R. (2015), 'Estijos Dainų šventė semiotiniu požiūriu', in R. Repšienė (ed), *Dainų šventė. Tapatybės savastis ir modernybės trajektorijos* (Vilnius: Lietuvos kultūros tyrimų institutas), 38–53.
Whitehead, C., U. Kockel and M. Nic Craith (2018), Reflexive introduction to *Rivers of our Being*. Folk oratorio composed by Valdis Muktupāvels as part of the Horizon 2020 project *CoHERE*, performed 30 November 2018, Scottish Storytelling Centre, Edinburgh.
Your Friend in Riga (2010), 'The land that sings = Best enjoyed slowly'. Available at: http://friendinriga.blogspot.com/2010/12/land-that-sings-best-enjoyed-slowly.html (accessed 15 May 2018).
Zubrickas, B. (1999), *Pasaulio lietuvių chorvedžiai: enciklopedinis žinynas* (Vilnius: Lietuvos liaudies kultūros centras).

# 4 The construction of belonging and Otherness in heritage events

*Cristina Clopot and Catherine McCullagh*

An increased awareness of tourism benefits for developing localities across Europe (Kozorog 2011) has been correlated with an increase in the allure of heritage festivals (Testa 2017) and the 'the proliferation of smaller-scale and specialised festivals in different national and local settings' (Sassatelli 2008: 7). Apart from local economic development (Graburn 2015), it is now readily accepted that festivals facilitate identity-building (Frost 2016) and can foster cohesion (Kuutma 1998). For migrants, representatives of minority groups and those inhabiting fragile environments, the sustainability of such events, interpreted here as intangible cultural heritage (ICH) practices (see *inter alia* UNESCO 2003; Bortolotto 2007; Taylor 2016), is vital for transmitting such practices and for sustaining feelings of belonging (Cornish 2016). Critically, festival performativity can also embody processes of 'Othering', suggesting the mobilisation of Authorised Heritage Discourse (AHD) (Smith 2006) and inviting engagement with their potential for maintaining alterities. It can also inhibit more holistic expressions of ICH and hinder the sustainable development of interactivity between people and places (see Council of Europe 2005).

Through analysing two seemingly unrelated festival settings, we exemplify some common themes and challenges faced by communities, groups and individuals across heterogenous European settings, including the various effects of migration. Our case studies include festivals from Scotland and Romania and their processes of inclusion and exclusion. We conclude our analysis with considerations on the differential implications of safeguarding and/or of rights-based approaches to the heritages expressed in each of the festivals analysed.

## 4.1 Belonging, 'Otherness' and liminality

This chapter builds on concepts of identity-work that reflect a binary process (Kockel 2007) of expressing self-identification, and thus belonging, while simultaneously drawing borders (Barth 1969) from 'Others'. Here, states of 'Otherness' are understood as manifesting phenomenological, intersubjective processes through which people construct identities of 'selves' and 'aliens' (see Husserl 1960). The processes of constructing 'belonging' and 'Othering' are conceptualised as co-constitutive community processes, whereby individuals ascribe objectivity to their subjective experiences when associating with others (Husserl 1960). Ascriptions of 'belonging' or being 'Other' can be changed through direct experience and are malleable to performativity during festivals. Acknowledging that such identity-making is active and ongoing, the ideas that guide our reflections here are progressed through the well-established recognition that heritage is political and that it is a form of 'social action' (Byrne 2008), which enables people to build and assert place-based identities.

Harrison (2013: 245) has noted that ICH practices, including festivals, are activities during which people engage with 'producing culture' and, on occasion, transforming their localities. This can support 'place-belongingness' – an 'intimate feeling of being 'at home' in a place' which is 'also unavoidably conditioned by the working of power relations (politics of belonging)' (Antonsich 2010: 652–653). Festival performances, the work of the politics of belonging (Yuval-Davis 2006), can both cement or rebuff adherence to a group. Understanding the festival as a liminal period (Matheson and Tinsley 2014), following Turner (1969: 96), and its performances as interruptions of regular social life, moments 'in and out of time', offers a useful frame for exploring such complexities. In Turner's[1] triadic understanding of the rites of passage, the liminal phase, the threshold between two conditions of stasis, induces transformation. In his model, 'initiands' forge bonds of extraordinary belonging, 'communitas', through sharing participation in the ritual. Understanding the festival's rites as expressions of communitas helps us consider the discourses and experiences that generate feelings of belonging and to assess the normative inclusion and exclusion of certain participants.

Festivals and heritage practices can be identified as expressions of AHD (Smith 2006), becoming the target of heritage policies at a national and transnational level (Noyes 2015). Of particular interest for us here is the interplay of official authentifications with performances of apparently unofficial, localised practices, forms of 'heritage from below' (Robertson 2012).

The analysis presented here draws on each author's own fieldwork. Cristina Clopot undertook participant observation and ethnographic interviews and used archives to evaluate ethnic heritage-making practices in Romania's *Proetnica* festival. Catherine McCullagh mobilised participant observation and interviews alongside visual ethnography to consider identity-building through Shetland's *Up-Helly-Aa* festivals in Scotland's Northern Isles. Bringing together two distinct settings, from different corners of Europe, has afforded useful, mutually informative comparisons and contrasts for our inquiries into the politics of festival performances. We are inspired by Byrne's (2008: 163) arguments that 'it is critical for any assessment of the social significance of heritage places and landscapes that inter-generational transmission and change be treated seriously' and that communities be given the space and power to do their own heritage work. Given this framing of the significance of festivals as heritage-making, identity-building actions, we present these case studies as examples

*Figure 4.1* Proetnica Festival in Sighişoara, Romania (Photo: Cristina Clopot, 2018)

of the various ways in which festivals can appear to mobilise 'heritage from below' (Robertson 2012) to facilitate feelings of belonging and experiences of communitas (Turner 1969) across diverse spaces.

## 4.2 *Proetnica* Festival in Romania

Situated in the heart of the most eastern and relatively recent member of the European Union, Romania, the *Proetnica* Festival has been taking place for fifteen years (see Figure 4.1). Each summer, during a week in August, representatives of ethnic groups in Romania travel to Sighisoara during peak tourist season. In this walled UNESCO World Heritage citadel, over 600 members of officially recognised minorities gathered to celebrate multiculturalism and create opportunities for intercultural dialogue. The festivities include a mixture of performances of ethnic heritage and identity, presentation booths and displays. ICH is on display through dances and songs performed by amateur groups. A parallel scientific stream was organised with talks and debates on issues of interest as well as an intercultural academy for young people.

The festival is organised by a German ethnic NGO and began as an initiative of the German Forum in Romania aiming to bring together all the ethnic groups that enjoy official protection under Romania's legislation. The festival is held with the support of the government and its dedicated Department for Intercultural Relations.

Sighisoara sits centrally in Transylvania, an area which has become a major tourist attraction in recent years. For one week though, the attention of locals and tourists alike is diverted to ethnic heritages, whereby 'heritage from below' (Robertson 2012) foregrounds otherwise invisible narratives (Harrison 2013). Speaking at the opening ceremony, a representative of the Culture Ministry said:

> *Proetnica* Festival has become a valuable tradition in the Romanian cultural landscape, as the most important cultural event of all ethnic minorities from our country, a real celebration promoting intercultural dialogue, diversity of culture, art and spiritual life.
>
> [Redactia 2018]

In 2018, as national debates and events focussed on the 100th anniversary of the creation of Romania, the core theme of the discussions revolved around the contribution of minorities to this national heritage. Claiming their place in heritage narratives of the past (Whitehead and Bozoğlu 2017), representatives of the national minorities have been engaged in heritage-making, as characterised by Byrne (2008: 165), that is 'the self-conscious, reflexive business of producing their heritage'. The difficulties in accommodating ethnic/minority heritage in national narratives have been discussed within and beyond heritage studies (see, for instance, Harrison 2013; Hall 1999). Given the range of complexities identified, it is unsurprising that ethnic minorities feel their voices are not represented in national celebratory events. Onstage, at *Proetnica*, it was emphasised repeatedly that promoting minorities' heritage is promoting Romania. Offstage, in the scientific programme, discussions revolved around ethnic minorities' contribution to Romanian history and the development of the state and other themes.

### 4.3 Shetland's *Up-Helly-Aa* Festivals

At 60 degrees north, Shetland is the British Isles' northernmost archipelago. Lying equidistant between mainland Scotland and Norway, it bears the cultural legacies both of having been under the jurisdiction of the latter until the late fifteenth century and of being positioned as periphery of the former since then. Relatively economically buoyant since the 1970s, due to revenues generated through its use as a North Sea oil terminal, the vulnerability of Shetland's open economy is re-emerging. A downturn in fossil fuel prices, governmental austerity and the uncertainties of Brexit have promoted fiscal concerns leading to intensifying interest in tourism development, including the active promotion of Shetland as a year-round holiday destination, despite the inclemency of its North Atlantic climate in any period from November to March.

Each year, between January and March, people across Shetland observe a series of twelve fire festivals called *Up-Helly-Aa*s. The origins of these unique celebrations, and of their naming, have been debated for many years. Varied accounts, including folklore suggesting that they date back to Shetland's past as a dominion of Norway (Brown 1998), are now set aside in favour of

*Construction of belonging and Otherness* 51

*Figure 4.2* Lighting up ceremony, Lerwick *Up-Helly-Aa* (Photo: Catherine McCullagh, 2018)

local scholarship tracing *Up-Helly-Aa*'s customs to the 'spontaneous popular creation[s]' (Smith 1993: 24) of radical movements formed by Shetlanders during the late nineteenth century (Brown 1998; Smith 1993).

Every *Up-Helly-Aa*'s 'front-stage' performances (Goffman [1969] 1990) are impressive. They include carnivalesque suspension of quotidien activities, making way for parades of 'misrule'. Public spaces are given over to representatives of the common populace: the *Jarl's* or 'Earl's' Squad, who, dressed as Vikings, are first among equals, leaders of numerous other troupes, comprising up to thirty costumed participants, or 'guizers'. At every *Up-Helly-Aa*, these squads process with flaming torches (see Figure 4.2), marching to hand-built wooden galleys, which they ignite – an astonishing finale to each festival's public spectacle.

*Up-Helly-Aa*'s sensory immersions are captivating: exposure to extreme cold; disorientation in crowded, darkened streets; and the embodied enchantment of the 'collective' as the processions accelerate through their repertoires. Almost all of the islanders who contributed to this research shared how their sensations of *Up-Helly-Aa* manifests their ideas of 'place, history, tradition and belonging' (Whitehead and Bozoğlu 2017: 1), strengthening their connection to Shetland: 'It's a real moment of pride in being a Shetlander'.

This is apparently active identity-building. It is heritage-making as defined in the Council of Europe's Faro Convention, affording expressions of 'values, beliefs, knowledge and traditions'; reflecting synergy between people and place, through time (Council of Europe 2005: Art. 2a). It emphasises ICH and ordinary people as its identifiers and transmitters (Nic Craith 2008). As one

Shetlander, and *guizing* squad member, put it: 'You could say [it's] a bit like democracy: for the people and by the people'.

This positioning of *Up-Helly-Aa*s, as 'heritage from below' (Robertson 2012), contrasts it with a darker aspect of the archipelago's heritage, a history of elites who instrumentalised the islands' *folk*, the Shetland dialect term for 'people', as non-free labour in the industrialisation of the North Atlantic fisheries (Fenton 1997). Ethnologist Ullrich Kockel (2008) proposes that this peripheralisation of 'folk' is a recurrent theme in European cultural history, reaching a hegemonic zenith when displays of the folk in such spaces replace the dynamic specificity of ordinary people in places and times. *Up-Helly-Aa*s appear to revoke such displacement. The festivities, presented locally as sustaining traditions of local radicalism (Brown 1998), are invoked as 're-investitures' of people and place – of Shetlander's own Selves: 'it's no$^2$ about you, it's about wiz [us]!'

## 4.4 Belonging – *Proetnica*

The *Proetnica* estival's core is centred around staged performances, which generate a sense of belonging as discussed further. Groups of men, women and children rotate in a dizzying spectacle of diversity in the citadel's main square for days in a row. Dressed in traditional costumes, people, to quote Barbara Kirshenblatt-Gimblett (1998: 377), 'become living signs of themselves'.

Groups representing each minority present themselves on stage articulating their identities through the performances. Materiality (Clopot 2016) plays a key role in this, with each group donning their ethnic costumes. The communicative event included either a dance or a song performed in a traditional manner by an amateur group. A standardised pattern was used with the dancers afforded twenty minutes for stage performances followed by one or two dances in front of the stage with festival participants. The performances, as one of the speakers at the opening ceremony observed, aimed to reflect the 'spirit of a shared European cultural diversity'. References to the desired commonality, to creating shared experiences through performances, were a repeated slogan throughout each day. As one speaker mentioned, the spirit of friendly competition, enacted through putting forward the best performance, 'maintains the vitality of each ethnic group'. Heritage practices, instrumentalised and objectified as each ethnic group's 'best assets', were meant not only to reflect the group's celebrations of ICH but also generate 'tolerance for the identities of the other', as another speaker put it.

A conscious effort was made to involve locals and tourists in these performances. This was done, as the organisers mentioned, in order to share experiences and encourage intercultural interaction. Moreover, organisers noted that they had purposefully asked that guards stand behind the stage so that the performance area was a space of interaction rather than a separate space.

Exposure to extreme difference can result in downplaying variances between ethnic groups, a sign of what Kirshenblatt-Gimblett (1998: 77) calls the 'banality of difference'. There was certainly a sense of this when one of the Jewish speakers in a debate organised for the festival's scientific section mentioned the performances from the previous day. He recalled only two of the ethnic groups and continued by referring to the others as 'whoever else there was there also'. The fast rotation of groups (20 minutes per performance and at least ten groups per day) and their poor introduction – only by ethnicity, name and locality – did not help the case.

The act of celebrating ICH through performance brought a sense of communitas (Turner 1969) for participants who emphasised their histories of attending the festival and connections made throughout the years: 'A real synergy is created around the stage', explained one organiser. Groups, sharing space in the same hostel, dance and sing together personifying interculturalism. Another organiser, though, asked about the opportunities and willingness of the groups for interaction with each other, mentioned a past attempt to organise an ethnic minorities ball during the festival only to have no one show up. At first sight, the offstage effects of communitas (Turner 1969) were difficult to observe. However, as the festival advanced, and audiences multiplied, there was increased inter-mixing between groups, particularly during the participative section of performance. Towards the end, the groups that joined the shared dancing sessions became so large that several circles of dancers were formed, and the dedicated space in front of the stage was overcrowded. At those points, the mechanism of communicating ICH through performance and the embodied act of 'practicing culture' (Colomer 2018: 210) seemed to enhance the sense of belonging to a community of equals.

## 4.5 'Othering' selves – proscribing belonging at *Up-Helly-Aa*s

In January 2018, in Lerwick, Shetland's capital, home to around one-third of the archipelago's population of 23,000, 5,000 onlookers watched as 1,000 costumed men performed the festival's public spectacle. People cheered and then gasped as the guizers flung flaming torches into the dragon-headed galley. Walking through the dispersing crowds, a new campaign, promoting *Up-Helly-Aa* season to prospective tourists (Promote Shetland 2018) formed the topic of discussion with Catherine's companions. They considered the outsider's gaze (see Urry 2002) looking to Lerwick, the largest, most famous *Up-Helly-Aa*, and the only one that prevents women from joining the guizer squads.

In later conversations, participants in the research shared knowledge and experiences of ten of the remaining eleven *Up-Helly-Aa*s, sharing that these also place constraints on women's public participation, prohibiting post-pubescent women from their joining *Jarl's* Squads. This variability of practices was articulated in nuanced terms, suggesting layered negotiations and expressing varying degrees of comfort along the festivals' exclusion/inclusion axes.

Contemporary feminist historians Lynn Abrams and Elizabeth Ewan (2018: 2) portray Scotland's past as a landscape populated with the normative ever-presence of men – their activities unscrutinised regarding their suitability to meet gendered 'expectations'. These commentators propose that such 'hegemonic masculinity' succeeds because of its mutability. It is contestable but also vigorously variable and, thus, independent of its 'assumed opposite': 'femininity' (Abrams and Ewan 2018: 2). In 2018, at Lerwick, the most evident 'folk' were certainly men, emplaced centre-stage. Their march traversed every route connecting the civic, ecclesiastical and commercial nodes of the town. Their guizing under fluid masculinities, represented as superheroes, rock stars and astronauts, was performed through costumes, including animal heads, false breasts and blackened faces. Read non-critically, these transformative enactments invoke *Up-Helly-Aa*s as the ultimate-North *Mardi Gras*; it's *Jarl*'s Squad 'Lords of Misrule', reversing the status quo and implementing a people's coup (see Brown 1998). But not everyone feels represented in this folk rule performance.

South Mainland[3] *Up-Helly-Aa* Committee's decision to elect a woman as *Jarl* in 2015 has intensified what one informant described as Shetland's 'big chat about equality'. Local print and social media platforms increase the visibility and pace of this discourse. One interviewee's comment, exemplifies observable perspectives that position *Up-Helly-Aa* performances as processes of making 'Others' from fellow selves: 'It all just seems excessively masculinist to me. Although there are women involved in some of them'. Notably, none of the interviewees expressed concern about men appearing to caricature objectified femininity while proscribing women's participation. Indeed, temporary transvestism was often perceived as simple pantomime, much the same, for some observers, as the *Jarl's* Squads' Viking costumery: '[T]hey dinna often look like Vikings, not the historical image that I have'.

What was made clear by female informants was that being excluded from full participation in these performances was what really mattered. It contravened their idealisations of *Up-Helly-Aa* as identity-work that should be made by and for 'the whole community', the social work mentioned above (Byrne 2008). Some expressed that they recognised this most clearly once they had experienced being included as guizers, beyond Lerwick, in the 'country' *Up-Helly-Aa*s.[4]

### 4.6 Othering and exclusion – *Proetnica*

The *Proetnica* Festival played down gendered differences, otherwise not uncommon in the lifeworlds of ethnic groups in Romania (Clopot and Nic Craith 2018). It reflected instead a different axis of inclusion–exclusion: that between the majority/minority population. Whereas discourses during the festival emphasised the aims to contribute to a pluralistic democratic society and send positive messages such as 'together we can' to Europe, the ability of the festival to achieve such ambitious aims was short-circuited by the social realities. A striking difference was noted by the fact that events onstage were gaining a lot of attention, with hundreds of locals and visitors watching and participating in the dances. Events offstage were poorly attended, and organisers lamented the lack of official representation, including dedicated legislative representatives or delegates representing the majority population. Whereas the onstage celebration was held in a positive key, akin to the folkloric performances of the past with an enhanced tone of festivalisation, the scientific session foregrounded Othering and intra-ethnicities friction(s).

Romania's complex ethnic landscape is a testament to the limits of accommodating multiculturalism at a national level (Hall 1999). *Proetnica* takes place in an area where ethnic tensions are fuelled by nostalgic claims (Clopot 2017) to a past when borders were traced differently. Equally, treatment of the Roma population has generated significant debates. These concerns shadowed debates during the festival, although not all were explicitly addressed. Discussions revolved around present problems faced by ethnic members in exercising their rights and transmitting ICH practices. Dialogues in the scientific session also revealed the tensions and problems that ethnic groups experience, including prejudices, stereotyping and a lack of access to rights, even when legislative measures are in place.

Tensions between different ethnic groups surfaced offstage too, notably during a Roma group recital. A group of local Roma, some under the influence of alcohol, were enjoying the music and dancing frantically in front of the stage as others looked on in both amazement and condescension. The guards kept a low profile, while other participants danced away from the Roma, marking spatially and symbolically the tensions that this ethnic group face in the country. Yet, organisers, and some of the guests in the scientific sessions, lauded the peaceful cohabitation of ethnic groups in Romania today, characteristics also noted by some researchers (see, for instance, van Assche and Teampău 2009), proposing that Romania should serve as a model for the European Union. *Proetnica*'s layers of Othering, and inclusion/exclusion were present not only along majority/minority lines but also between ethnic groups.

## 4.7 Restricting or widening belonging – 'Communitas' in *Up-Helly-Aa*s

Considering the apparent gendered dichotomisation in some *Up-Helly-Aa*s requires a following of 'plots' and 'conflicts' (after Marcus 1998) that go beyond front-stage performances of parades and media debates to the festivals' hidden rites. These take place in what Shetlanders call the 'halls': civic buildings that are given over to every *Up-Helly-Aa* for what has been termed a 'ritualised socialisation' (Brown 1998: 9) that will last throughout the night. Every hall holds an assembly of Shetland residents who have accessed entry by offering to serve refreshments. They are joined by relatives and friends from the 'South', and further abroad, and, more usual now, by tourists in groups organised through local associations. Between twenty and fifty squads will visit each hall during *Up-Helly-Aa* night. In each, every squad performs a satirical sketch or dance, often based on locally topical events. After, the guizers join their families and friends to drink and eat together in a decorated side-room. Following this they all return to the main hall and, as the band plays a traditional tune, the squad and their hosts dance together. The guizers then move to the next hall on their itinerary, and a new squad enters, beginning the process again. For the guizers interviewed, performing at the halls generated feelings of belonging with people and place.

Through applying Victor Turner's refinements of the rites of passage model (Turner 1969; 1974) to these backstage traditions, it is possible to observe three distinct rites. These are: separation from the community during months of secret preparations; liminality, during the guizers ludic performances both as subjects and provocateurs of ridicule; and, finally, reintegration, through sharing food, drink and dancing. In Turner's (1969) conceptualisation of such rites, it is those who share the liminal stages, adopting a collective status as ritualised 'fools', who access the ritual's most potent outcome: the development of communitas, bonding them as peers in mutual solidarity. Using such analysis lends thickness to descriptions of much of the *Up-Helly-Aas'* powerplay, used to maintain wider societal alterity. For example, while all informants agreed that both hosts and guizers participate in *Up-Helly-Aa* night, most of the women interviewed also shared their frustration at the restrictions placed around how they participate, intensified when they alone served the refreshments, while men shared the bonds of guizing.

'It's tradition, it's in our blood', explained one younger member of Lerwick's *Jarl's* Squad. Historically, the culturally specific gendered divisions of men working at sea and women labouring onshore that predominated in Northern Europe's commercial fishing economies (Byron 1994) also defined lifeways in Shetland. Since the late twentieth century, these traditions of the 'joint maritime household' have altered in response to socioeconomic changes (Byron 1994). Similarly, extrinsic forces have also affected *Up-Helly-Aa*s. For example, in the 1970s, following an influx of people coming to develop the archipelago's oil pipeline terminal, some Shetlanders feared that their culture would demise. The Lerwick *Up-Helly-Aa* Committee introduced a five-year residency rule, for the first time prohibiting migrant male workers from participating in the squads (Brown 1998). In this century, the welcome of women guizers at the country *Up-Helly-Aa*s, including South Mainland's election of a female *Guizer Jarl*, demonstrates local reflexivity. Both responses evidence Shetland residents adapting to changes in context in order that *Up-Helly-Aa*'s identity-work can continue to be transmitted.

Following the festivities, discussion with companions returned to the increased promotion of *Up-Helly-Aa*s. There is concern that far from stimulating change, the wider world's gaze may contribute to maintaining stasis. The marketisation of the Lerwick's *Jarl's* Squad as ambassadors for their isles,[5] attending national and international events, commodifies their communitas and reifies their representation of masculinity as the normative form for Shetland identity: men as '*wiz*'. Might people in Shetland lose endogenous agency in adapting and changing their own identity inscription?

When responding to questions about whether Shetland residents see *Up-Helly-Aa*s reflecting the values that they are forming around their present-day identities, one person shared how they had felt empowered to bring their deliberation of such values to the community after witnessing what they perceived as ridiculing homosexuality during some *Up-Helly-Aa* performances: '[I]t was well below acceptable [...] I wrote to the committee and complained about it'. Other informants also mentioned how the enactments performed during the liminal stages of *Up-Helly-Aa*'s rituals sometimes extended beyond lampooning the public acts of authority figures. Complaints were made to the organising committees, and, as one person said, 'that being personal side of it has changed', people 'are saying "we are getting offended by this"'. Such endogenous agency is central to *Up-Helly-Aa* heritage-making. It is evident in the stories about the festivals' origins in home-grown radicalism. It is active in the adaptation of the festivals to suit changing contexts. Kockel (2008) reminds us that this being able to change from within builds capacity for sustainably and regeneratively transmitting culture. In Shetland, the archipelago's residents' practices of publicly and/or collaboratively deliberating the values that form around local identity-work can be seen in the contests around the complexities in the *Up-Helly-Aa* festival tradition.

## 4.8 Shared learnings in different contexts

The case studies discussed here reflect shared themes, albeit manifested differently. There is much to be shared across the two cases, in spite of their seeming dissimilarities. Both case studies afford opportunities to consider the transmission of ICHs as manifested through ordinary people. Materiality (especially costume) plays a key role in both cases. Costumes emphasise identities in the case of *Proetnica*, whereas in *Up-Helly-Aa*s, they are central for the guizing experience. Moreover, as each of the sections has shown, both festivals emphasise the role of participation, a key theme that was repeatedly emphasised by partakers, as active heritage-making. Participation, however, was also problematised in the two case studies as it brought to the fore the politics of the festivals and the two main themes of concern for us, belonging and Otherness. We briefly summarise the discussion of the two main themes in Table 4.1.

As previously discussed, the liminal state of the festival affords participants a sense of belonging. In the case of *Proetnica*, this reinforces intra-group belonging of singers and dancers as well as a sense of communitas that is inclusive of other ethnic groups and, temporarily, for the liminal period of the performance, of tourists and local viewers. Similar feelings of belonging are shared through participation in the guizing and halls for socialisation in the different *Up-Helly-Aa* locations.

*Table 4.1* Summary of themes discussed in the case studies

| Theme | Proetnica | Selected Up-Helly-Aas |
|---|---|---|
| Belonging | Singers and dancers | Guizers, Jarl's squad |
| Belonging | Minorities (ethnic groups) | Hosts |
| Otherness | Majority population | Women (post-pubescent) |
| Otherness | Across ethnic groups | New migrants |

The second theme that is highlighted is that of exclusion, or Othering. Conflict between diverse participants in heritage processes has been theorised in heritage studies for decades (see *inter alia*, Meskell 2002; Ashworth, Graham and Tunbridge 2007; Silverman 2011). Tunbridge and Ashworth's (1996: 20–21) argument that dissonance arises because 'all heritage is someone's heritage and therefore logically not someone else's' remains compelling as is the alterity implied by Smith (2006) in her conceptualisation of AHD. Both commentaries provide useful frameworks for understanding reasons and uses for the regulation of women and migrants' participation in *Up-Helly-Aa*s. These reflections also provide useful ground to understand the processes at *Proetnica* Festival in Romania, where ethnic boundaries are negotiated through reference to the majority population but also among different groups.

Although this short summary might seem to give a sense of neatness to the politics of these festivals, the close look (as presented in the previous sections) analysis suggests that Othering and belonging dynamics are not only layered but also malleable and dependent upon context in both cases. This flexibility gives festivals a transformative potential and could serve as a fertile ground for rights-based approaches as we discuss below.

### 4.8.1 Towards rights-based approaches

These concerns and the experiences of dissonance raised in the case studies in this chapter inspire us to key questions for our own research and for all engaging in critical studies of heritage. How do we develop useful praxes with people who are assembling and transmitting their cultural expressions of place, history, tradition and belonging, now, and for their futures, and support these heritages from below as important social action?

The tensions we have experienced in the two case studies seem to contravene key articles in the Faro Convention aimed at ensuring that partaking in heritage be understood as 'cultural participation as defined in the Universal Declaration of Human Rights' and that member states guarantee to use heritage to construct 'peaceful and democratic' societies (Council of Europe 2005: Art 2a and 2d). While at the time of writing the United Kingdom's status as a European member state is uncertain, the convention's articles could still provide recourse for those, who, as one interviewee put it, would like *Up-Helly-Aa* 'to be for everybody' and not just 'for everybody to watch'.

In a similar manner, the ethos of *Proetnica*, inspiring intercultural dialogue and enhancing awareness and participation in diverse heritages, falls short of its aims. Whereas legislation such as the European Charter for Regional or Minority Languages or the contentious Framework Convention for the Protection of National Minorities, as well as provisions in international human rights instruments[6] ensure such events can take place, their implementation in different nations is not equal (see also Kaina and Karolewski 2009 on difficulties of establishing a common identity). As Laia Colomer (2018: 213) has argued recently, 'the core of the controversy lacks an articulate definition (at least in European countries) of what exactly is meant by "multicultural discourses of culture'". This ambiguity resonates with Romanian ethnic groups' experiences and their feelings of exclusion along the majority/minority lines but also in the frictions between ethnicities.

One possible approach to mitigate such shortcomings would be to develop rights-based approaches. For instance, William Logan's (2014, among others) work exemplifies and advocates for situated, broad-based, educative and collaborative approaches to heritage management, aimed at facilitating effective and democratic context for safeguarding principles and their implementation.

Adopting rights-based approaches can also be problematic. Just as the contestability of heritages inspires critical engagement, so too do the intersections between heritages and human rights, particularly following UNESCO's adoption of the Convention for the Safeguarding of ICH (UNESCO 2003; Silverman and Ruggles 2007), emphasising human rights and local perspectives over international legislations (Hill, Nic Craith and Clopot 2018). Regardless that the convention has not been ratified by the United Kingdom, rendering its provisions inapplicable for those deliberating *Up-Helly-Aa* practices, its suitability as a framework for generating greater equity may also be contested. For example, anthropologist, Marilyn Strathern posits that human rights as constructs of a 'Western' 'constitutional model' of what a human being should be (Strathern 2016: 196) inspire a polarising discourse, depicting people in perpetual combat, fighting to win their rights above the rights of others. Such an approach thus necessarily needs to be sensitive to the needs of the communities and the wider social patterns in a society. With all their shortcomings, when dealt with sensitively, such approaches can support communities, as we reflected at the beginning of this chapter, to do their own heritage work and sustain 'heritage from below' (Robertson 2012).

Our comparative analysis has shown that two unrelated festival types, in two very different contexts in Europe, can demonstrate similar patterns and offer diverse communities occasions for strengthening belonging. They also show that such apparently inclusive performances can, by contrast, be used to proscribe the participation of selected groups, all the while with official sanction. The learnings from this analysis of these two festival types that seem worlds apart can help communities reconsider their practices.

## Acknowledgement

This publication is a result of the European Union–funded Horizon 2020 research project: CoHERE (Critical Heritages: performing and representing identities in Europe). CoHERE received funding from the European Union's Horizon 2020 research and innovation programme under grant agreement No. 693289.

## Notes

1 It is often acknowledged that Turner has developed the ideas of Arnold van Gennep.
2 The analysis of the *Up-Helly-Aa* festivals includes quotes given in Shetland dialect, a form of the Scots language. The authors uphold the argument that Scots spellings are not

contractions of English, and therefore the phenomenon of an 'apologetic apostrophe' is not used here.
3 The southern part of Shetland's largest island, called 'Mainland', is a narrow peninsula, extending some 25 miles from Lerwick. Here, the dispersed communities rotate the responsibility for hosting the 'SMUHA' parade and galley burning.
4 Outside of Lerwick *Up-Helly-Aa*, the remaining eleven festivals do permit women to participate as guizers, taking part in the parades and squad performances in the halls. However, only the South Mainland *Up-Helly-Aa* allows adult women into its *Guizer Jarl's* Sqaud.
5 As well as attending events throughout the United Kingdom, the Lerwick *Guizer Jarl's* Squad are regularly invited to participate in New York City's 'Tartan Day' parade, an event designed to promote Scotland to prospective tourists (see *inter alia* Shetland News 19 March 2003).
6 See, for instance, the 1966 International Covenant on Civil and Political Rights or the 1992 Declaration on the Rights of Persons Belonging to National or Ethnic, Religious and Linguistic Minorities.

# References

Abrams, L. and E. Ewan (2018), *Nine centuries of man, manhood and masculinities in Scottish history* (Edinburgh: Edinburgh University Press).
Antonsich, M. (2010), 'Searching for belonging – An analytical framework', *Geography Compass* 4(6): 644–659.
Ashworth, G., B. Graham and J. Tunbridge (2007), *Pluralising pasts: heritage, identity and place in multicultural societies* (London: Pluto).
Barth, F. (1969), 'Introduction', in F. Barth (ed.), *Ethnic groups and boundaries: the social organisation of culture difference* (London: Allen & Unwin), 9–38.
Bortolotto, C. (2007), 'From objects to processes: UNESCO's "intangible cultural heritage"', *Journal of Museum Ethnography* 19: 21–33.
Brown, C. (1998), *Up-Helly-Aa: custom, culture and community in Shetland* (Manchester: Manchester University Press).
Byrne, D. (2008), 'Heritage as social action', in G. Fairclough, R. Harrison, J. Jameson and J. Schofield (eds), *The heritage reader* (London: Routledge), 149–173.
Byron, R. (1994), 'The maritime household in Northern Europe', *Comparative Studies in Society and History* 36(2): 271–292.
Clopot, C. (2017), 'Ambiguous attachments and industrious nostalgias: heritage narratives of Russian Old Believers in Romania', *Anthropological Journal of European Cultures* 26(2): 31–51.
Clopot, C. (2016), 'Weaving the past in a fabric: Old Believers' traditional costume', *Folklore. Electronic Journal of Folklore* 66: 115–132.
Clopot, C. and M. Nic Craith (2018), 'Gender, heritage and changing traditions – Russian Old Believers in Romania', in W. Grahn and R. Wilson (eds), *Gender and heritage: performance, place and politics* (London: Routledge), 48–61.
Colomer, L. (2018), 'ICH and identity: the use of ICH among global multicultural citizens', in C. Waelde, C. Cummings, M. Pavis and H. Enright (eds), *Research handbook on contemporary intangible cultural heritage – Law and heritage* (Cheltenham: Elgar), 194–215.
Cornish, H. (2016), 'Not all singing and dancing: Padstow, folk festivals and belonging', *Ethnos* 81(4): 631–647.

Council of Europe (2005), *Framework convention on the value of cultural heritage for society*. Available at: www.coe.int/en/web/conventions/full-list/-/conventions/rms/0900001680083746 (accessed 14 August 2018).
Fenton, A. (1997), *The Northern Isles: Orkney and Shetland* (East Linton: Tuckwell).
Frost, N. (2016), 'Anthropology and festivals: festival ecologies', *Ethnos* 81(4): 569–583.
Goffman, E. ([1969] 1990), *The presentation of self in everyday life* (Harmondsworth: Penguin).
Graburn, N. (2015), 'Ethnic tourism in rural China: cultural or economic "development"', in A. Diekmann and M. Smith (eds) *Ethnic and minority cultures as tourist attractions* (Bristol: ChannelView), 176–187.
Hall, S. (1999), 'Whose heritage? Un-settling "the heritage", re-imagining the post-nation', *Third Text* 13(49): 3–13.
Harrison, R. (2013), *Heritage: Critical Approaches* (London: Routledge).
Hill, E., M. Nic Craith and C. Clopot (2018) 'At the limits of cultural heritage rights? The Glasgow Bajuni Campaign and the UK Immigration System: a case study', *International Journal of Cultural Property* 25(1): 35–58.
Husserl, E. (1960), *Cartesian meditations: an introduction to phenomenology* (The Hague: Nijhoff)
Kaina, V. and I. Karolewski (2009), 'EU governance and European identity', *Living Reviews in European Governance* 4(2): 5–41.
Kirshenblatt-Gimblett, B. (1998), *Destination culture: tourism, museums, and heritage* (Berkeley, CA: University of California Press).
Kockel, U. (2008), 'Putting the folk in their place: tradition, ecology and the public role of ethnology', *Anthropological Journal of European Cultures* 17(1): 5–23.
Kockel, U. (2007), 'Heritage versus tradition: cultural resources for a new Europe?', in M. Demossier (ed), *The European puzzle: the political structuring of cultural identities at a time of transition* (Oxford: Berghahn), 85–101.
Kozorog, M. (2011), 'Festival tourism and production of locality in a small Slovenian town', *Journal of Tourism and Cultural Change* 9(4): 298–319.
Kuutma, K. (1998), 'Festival as communicative performance and celebration of ethnicity', *Folklore: Electronic Journal of Folklore* 7: 79–86.
Logan, W. (2014), 'Heritage rights – avoidance and reinforcement', *Heritage and Society* 7(2): 156–169.
Marcus, G. (1998) *Ethnography through thick and thin* (Princeton, NJ: Princeton University Press).
Matheson, C. and R. Tinsley (2014), 'Layers of passage: the ritual performance and liminal bleed of the Beltane Fire Festival, Edinburgh', in J. Laing and W. Frost (eds), *Rituals and traditional events in the modern world* (London: Routledge), 151–168.
Meskell, L. (2002), 'Negative heritage and past mastering in archaeology', *Anthropological Quarterly* 75(4): 557–574.
Nic Craith, M. (2008), 'Intangible cultural heritages: the challenge for Europe', *Anthropological Journal of European Cultures* 17(1): 54–73.
Noyes, D. (2015), 'From cultural forms to policy objects: comparison in scholarship and policy', *Journal of Folklore Research* 52(2): 299–313.
Promote Shetland (2018), *Up-Helly-Aa*. Available at: www.shetland.org/things/events/culture-heritage/up-helly-aa (accessed 14 August 2018).
Redactia (2018), 'A început Festivalul Intercultural ProEtnica 2018, "un dar adus de mulţi oameni"', *Zi de Zi*, 23 August. Available at: www.zi-de-zi.ro/2018/08/23/a-inceput-festivalul-intercultural-proetnica-2018-un-dar-adus-de-multi-oameni/ (accessed 1 October 2018).

Robertson, I. (2012), 'Introduction: heritage from below', in I. Robertson (ed), *Heritage from below* (Aldershot: Ashgate), 1–19.

Sassatelli, M. ed. (2008), 'European public culture and aesthetic cosmopolitanism', Euro-festival Project, Deliverable 1.1. Available at www.euro-festival.org (accessed 10 May 2018).

Shetland News (19 March 2013) 'Vikings go Tartan in New York', *Shetland News*. Available at www.shetnews.co.uk/features/fire-festival-2013/6488-vikings-got-tartan-in-new-york (accessed 9 October 2018).

Silverman, H. (2011), *Contested cultural heritage* (New York, NY: Springer).

Silverman, H. and D. Ruggles (2007), Cultural heritage and human rights (New York, NY: Springer).

Smith, B. (22 January 1993), 'Up-Helly-Aa – Separating the facts from the fiction'. *The Shetland Times*.

Smith, L. (2006), *Uses of heritage* (London: Routledge).

Strathern, M. (2016), *Before and after gender: sexual mythologies of everyday life* (Chicago, IL: HAU).

Taylor, D. (2016), 'Saving the "live"? re-performance and intangible cultural heritage', *Études Anglaises* 69(2): 149–161.

Testa, A. (2017), '"Fertility" and the carnival 1: symbolic effectiveness, emic beliefs, and the re-enchantment of Europe', *Folklore* 128(1): 16–36.

Tunbridge, J. and G. Ashworth (1996), *Dissonant heritage: The management of the past as a resource in conflict* (Chichester: Wiley).

Turner, V. (1974), 'Liminal to liminoid, in play, flow, and ritual: an essay in comparative symbology', *Rice Institute Pamphlet-Rice University Studies* 60(3): 53–92.

Turner, V. (1969), *The ritual process: structure and anti-structure* (Chicago, IL: Aldine).

UNESCO (2003), *Convention for the Safeguarding of the Intangible Cultural Heritage* (Paris: UNESCO).

Urry, J. (2002), *The tourist gaze: leisure and travel in contemporary societies* (London: Sage).

van Assche, K. and P. Teampău (2009), 'Layered encounters: performing multiculturalism and the urban palimpsest at the "gateway of Europe"', *Anthropology of East Europe Review* 27(1): 7–19.

Whitehead, C and G. Bozoğlu (2017), 'Heritage and memory in Europe: a review of key concepts and frameworks', *CoHERE Critical Archive*. Available at: http://cohere-ca.ncl.ac.uk/#/grid/319 (accessed 2 October 2018).

Yuval-Davis, N. (2006), 'Belonging and the politics of belonging', *Patterns of Prejudice* 40(3): 197–214.

# 5 Nostalgic festivals

## The case of Cappadox

*Babak Taheri, Martin Joseph Gannon and Hossein Olya*

It is broadly acknowledged that cultural festivals serve as powerful, interactive venues imbued with the potential to stimulate feelings of nostalgia (Kim 2005; Li, Huang and Cai 2009). The festival setting therefore represents a core cultural space, where individuals can engage in the process of 'sense-making', 'self-exploration', 'self-discovery' and 'yearning for the past', all buttressed by the inherent exposure to interactive sociality that a festival's tangible and intangible offering provides. To explore this heady nexus of past and present, this study considers the consumer experience at one of Turkey's most novel and popular contemporary festivals, Cappadox. Hosted annually in the distinguished geographic region of Cappadocia, this cultural festival offers visitors the opportunity to engage in contemporary consumption couched within an historic setting (Taheri et al. 2018).

Firmly established in the land where 'East' meets 'West', the Cappadox festival is positioned as an unmissable, under-the-radar European arts festival, attracting a wide range of European performers and visitors alike, while retaining a programme keen to celebrate modern Turkish culture (Coldwell 2018). Here, visitors' personal identity conception salutes the contemporary formation of a 'festival' as a product of consumer experience (cf. Jafari, Taheri and vom Lehn 2013; Lau and Li 2019; Nic Craith 2012). Therefore, such cultural festivals are 'considered as social construction processes that are conditional not only to the level of penetration of globalisation but also to the way in which these processes are mediated through local processes of place making' (Lau and Li 2019:45). As such, several intangible characteristics (such as consumer experience and consumer engagement) extend the tangible aspects of festival consumption. It is also important to recognise that many festivals are closely associated with historic and cultural representations of the nation in which they are hosted, and 'intangible heritage [e.g., festival events] manifests diverse symbolic meanings and national embodiments, often grounded in the material and tangible remnants of the past' (Park 2011: 521).

Festivals can thus provide visitors with the opportunity to come together with likeminded individuals in order to experience the tangible and intangible festival offerings and bask in the nostalgic and transformative experience of the art and culture showcased therein (cf. Gonzalez 2008; Lau and Li

2019; Nic Craith 2008; Nic Craith and Kockel 2015; Tan et al. 2018). As such, the main objective of this chapter is to draw the attention of marketing and consumer behaviour scholars to the 'transformative' and 'nostalgic' nature of festivals in our ever-changing, experiential societies (Jones 2012). In doing so, data was collected from European visitors to different cultural events, concerts and proceedings (e.g., music, dance, art) at the Cappadox Festival, Turkey. Since 2015, the Cappadox festival has served as a top cultural heritage attraction for European visitors eager to experience its varied programme and otherworldly landscape (Taheri et al. 2018). This study follows an inductive qualitative approach, with several implications drawn from the findings and pertinent directions for future research provided. In festivals, the consumption experience extends beyond the offering's core consumption stage; it provides the aforementioned *transformative* experience as festivalgoers feel nostalgia for satisfactory experiences (e.g., emotional outcomes, strong nostalgic memories) and discuss their experience with others (e.g., participative interaction, Word of Mouth (WoM)). This is likely influenced by the level of entertainment, escapism, flow and learning dimensions that the festival offers. In other words, festival consumption experiences may carry symbolic value and engender interpersonal meanings for consumers, over and above their functional value as entertainment arenas.

Yet it is also established that cultural consumers' experiences are often transient as they seek to see everything a cultural experience or site has to offer within a limited timeframe (cf. Bourdieu and Darbel 2008; Leinhardt, Knutson and Crowley 2003). Here, they may embrace cultural tastes obtained through past experiences, stimulated by feelings of nostalgia within the consumption contact zone. For instance, important questions concerning 'who we are with?' and 'how much do we know about the site we are visiting?' significantly affect visitors' experiences of cultural heritage (Gannon et al. 2017). While this is consistent for both new and first-time visitors, locals also consume cultural heritage, most of whom have considerably more entrenched knowledge, memories and emotional feelings for the objects, experiences and interactions manifest within their local cultural consumption spaces (Belk 1990; Black 2009; Kotler, Kotler and Kotler 2008). Regarding those with prior knowledge cultural places, the visiting experience becomes more enjoyable as their level of engagement increases; they go beyond merely interacting with objects contained within cultural heritage sites, with their sense of engagement extended by creating bonds with others who share similar feelings towards the context and content contained therein (Gannon et al. 2017). This study contends that this social bond can intensify the nostalgic feelings visitors experience towards objects found within cultural heritage sites. Further, the analysis of thirty-two in-depth interviews with European consumers attending the Cappadox festival, Cappadocia, Turkey, demonstrates the reciprocal nature of this relationship, whereby interaction with cultural objects creates a sense of nostalgia, which in turn stimulates the pursuit of social interactions within the cultural festival context.

As such, this chapter addresses recent calls (e.g., Black 2009; Falk and Dierking 1997; Hooper-Greenhill 2007; Taheri, Jafari and O'Gorman 2014; Jafari, Taheri and vom Lehn 2013) to further investigate the factors that influence consumers' engagement within the cultural heritage context. The focus is therefore on the interplay between the concepts of nostalgia and social interaction. It examines the way in which feelings of the past influence visitors' engagement in the present. The key contribution stems from the demonstration of how feelings of nostalgia shape social bonds and interaction among cultural heritage consumers. It is hoped that the findings will extend extant understanding of consumption within the cultural heritage and festival contexts. The chapter begins by outlining the theoretical underpinning, before the research design and methodology is explained. Next, the findings are discussed, followed by concluding remarks centred on providing suggestions for future research.

## 5.1 Nature of engagement

Engagement generally refers to a sense of involvement stemming from an adequate response to stimuli; it can emerge either alone or when participating in communal and social consumption activities (Abdul-Ghani, Hyde and Marshall 2011; Taheri, Jafari and O'Gorman 2014). Within consumption literature, engagement is defined as 'a state of being involved, occupied, fully absorbed, or engrossed in something (i.e., sustained attention)' (Higgins and Scholer 2009: 102), with focus on 'commitment to an active relationship with a specific market offering' (Abdul-Ghani, Hyde and Marshall 2011: 1061). Whatever definition we take, engagement refers to the level and type of interaction and involvement individuals experience during consumption (Taheri, Jafari and O'Gorman 2014). Engagement contributes heavily to the value derived from experiential consumption and the extent to which consumers feel truly 'part of' an experience (Grant 2000; Higgins 2006). Mollen and Wilson (2010) classify engagement based on extant literature in three fragments: (1) the mental state accomplished by active, sustained cognitive processing; (2) the satisfying of utility and relevance; and (3) emotional bonding or impact. Hollebeek (2010) views engagement as a two-way interaction between 'engagement subjects' (i.e., consumers/customers) and 'engagement objects' (i.e., products, brands or services). Based on this, engagement could be seen as an interaction between visitors or tourists (engagement subjects) and visitor attractions (engagement objects).

Interest in the concept of engagement spans multiple disciplines, including consumer psychology, education, leisure, tourism, and heritage, with diverse definitions (Cordina, Gannon and Croall 2018). For instance, it is argued that via interaction with objects, products and brands (Edmonds, Muller and Connell 2006), consumers can construct meaning by experiencing involvement (Higgins 2006), representational action (Herrington, Oliver and Reeves 2003), the cognitive activity of delivering extra-textual perspectives (Douglas and Hargadon 2000), commitment (Mollen and Wilson 2010) and/or an emotional connection to consumption (Rappaport 2007). More specifically, with regards to cultural consumption and tourism, the concept of engagement has long interested scholars. A substantial body of literature has examined how the supply side influences cultural heritage site visitors' consumption patterns, stressing the importance of the cultural environment. Here, specific reference is made to the design of cultural heritage site' intangible offerings (Nic Craith and Kockel 2015;Yalinay et al. 2018) and how this encourages visitors to engage and interact with objects and artefacts therein (Falk and Dierking 1997; Hooper-Greenhill 2007; vom Lehn 2006).

Within this context, Edmonds, Muller and Connell (2006) identify three salient categories of engagement: 'attractors' drawing visitor attention towards an exhibit; 'sustainers' lengthening the duration of visitors' engagement; and 'relaters' fostering deeper visitor–exhibit relationships, thus encouraging future visits. Further, Hooper-Greenhill (2007) regards engagement as pivotal to both the educational and recreational roles of modern cultural heritage sites. Edmonds, Muller and Connell (2006: 316) note that offerings that achieve this triumvirate 'meet the highest approval in the world of cultural heritage sites and art galleries.' Consequently, the success of cultural heritage offerings is often measured in relation to the average time spent on-site and the perceived level of interactivity, as well as the ease with which visitors can interact with tangible heritage therein. Such measures reflect the increasingly high-tech forms of 'edutainment' argued to underpin engaging cultural heritage sites. However, some authors note a degree of backlash against the dumbing-down of cultural heritage, where the focus is on entertaining visitors rather than educating them or stimulating them mentally (Goulding 2000). In other words, the level of interactivity of an exhibit is not necessarily correlated with levels of satisfaction, enjoyment and learning in the case of all cultural heritage consumers.

Further, the demand side considers how visitors' own characteristics influence their engagement within cultural consumption contexts. Here, typologies originally distinguished between the 'psychocentric' and 'allocentric' tourist (Plog 1974). While the former typically values familiarity, the latter is more interested in engaging with the novel or the unknown. Moscardo (1996) extends this categorisation by positing the notion of 'mindful' and 'mindless' visitors. Mindful tourists experience greater learning and understanding (alongside higher levels of satisfaction) than mindless visitors, who typically experience lower levels of engagement. Pattakos (2010), meanwhile, contends that visitors' levels of engagement exist within a continuum, with those at the highest level being proactively engaged in their experiences. Elsewhere, Edmonds, Muller and Connell (2006) demonstrate how active and passive visitors interact with exhibits in an art gallery where technological means (e.g., light and sound effects, computer programs and sensors) facilitate engagement.

Within the cultural heritage sector, visitor engagement has also been classified with particular reference to the objects contained within a site (Kolar and Zabkar 2010). Here, Edmonds, Muller and Connell (2006) identify four core categories of interaction between visitors and objects, namely static, dynamic-passive, dynamic-interactive and dynamic-interactive (varying). At the highest level of interaction, dynamic-interactive (varying), visitor–object relationships emerge when the experience is influenced by both players and changes over time as a direct result of the history of these interactions. It is also argued that nostalgic feelings and social interaction are the key drivers of local visitors' behaviour in cultural heritage sites particularly in Turkey, from the perspective of engaging with exhibits (Brown and Humphreys 2002; Karanfil 2009). The following section explores literature shedding further light on these factors and the nature of their relationship with visitor engagement.

## 5.2 Nostalgia and social interaction

The importance of nostalgia in shaping the way in which visitors engage with destinations and attractions is established, with its influence recognised from early perspectives on pathological conditions to more recent work on sociological phenomena and identity development and maintenance (Davis 1979; Holak, Matveev and Havlena 2008; Jafari and Taheri 2014). While often difficult to isolate, Belk (1990: 670) defines nostalgia as 'a wistful mood that may be prompted by an object, a scene, a smell, or a strain of music'. Further, Sierra and McQuitty (2007: 106) consider it 'a yearning for the past, or a fondness for tangible or intangible possessions and activities linked with the past, and is experienced when individuals feel separated from an era to which they are attached'. Nonetheless, despite this abstract conceptualisation, the majority of individuals have felt nostalgia at some point in time. This may be manifest in a number of ways, or in a number of places, such as at work, when visiting a memorable place, drinking in a café or pub, tasting a particular food, watching a film, listening to music, dancing with partners, talking with childhood friends or even walking the streets of our formative years (cf. Goulding 1999; Holbrook and Schindler 1991; Jafari and Taheri 2014).

As such, nostalgia has several meanings. It can be described as aiming to bring again what previously was; feelings of contentment with the past, even if modified; and the reappropriation of symbols that create ownership of symbolic capital (Gvion 2009). Holbrook and Schindler (1991: 330) also note that nostalgia can be manifest as 'a preference (general liking, positive attitude, or favorable affect), toward objects (people, places, or things) that were more common (popular, fashionable, or widely circulated) when one was younger (in early adulthood, in adolescence, in childhood, or even before birth)'. Holbrook (1993) explores these characteristics further, positing four main features of nostalgia. He contends that 'preference' refers to consumers' tastes towards a variety of objects used in consumption; 'objects' refer to both popular and highbrow culture; and finally, 'when one was younger' refers to an individual's 'personally experienced past' and the wider context this exists within (Davis 1979).

Therefore, as per Holak, Matveev and Havlena (2008: 172f.), nostalgic experiences may differ in two key ways: '1) the personal versus collective nature of the experience and 2) the basis of the feeling in direct versus indirect experience'. Personal experiences refer to memories which differ across people, while collective experiences refer to cultural events that members of society share (Holak, Matveev and Havlena 2008; Jafari and Taheri 2014). Further, Sierra and McQuitty (2007: 100) stress that 'for people to have nostalgia-related responses (e.g., a yearning for the past), they must have memories of the past, either lived or learned'. Thus, nostalgia and its effect on cultural consumer patterns are linked to past experience or, at least, knowledge of how things once were (Davis 1979; Goulding 2001). Havlena and Holak (1996) identify four types of nostalgic experience: personal nostalgia (i.e., direct individual experience); interpersonal nostalgia (i.e., those which combine other people's experiences with the individual's interactions with that person); cultural nostalgia (i.e., when members of society share the same historic values and create a cultural identity); and virtual nostalgia (i.e., emotion emerging from collective (yet indirect) experiences). Given this, Goulding (2001) suggests that nostalgia can influence the myriad of factors affecting consumption choices within the cultural heritage context, with this nostalgia deeply rooted in the cultural experiences of the consumer's youth (Holbrook 1993; Jafari and Taheri 2014).

Further, nostalgia has a close relationship with identity, where consumers may make sense of who they are through recognising and understanding their past (Gvion 2009; Jafari and Taheri 2014). Cultural consumers may generate attachment from the past (e.g., memories from their childhood about particular cultural heritage sites), or they may have indirect nostalgic feelings based on external sources. Some consumers also symbolically, tangibly or intangibly link their past memories to contemporary consumption experiences (Schindler and Holbrook 2003; Sierra and McQuitty 2007). Nostalgia can contribute to individuals' sense of identity based on shared heritage and memories, where self-identity provides consumers with the push to purchase a product or service (i.e., engage with a cultural heritage sites). For instance, a consumer who positively recalls visiting a cultural heritage site with friends in his/her youth is likely to experience positive emotions when talking with friends about the same kind of cultural heritage sites (Goulding 2001; Reed 2002).

Moreover, Falk and Dierking (1997) argue that most visitors go to cultural heritage sites in a group and that those who visit alone nonetheless invariably come into contact with other visitors and staff. Therefore, the perspective and experience of these consumers is influenced by the social context. In this regard, McLean (1999) highlights how other visitors, not just exhibits and object contained therein, are likely to impact upon how memorable visitors perceive cultural heritage site consumption to be. Additionally, cultural consumers are not passive, but skilful, performers. Aiming to access new avenues of social capital and knowledge, they are subject to steady levels of engagement with cultural products, while simultaneously forming ties that are adjusted to the scene of the performance of others (Bagnall 2003; Putnam 2000; Jafari, Taheri and vom Lehn 2013). Hein and Alexander (1998) and Falk and Dierking (1997) therefore stress the important role of social interaction in consumers' cultural heritage site experiences and the influence this has over the enjoyment and learning derived therein.

As such, the interplay between consumption, engagement, social interaction and nostalgia brings to mind social capital concerns, such as strong/weak social ties and bonding/bridging theories (Putnam 2000). Social capital theory can be used to understand 'within society' relations and 'outside society' relations. For instance, when a group of people visit cultural heritage sites, they mostly talk about the characteristics of the place and their past experiences. Essentially, visitors participate in a social manner, changing and influencing the experience of others, within this cultural consumption setting (Blumer 1969; Bourdieu and Darbel 2008; Goffman 1990; vom Lehn and Heath 2005). As such, visitors do not typically experience cultural heritage sites in isolation, instead processing their experiences tinged by the influence of social interactions therein. Jafari, Taheri and vom Lehn (2013) also contend that there is symbiotic interplay between consumption and sociality, suggesting that consumption nourishes sociality (e.g., leisure and brand communities) and sociality influences consumption (e.g., consumption of food and drinks). Driven from any interplay between consumption and sociality, sociality can strengthen existing ties, establish new ties and extend online and offline environments. To this end, social interaction within cultural spaces has long been argued to influence the nature of consumption, visitor behaviours, and ultimately engagement (Falk and Dierking 1997; Hooper-Greenhill 2007; vom Lehn 2006; Jafari, Taheri and vom Lehn 2013).

## 5.3 Methodology

For this study, data was sought from European visitors to the Cappadox cultural festival hosted annually in Cappadocia, Turkey. This multi-day festival emphasises participation, interaction and entertainment and offers visitors the opportunity to experience a comprehensive corpus of cultural workshops and events centred on demonstrating contemporary Turkish traditions and intangible heritage (Coldwell 2018). The Cappadox Festival has quickly become a mainstay of the Turkish cultural heritage scene, attracting a large number of domestic and international visitors and a range of globally recognised corporate partners and sponsors (Cappadox 2018). Hosted within the confines of the Cappadocia UNESCO World Heritage Site, the Cappadox Festival is also noted for its scenic surrounds. Here, the site's distinctiveness is manifest in the troglodyte architecture, inhabited cave-dwellings and underground caverns reflective of the wider region (Taheri et al. 2018). However, irrespective of Cappadocia's reputation as a visitor site of cultural significance, the Cappadox Festival provides a less established consumption experience; 2018 represents only the fourth time it has welcomed visitors to the region (Taheri et al. 2018). As such, the festival represents an interesting vehicle for the study of nostalgia, social interaction and engagement in a cultural consumption context. It is not constrained by the ingrained nature of better-established festivals, yet exists in a location well recognised throughout the region and further afield and that is popular with a wide range of cultural visitors.

As such, in order to explore the interplay between the aforementioned concepts (e.g., consumption, engagement, interaction, and nostalgia), semi-structured interviews with festival attendees were conducted. Each interview lasted around 30 minutes and was recorded and transcribed for posterity. Overall, thirty-two participants between the ages of 20 and 58 were interviewed. In order to explore these visitors' opinions and perspectives of their cultural festival experience, two initial interviews adopted an open-ended conversation approach. Further, given the lack of consistency with regards to the language interviews were conducted in, the study adopted the translation theory approach of Hogg, Liao and O'Gorman (2014). Here, the research team ensured that an appropriate level of focus was afforded to translating interview responses into English. Following data collection, the thematic approach was used to conduct data analysis (Wells et al. 2016).

## 5.4 Results

Arguably, a core dilemma within contemporary society concerns the interplay between identity and social interaction (Goulding 1999; Jafari and Taheri 2014). Nostalgia-based heritage sites are typically endowed with characteristics that offer visitors the opportunity to engage with others in interactive environments (Jafari and Taheri 2014). This therefore emphasises the opportunities for communal consumption available to visitors therein. The findings reveal that the festival servicescape in some way contributes to this (Yalinay et al. 2018). Here, physically walking through the heritage site arouses nostalgic feelings in visitors and provides them with the imaginative stimuli required to 'walk into the past', particularly if the environment satisfies visitors' extant cultural motivation:

> I have been coming to this place for the last couple of years. It still has the same smell and same feeling. It reminds me of the past and history in a modern representation. I used to come here with my mum when I was a little girl. The place has been changed a lot. I think the festival has helped as well ... I feel I have gained a lot from my experience. I am totally satisfied!
> [Female, Married, Shop Assistant, Turkish, 44 years old]

Even when focus is on education, cultural accuracy, and individual discovery, the importance of social interaction (with family and friends) and interactive storytelling looms large. Indeed, our participants suggested that social interaction and the communal aspects of cultural consumption helped them to discover the culture(s) portrayed within the contemporary festival context. Social interaction in such cultural places 'in the now' stimulated feelings of nostalgia for familial interaction 'in years gone by', where the social aspects of cultural heritage consumption brought about favourable memories of 'consumption past', demonstrating the cross-generational, temporal importance of communal cultural consumption:

> You know we interact with Cappadocia through the festival. It is like having fun with your friends in a historical area. I used to come here when I was a kid with my father and grandfather. It is still inspiring.
> [Male, Divorced, Office worker, Turkish, 45 years old]

Such interaction may increase the level of visitors' satisfaction, and the majority of the participants stated that the social aspects of cultural heritage consumption in the festival context encouraged them to share their festival site experience with their contacts on social networking sites. This echoes extant research, where Jafari, Taheri and vom Lehn (2013) note that visitors' sociality can be extended beyond the tangible heritage and festival boundaries:

> The last couple of years have been great. I come here with my friends and enjoy it! There is a desire to portray different aspects of the village, the caves, the people and the history. It's all there. The festival helps us to discover these more. It is like personally interpreting the past. I feel I have converted to the historical area ... I will tell my friends to visit this place. I put a lot of photos on my Instagram page.
> [Female, Single, Student, French, 30 years old]

As such, festival sites cannot be considered simple object-endowed places; they must also be considered as people-oriented social spaces (Jafari and Taheri 2014; Taheri and Jafari 2012). Festivals and heritage sites have the capacity to stimulate connections between individuals by achieving mutual benefits through strengthening existing ties (Jafari, Taheri and vom Lehn 2013; Putman 2000; Simon 2010). In the case of Cappadox, some of the festival visitors interviewed explicitly mentioned this, while also highlighting the nostalgic value of the strengthening of existing social ties, particularly when familial in nature:

> I came here ten years ago. It is still the same place – I feel déjà vu ... My partner and I are going through a difficult time, and I thought I should take her here as we came here ten years ago! ... I talked a lot with my partner after a log day of activities ... I love the place and I think the festival plays an important role here ... I'm so happy about all the memories and flashbacks during my visit.
> [Male, Engaged, Shop Assistant, Turkish, 32 years old]

In cultural sites, 'we learn about who we are, our history and our culture through stories and by telling stories' (Shankar, Elliott and Goulding 2001: 431). Such stories and social interactions make festival experience entertaining by 'using consumption objects as resources to interact with fellow consumers' (Holt 1995: 9). This consumption is varied and can be manifest in many forms in the festival context. However, the contemporary visitor experience does not need to be analogous with a visitor's memories in order to stimulate feelings of nostalgia. Here, embodied practices such as music and intangible heritage serve as aesthetic and social experiences (Nic Craith and Kockel 2015; Taylor 2016). Those visiting Cappadox experienced various representations of cultural heritage (e.g., through music and heritage workshops), representing the performance and re-performance of traditions for the purpose of cultural consumption, with the aesthetic and social elements combining to turn such performances into an engaging product (Taylor 2016). Indeed, reimagined cultural heritage sites can go some way to engaging visitors by retaining core sources of value presented and maintained in a contemporary manner, with one participant stating:

> I came here for a school trip when I was a little kid. It is still the same place. Yes, it has been modernised for tourists, but it is still beautiful. I remember we walked around and enjoyed the history and food. Yes, the food is still amazing here. We went to my favourite restaurant, and it reminded me of my childhood … the festival helped a lot with changes as well. There are a lot of activities here, and I can take a lot from them.
> 
> [Male, Divorced, Security, Turkish, 42 years old]

As such, the cultural heritage festival concept represents a compelling and novel context for demonstrating the complex interplay between engagement, interaction and nostalgia. Here, the festival's value is not necessarily derived from its tangible offering but instead from its more intangible characteristics – a place offering memorable experiences, opportunities for significant social interaction and the strengthening of existing bonds – each of which have the power to live long in the visitor's memories. Therefore, cultural heritage festival consumption can nourish sociality as 'through consumption, people build up social ties with each other and even feel a sense of belonging to a wider social group or community' (Jafari, Taheri and vom Lehn 2013: 1731). As such, some participants contend that the festival serves as a catalyst to develop social interactions and strengthening existing ties. Here, the findings suggest that the depth of detail contained within any visitor's memories borders on the irrelevant – it is the nostalgic significance derived from whom is being remembered and their links to the cultural setting that holds the greatest value:

> I am here again after many years. It is still very beautiful. The festival is amazing too. We used to come here for school trips. We had a nice history teacher with us. My grandfather joined us as well. Both passed away. However, I can still feel them here. This is a beautiful memory. I will send some photos to my grandmother. She will love this place. She could not make it when we came here with my grandfather. I love festivals – particularly the live music bands.
> 
> [Male, Divorced, Office worker, Turkish, 45 years old]

## Discussion and conclusion

This chapter explores the interplay between notions of nostalgia, social interaction and the interactive engagement experiences for a sample of European visitors to a contemporary festival in a world-renowned cultural destination. In this festival context, cultural consumers directly interact with the cultural sites through their prior knowledge as well as static and visual facilities provided more generally within the cultural site (cf. Kotler, Kotler and Kotler 2008; Taheri and Jafari 2012; Jafari and Taheri 2014; Jafari, Taheri and vom Lehn 2013). This study demonstrates how the intangible heritage experience (and its associated offerings) can provide both consumers (and indeed cultural festivals) with a valid source of identity. In doing so, the interplay between nostalgia and identity can stimulate feelings of engagement in consumers. In addition, the findings reveal that cultivating tangible and intangible heritage is vital in developing cultural identity, particularly for festivals showcasing national culture and identity, as they can result in destination loyalty and nostalgic feelings for visitors (cf. Nic Craith and Kockel 2015; Taylor 2016). Here, shared experiences and communal nostalgia serve as intangible heritage, and are of vital significance in stimulating engaging cultural consumption.

This interaction is underpinned by the sense of nostalgia visitors feel toward cultural sites, bolstered by performances, workshops and events comprising the contemporary festival context. Here, European visitors elect to interpret their own experiences and engagement, alongside their social interactions with others, as the wide programme offered by the Cappadox festival can be interpreted, enjoyed and engaged with in multiple ways. For our European visitors, the pursuit of nostalgia is not solely symptomatic of missing the past or returning back to days gone by but also 'simply an emotional manifestation that reminds tourists of their younger days, reflecting nostalgic longing for a romanticised or idealised past' (Zhao and Timothy 2017: 101). Nostalgia therefore becomes a shared experience, which creates the basis for bonding with likeminded individuals and romanticising the past within such settings. New facilities and new ways of engaging visitors can thus be seen to mediate the relationship between cultural sites and the nostalgic experience of visitors. Visitors seek new information and create new links to their pre-existing knowledge and experiences in order to learn meaningfully (i.e., determining what we learn from such experiences). Here, the European visitors held strong connections with the objects and exhibits (i.e., tangible heritage) that could correspond to their sense of nostalgia. Replacing such memory- and meaning-laden objects may introduce fresh concepts within the domain of cultural consumption, but for a particular group of individuals, the link between the present and past is cut-off. In such instances, the creation of social bonds among individuals becomes less likely.

Nonetheless, this study contends that cultural heritage festivals represent important avenues for social interaction (both online and offline), particularly for visitors with extant interest in culture and heritage (Kolar and Zabkar

2010). A study by Stamboulis and Skayannis (2003: 41) also stresses that 'the tourist may go on interacting with it (the intangible heritage) long after he/she has departed'. To this end, tourism and heritage developers and planners should preserve the integrity of tangible heritage, which ultimately serves as the main selling point of Cappadocia, by carefully managing the physical heritage components therein. They must also deliver an interactive bespoke festival package by presenting intangible cultural heritage through attractions that closely match the tangible setting. Here, factors influencing the traditional lifestyle of local residents need to be considered in order to gain a better understanding of the community's culture and history. This interaction between tangible and intangible heritage can therefore enhance tourists' perceptions of both the destination and the festival, thus contributing to their pursuit of their true selves. In doing so, promotional literature and materials should be designed cognisant of this. Here, communication strategies should reflect the interactive, communal and participative experiences required to stimulate engagement in order to appeal to visitors. For example, an emphasis should be placed on information sharing (i.e., through interactive blogs and forums), with visitors encouraged to share their nostalgic experiences. As such, this study echoes Jafari, Taheri and vom Lehn (2013) in stressing the importance of interactive sociality and the interactive consumption process. Managerial impetus should therefore be placed on designing heritage sites and festivals in a way that allows visitors to experience 'meanings and feelings – through experiences of cultural consumption – with one another' (Jafari, Taheri and vom Lehn 2013: 1745), with the opportunity for this emphasised in promotional materials. As such, managers must understand the importance of *'third'* spaces (Jafari, Taheri and vom Lehn 2013) (e.g., festival and heritage sites) as platforms for social interaction, and design servicescapes cognisant of this (Yalinay et al. 2018). In addition, the results may serve as a reference for other European festivals by showing how engagement and social interaction can influence visitors' experiences. Recognising this may also contribute to the sustainability of intangible cultural heritage. European festivals developers and organisers should try to build trust, amass a sense of 'power sharing' and educate the local community on the benefits and threats of hosting cultural festivals (cf. Freitag and Bühlmann 2009; Kaina and Karolewski 2009).

Finally, in order to stimulate nostalgia and engagement, the choice of sponsorship must be cognisant of the unique cultural offering and intangible heritage contained within the consumption space. For example, if the festival has a particular theme (e.g., folk music), the thematic content (e.g., musical performance) should be high quality and supported by appropriate music sponsors. The results indicate that social interaction and engagement are important attributes for increasing level of nostalgic feelings; thus, European festivals should have interesting programs and activities that reflect the tangibility and intangibility of heritage sites with a particular European significance (i.e., *'placing heritage'* 'affixing the idea of a European cultural heritage to certain places in order to turn them into specific European heritage sites'

(Lähdesmäki 2016: 766)). Hence, festival marketers must consider the value of their tangible and intangible heritage offerings and the cost of admissions and on-site activities. As such, planning a successful festival with loyalty-building attributes (e.g., nostalgia and social interaction) may motivate tourists to visit destinations with the express intention of consuming such identity-building, social experiences.

## References

Abdul-Ghani, E., K. Hyde and R. Marshall (2011), 'Emic and etic interpretations of engagement with a consumer-to-consumer online auction site', *Journal of Business Research* 64(10): 1060–1066.

Bagnall, G. (2003), 'Performance and performativity at heritage sites', *Museum and Society* 1(2): 87–103.

Belk, R. (1990), 'The role of possessions in constructing and maintaining a sense of past', in M. Goldberg, G. Gornand and R. Pollay (eds), *Advances in consumer research*, vol. 17 (Provo, UT: Association for Consumer Research), 669–676.

Black, G. (2009), *The engaging museum: developing museums for visitor involvement* (London: Routledge).

Blumer, H. (1969), *Symbolic interactionism: perspective and method* (Berkeley, CA: University of California Press).

Bourdieu, P. and A. Darbel (2008), *The love of art: European art museums and their public* (Cambridge: Polity).

Brown, A. and M. Humphreys (2002), 'Nostalgia and the narrativization of identity: a Turkish case study', *British Journal of Management* 13(2): 141–159.

Cappadox (2018), 'Cappadox'. Available at: http://cappadox.com/ (accessed 2 Oct 2018).

Coldwell, W. (2018), '10 of the best under-the-radar music festivals in Europe'. Available at: www.theguardian.com/travel/2018/apr/06/10-best-music-festivals-europe-probably-never-heard-of (accessed 15 October 2018).

Cordina, R., M. Gannon and R. Croall (2018), 'Over and over: local fans and spectator sport tourist engagement', *The Service Industries Journal* DOI: 10.1080/02642069.2018.1534962.

Davis, F. (1979), *A yearning for yesterday: a sociology of nostalgia* (London: Collyer MacMillan).

Douglas, J. and A. Hargadon (2000), 'The pleasure principle: immersion, engagement, flow' Paper presented at the 11th ACM on Hypertext and Hypermedia, San Antonio, TX, USA, 30 May–3 June.

Edmonds, E., L. Muller and M. Connell (2006), 'On creative engagement', *Visual Communication* 5(3): 307–322.

Falk, J. and L. Dierking (1997), *The museum experience*. Washington, DC: Whalesback.

Freitag, M., and M. Bühlmann (2009), 'Crafting trust the role of political institutions in a comparative perspective', *Comparative Political Studies* 42(12): 1537–1566.

Gannon, M., I. Baxter, E. Collinson, R. Curran and R. Maxwell-Stuart (2017), 'Travelling for Umrah: destination attributes, destination image, and post-travel intentions', *The Service Industries Journal* 37(7–8): 448–465.

Goffman, E. (1990), *Presentation of self in everyday life* (London: Penguin).

Gonzalez, M. (2008), 'Intangible heritage tourism and identity', *Tourism Management* 29(4), 807–810.

Goulding, C. (2001), 'Romancing the past: heritage visiting and the nostalgic consumer', *Psychology and Marketing* 18(6), 565–592.

Goulding, C. (2000), 'The museum environment and the visitor experience', *European Journal of Marketing* 34(3/4): 261–278.
Goulding, C. (1999), 'Heritage, nostalgia, and the "grey" consumer', *Journal of Marketing Practice: Applied Marketing Science* 5(6/7/8): 177–199.
Grant, J. (2000), *The new marketing manifesto: the 12 rules for building successful brands in the 21st century* (UK: Thomson).
Gvion, L. (2009), 'Organised leisure as promoting nostalgia: Israeli senior citizens singing in Yiddish', *Leisure Studies* 28(1), 51–65.
Havlena, W., and S. Holak (1996), 'Exploring nostalgia imagery using consumer collages', *Advances in Consumer Research* 23: 35–42.
Hein, G., and M. Alexander (1998), *Museums places of learning* (Washington, DC: Technical Information Service).
Herrington, J., R. Oliver and T. Reeves (2003), 'Patterns of engagement in authentic online learning environments', *Australasian Journal of Educational Technology* 19(1), 59–71.
Higgins, E. (2006), 'Value from hedonic experience and engagement', *Psychological Review* 113(3): 439–460.
Higgins, T. and A. Scholer (2009), 'Engaging the consumer: The science and art of the value creation process', *Journal of Consumer Psychology*, 19(2): 100–114.
Hogg, G., M-H. Liao and K. O'Gorman (2014), 'Reading between the lines: Multidimensional translation in tourism consumption', *Tourism Management* 42: 157–164.
Holak, S., A. Matveev and W. Havlena (2008), 'Nostalgia in post-socialist Russia: Exploring applications to advertising strategy', *Journal of Business Research* 61(2): 172–178.
Holbrook, M. (1993), 'Nostalgia and consumption preferences: some emerging patterns of consumer tastes', *The Journal of Consumer Research* 20(2): 245–256.
Holbrook, M. and M. Schindler (1991), 'Echoes of the Dear Departed Past: Some Work in Progress on Nostalgia', in R. Holmanand and M. Solomon (eds), *Advances in Consumer Research*, Vol. 18 (Provo, UT: Association for Consumer Research), 330–333.
Hollebeek, L. (2010), 'Demystifying customer brand engagement: Exploring the loyalty nexus', *Journal of Marketing Management* 27(7–8): 785–807.
Holt, D. (1995), 'How consumers consume: A typology of consumption practices', *Journal of Consumer Research* 22(1): 1–16.
Hooper-Greenhill, E. (2007), *Museums and education: purpose, pedagogy, performance* (London: Routledge).
Jafari, A. and B. Taheri (2014), 'Nostalgia, reflexivity, and the narratives of self: reflections on Devine's "Removing the rough edges?"', *Consumption Markets and Culture* 17(2): 215–230.
Jafari, A., B. Taheri, B. and D. vom Lehn (2013), 'Cultural consumption, interactive sociality, and the museum', *Journal of Marketing Management* 29(15–16): 1729–1752.
Jones, C. (2012), 'Events and festivals: fit for the future?', *Event Management* 16(2): 107–118.
Kaina, V. and I. Karolewski (2009), 'EU governance and European identity, *Living Reviews in European Governance* 4(2): 5–41.
Karanfil, G. (2009), 'Pseudo-exiles and reluctant transnationals: disrupted nostalgia on Turkish satellite broadcasts, Media', *Culture, and Society* 31(6): 887–899.
Kim, H. (2005), 'Research note: nostalgia and tourism', *Tourism Analysis* 10(1): 85–88.
Kolar, T. and V. Zabkar (2010), 'A consumer-based model of authenticity: An oxymoron or the foundation of cultural heritage marketing?', *Tourism Management* 31(5): 652–664.
Kotler, N., P. Kotler and W. Kotler (2008), *Museum Marketing and Strategy: Designing Missions, Building Audiences, Generating Revenue and Resources*, 2nd ed. (San Francisco, CA: Jossey-Bass).

Lähdesmäki, T. (2016), 'Politics of tangibility, intangibility, and place in the making of a European cultural heritage in EU heritage policy', *International Journal of Heritage Studies* 22(10): 766–780.

Lau, C. and Y. Li (2019), 'Analyzing the effects of an urban food festival: A place theory approach', *Annals of Tourism Research* 74: 43–55.

Leinhardt, G., K. Knutson and K. Crowley (2003), 'Museum learning collaborative redux', *Journal of Museum Education* 28: 23–31.

Li, M., Z. Huang and L. Cai (2009), 'Benefit segmentation of visitors to a rural community-based festival', *Journal of Travel and Tourism Marketing* 26(5–6): 585–598.

McLean, K. (1999), 'Museum exhibitions and the dynamics of dialogue', *Daedalus* 128(3): 83–107.

Mollen, A., and H. Wilson (2010), 'Engagement, telepresence and interactivity in online consumer experience: Reconciling scholastic and managerial perspectives', *Journal of Business Research* 63(9–10): 919–925.

Moscardo, G. (1996), 'Mindful visitors: heritage and tourism', *Annals of Tourism Research* 23(2): 376–397.

Nic Craith, M. (2012), 'Europe's (Un)common Heritage(s)', *Traditiones* 41(2): 11–28.

Nic Craith, M. (2008), 'Intangible cultural heritage: The challenges for Europe', *Anthropological Journal of European Cultures* 17(1): 54–73.

Nic Craith, M. and U. Kockel (2015), 'Re-building heritage: Integrating tangible and intangible', in W. Logan, M. Nic Craith and U. Kockel (eds), *A companion to heritage studies* (Malden, MA: Wiley), 53–62.

Park, H. (2011), 'Shared national memory as intangible heritage: re-imagining two Koreas as one nation', *Annals of Tourism Research* 38(2): 520–539.

Pattakos, A. (2010), 'Discovering the deeper meaning of tourism', in R. Wurzburger, T. Aageson, A. Pattakos and S. Pratt (eds), *Discovering the deeper meaning of tourism creative tourism: a global conversation* (Santa Fe, NM: Sunstone), 53–62.

Plog, S. (1974), 'Why destination areas rise and fall in popularity', *Cornell Hotel and Restaurant Administration Quarterly* 14(4): 55–58.

Putnam, R. (2000), *Bowling alone: the collapse and revival of American community* (London: Simon and Schuster).

Rappaport, S. (2007), 'Lessons from online practice: new advertising models', *Journal of Advertising Research* 47(2): 135–141.

Reed, A. (2002), 'Social identity as a useful perspective for self-concept-based consumer research', *Psychology and Marketing* 19(3): 235–266.

Schindler, R. and M. Holbrook (2003), 'Nostalgia for early experience as a determinant of consumer preferences', *Psychology and Marketing* 20(4): 275–302.

Shankar, A., R. Elliott and C. Goulding (2001), 'Understanding consumption: contributions from a narrative perspective', *Journal of Marketing Management* 17(3–4): 420–453.

Sierra, J. and S. McQuitty (2007), 'Attitudes and emotions as determinants of nostalgia purchases: an application of social identity theory', *Journal of Marketing Theory and Practice* 15(2): 99–112.

Simon, N. (2010), *The participatory museum* (San Francisco, CA: Museum 20).

Stamboulis, Y. and P. Skayannis (2003), 'Innovation strategies and technology for experience-based tourism', *Tourism Management* 24: 35–43.

Taheri, B. and A. Jafari (2012), 'Cultural heritage sites as playful venues in the leisure society', in R. Sharpley and P. Stone (eds), *The contemporary tourist experience: concepts and consequences* (New York: Routledge), 201–215.

Taheri, B., A. Jafari and K. O'Gorman (2014), 'Keeping your audience: Presenting a visitor engagement scale', *Tourism Management* 42: 321–329.

Taheri, B., M. Gannon, R. Cordina and S. Lochrie (2018), 'Measuring host sincerity: Scale development and validation', *International Journal of Contemporary Hospitality Management* 30(8): 2752–2772.

Tan, S-K., S-H. Tan, Y-S. Kok and S-W. Choon (2018), 'Sense of place and sustainability of intangible cultural heritage – The case of George Town and Melaka', *Tourism Management* 67: 376–387.

Taylor, D. (2016), 'Saving the "live"? Re-performance and intangible cultural heritage', *Études Anglaises* 69(2): 149–161.

vom Lehn, D. (2006), 'Embodying experience: a video-based examination of visitors' conduct and interaction in museums', *European Journal of Marketing* 40(11/12): 1340–1359.

vom Lehn, D. and C. Heath (2005), 'Accounting for new technology in museum exhibitions', *International Journal of Arts Management* 7(3): 11–21.

Wells, V., D. Gregory-Smith, B. Taheri, D. Manika and C. McCowlen (2016), 'An exploration of CSR development in heritage tourism', *Annals of Tourism Research* 58: 1–17.

Yalinay, O., I. Baxter, E. Collinson, R. Curran, M. Gannon and J. Thompson (2018), 'Servicescape and shopping value: the role of negotiation intention, social orientation, and recreational identity at the Istanbul Grand Bazaar, Turkey', *Journal of Travel and Tourism Marketing* 35(9): 1132–1144.

Zhao, S., and D. Timothy (2017), 'Tourists' consumption and perceptions of red heritage', *Annals of Tourism Research* 63: 97–111.

# 6 Events that want to become heritage

## Vernacularisation of ICH and the politics of culture and identity in European public rituals

*Alessandro Testa*

> 'Participatory festivals are neither simple drunken revels nor mystical survivals of ancestral rites but resonant forms of collective action in response to a global crisis of local communities'.
>
> (Noyes 2003: 12)

The scholarship about festivals, festive heritage and the politics of culture and identity during/around/based on such events has been expanding fast in the last few decades. Since this chapter cannot be exhaustive about the state of the art of any of those issues, I will focus on a limited set of problems, intersecting theoretical reflections with evidence taken from my own ethnographic fieldworks.

The 'events' I refer to in the title are structured forms of collective action (Handelman 1999; Noyes 2003), performances which have undergone a process of 'heritagisation' (or 'heritage-making') (Hafstein 2012; Hemme, Tauschek and Bendix 2007; Smith and Akagawa 2009; Logan, Kochel and Nic Craith 2015; Testa 2016a). More precisely, I focus on examples of 'public rituals', a category which here is used as a synonym for 'festivals' or 'public festive performances' – I prefer the term 'public ritual' in order to emphasise that there is always a ritual dimension in festivals, whereas there is not always a festive dimension in other types of rituals or performances (Testa 2014a). These are, in fact, among the types of phenomena once considered typically 'folkloric', in Europe at least, and which today, after a terminological and ontological shift that is very interesting to study *per se* (Testa 2016a), are often recognised as pieces of intangible cultural heritage (ICH) by UNESCO.

The European dimension of festive/ritual heritagisation has been the object of a precocious scholarly interest (Boissevain 1992). This tradition of studies intercepts and builds upon a socially transversal renewed interest in the past and for local traditions, and for new modes of social memory construction and expression, in connection with interwoven phenomena of ritualisation, re-enchantment and musealisation (Testa 2017a). These processes took place roughly between the 1960s and the late 1980s, peaking in the 1990s, and represent a trend that has its *raison d'être* in a rather complex cluster of socio-cultural factors affecting European societies in the post-Fordist, late modern era (Boissevain 1992; Hodges 2011; Macdonald 2013; Testa 2014b, 2017a).

The institutionalisation of these phenomena from about the 1990s and then their 'heritagisation' proper from the beginning of this century have brought about the necessity of a different kind of critical reflection, with a focus on the many existing relations between Europe, European identities and ICH. Studies have focussed not only on the 'top' and 'etic' level (the institutions and agencies, the functionaries and academics), as well as on the 'below' and 'emic' one (the local communities, the 'natives' or 'tradition-holders'), but also on the circulations, interactions and negotiations between these two conceptual poles (Macdonald 2013; Nic Craith 2008; Shore 2000; Wilken 2012; Taylor 2016). This stream of works is now solidly established within the broader field of the anthropology of Europe.

Critical studies about cultural heritage and/in Europe have generally been problematised with respect to collective identity/identities construction and expression (Delanty 1999; Johler 2003; Kuutma 2007; Nic Craith 2008; Niedermüller and Stoklund 2001) and the problem of their 'nestedness' (Herb and Kaplan 1999), an interesting aspect ethnographically observable at different levels (local, regional, national, European) and transversally across them. This has led to the theorisation of a specific 'memory-heritage-identity complex' (Macdonald 2013), which would characterise all European societies, albeit differently conjugated nationally, regionally and locally.

My interpretative endeavour stands on a critical and reflexive study of the issues previously outlined, in order to understand the relational and processual nature of heritage-making processes, the emergence of heritage poetics and discourses, and the establishment of heritage politics and practices at all levels (from local to global, at the upper and grassroots levels, and within all the gradations, intersections and intervals between these conceptual ends). In order to achieve this, I have chosen the 'methodological agnostic' approach as theorised by Brumann (2014), that is, 'an 'agnostic' study of heritage [that] does not posit a priori that heritage is an empty signifier, an entirely arbitrary and socially determined ascription, but takes people's heritage experience and beliefs seriously' (Brumann 2014: 180). I have also tried to reunite the somewhat artificial distinction, today considered almost self-explanatory, between tangible and intangible (Testa 2016a, forthcoming); therefore, I fully endorse the idea of an integrated or 'symbiotic' concept of heritage, 'one that merges the tangible with the intangible, and thus reinforces the indivisible nature of heritage, transcending the conventional dualism' (Nic Craith and Kockel 2015: 429).

With the idea of an event 'wanting' to become heritage, I intend to highlight the process of emergence of a heritage sensibility among various social groups and agents (locals, organisers, performers, public functionaries, aficionados, tourists or visitors, ethnologists, etc.), actually animating and shaping an event and participating or being otherwise involved in it. I refer both to festivals undergoing heritagisation and those which have already been officially recognised as heritage, in one form or another. This emergence is characteristic of UNESCO ICH applications and recognitions. However, as will be made evident in the forthcoming pages, it can also characterise other external or official recognitions (e.g. being enlisted in national or NGOs' lists) as well as less formalised or 'vernacular' ways of conceptualising festive events and public rituals, ways that are compatible, comparable or more or less associable with what is today categorised as ICH.

While referring to other cases taken from the literature, I will focus especially on three case studies that have been at the centre of my historical and ethnographic investigations in the last ten years, with the aim of operating a critical kind of comparison (i.e. a differential and relational as well as analogical type of comparison).

## 6.1 The case studies

In the revitalised carnival pantomime of the deer-man, in Castelnuovo al Volturno, a small village in the central Apennines (Testa 2014b, 2017a, 2017b, forthcoming), the process of heritage-making has acquired a peculiar form. This pantomime displays some rather archaic features, among which are a set of characteristic masks and the ritualised hunt for a man disguised as a deer. Like many others in the mountainous areas of Europe, this festival went through a period of neglect during the 1950s and 1960s, only to be reborn afterwards, from the late 1970s to the early 1990s, when it was revitalised, refunctionalised and charged with new forms, meanings and functions. The revival was associated with institutionalisation (in different forms) and also with the development of a heritage discourse around the revitalised tradition, which in the last few decades has become one of the 'cultural brands', identity markers and tourist attractions of the area. The fact of being associated with a primistivistic, magical and 'pagan' imaginary has fostered sentiments of authenticity, typicity and therefore the need for conservation and promotion through heritagisation. In fact, 'why does an "ancient" festival function more efficiently in the construction and the maintenance of the locality? Because the stretching of the temporal depth of the festival means the widening of its symbolic density and stratification' (Faeta 2005: 163). There have been extensive talks, in the last few years, about a possible application to UNESCO.

Every year for almost fifty years now, a very special carnival is celebrated in Solsona, in central Catalonia (Vilaseca and Trilla 2011; Testa forthcoming). After having been prohibited during Francoism, it became one of the vehicles of the Catalan reaction against the regime in the early seventies, a veritable symbol of political and cultural liberation, and a free expression of Catalanism – similar to the more famous 'Patum' festival in Berga (Noyes 2003), which was the first Spanish festival recognised by UNESCO, in 2004. In 1979, the Spanish government declared Solsona's carnival '*Fiesta de Interés Turístico Nacional*' ('Festival of National Touristic Interest'), despite its then emerging (and today explicit) anti-Castilian stance. This recognition, which has existed in Spain for more than half a century, is comparable to other early listings of folkloric/festive events in Europe, and can be considered, *mutatis mutandis*, a national precursor of the transnational UNESCO ICH scheme. After the recognition, during the 1980s, the festivity became the host of a series of ritualised acts and other performances, which structured a then still young event. In the last few decades, the festival has grown exponentially, becoming a mass event participated in by not only most of the townsfolk and visitors from surrounding areas and regions but also from Barcelona. Today, the Solsona carnival week and its inner rituals last for seven days, during which they occupy and hegemonise the public sphere completely. This festival bears a great significance for the local community and is participated in massively, with extreme enthusiasm and even rapture. It contributes to the configuration of the social fabric, structuring and formalising an entire set of interpersonal and intergroup relationships, mostly through the creation and reproduction of '*colles*' and '*comparses*' (two very specific kinds of network that function within, during and for the carnival). More importantly, it makes it possible for the people of Solsona to articulate and express their 'being Catalans' in central Catalonia.

The *Masopust* (Czech word for 'Carnival') in Hlinsko v Čechách in Bohemia is characterised by what in the English-speaking world is known as 'mumming' (i.e. door-to-door processions of masked men who perform dances and other pseudo-ritual actions to ensure, they claim, good luck and fertility) (Blahůšek and Vojancová 2011; Testa 2017a, 2017b, forthcoming). The *Masopust* in Hlinsko exhibits many features in common with other carnival-like festivals in the Czech Republic, Slovakia and elsewhere in central-eastern European Slavic countries. Unlike many similar manifestations, it was not prohibited during socialist times in Czechoslovakia, although the official position of the Communist Party towards this kind of events was one of discouragement, if not open condemnation (Testa 2016b). In any case, this festival also went through a phase of partial disinterest during the 1980s, but during the 1990s, with the political–economic transition that followed the fall of Communism, it acquired a new relevance and popularity, which has since continued to grow. This growth or re-growth in popularity was crowned by an important recognition: *Masopust* in Hlinsko and in three surrounding villages was included on the UNESCO Representative List of the Intangible Cultural Heritage of Humanity in 2010. The coming of UNESCO to Hlinsko and the heritagisation dynamics have initiated a set of changes both within the festival and in the broader social contexts in which it takes place. Several adjustments and alterations have affected the post-transition and post-UNESCO event, namely in its calendar structure, its local perception and in the ritual structure of the performances: as it has been written, 'by attempting to preserve spaces, practices, and objects, UNESCO experts and national heritage professionals effectively transform them' (Berliner 2012: 771).

## 6.2 Localisations, adjustments and transformations: the vernacularisation of ICH

Although many claims have been made about the risk of a homogenised and homogenising conception and application of the UNESCO ICH and, by metonymy, of other national or regional schemes that inevitably, in the current globalised arena, are influenced by its nomenclature and taxonomy, the now abundant ethnographic evidence about ICH and related matters tells a different story: local, vernacular variants of the ICH discourse and politics of culture – and of the concept of 'folklore' that lies, genealogically, beneath ICH (Testa 2016a) – have been emerging ever since the formalisation of the Convention in 2003. True, the universalisation of UNESCO heritage conception based on Western, liberal and upper-class criteria has led to the emergence of a veritable Authorised Heritage Discourse (Smith 2006), which has also been called the *'expression d'une économie morale idéologiquement occidentaliste et néolibérale'* (Bortolotto 2011: 21–22), and a 'worldwide mentality' (Bendix 2009: 257). Nevertheless, once situated in specific contexts, this discoursive, (geo)political and ideological framework can acquire different traits and even be re-thought and reconfigured. There are at least two levels in which this contextualisation can be observed and analysed: a comparative one, the (pan-)European dimension, with its specific stress on history, sense of European 'exceptionalism' and characteristic patterned forms of 'past-presencing' (Macdonald 2013), and the micro/local one, where vernacular forms of heritage, heritagisation and situated politics of culture manifest themselves as *'mises en pratique localisées de l'"idée de patrimoine" […] qui devraient être analysées comme des adaptations d'une certaine vision qui s'est diffusée à travers le monde'* (Bondaz et al. 2014: 10). Accordingly, ethnologists have attempted to draw a more detailed picture of the heritage discourse without losing sight of the broader framework (Adell et al. 2015), trying to capture the dynamicity of processes of circulation, hybridation, syncretism and crossed influences between different social actors and institutions operating on the ICH scene: different local groups and individuals, institutions and agencies and their tribes (UNESCO experts and personnel, public functionaries and bureaucrats, academics, experts and the like), aficionados, tourists, etc. It cannot be stressed enough that 'these connections cannot be characterised as linear or top-down, and they do not simply illustrate the entrance of international discourses on a local or national level. On the contrary, they symbolise the complex paths taken in the production of an intangible cultural heritage discourse' (Tauschek 2011: 55).

These local appropriations and vernacularisation happen at the linguistic/terminological level already: in the three case studies previously presented, the word 'heritage' and its correspondent in the respective languages (*'patrimonio'*, *'patrimoni'*, *'dědictví'*) is not the only one, and sometimes not the most important one, used at the emic level to refer to the heritagised events. In fact, in all of my ethnographic investigations, the expression 'intangible cultural heritage' (which still retains a certain technical connotation) is used mostly by functionaries and experts and only seldom by other categories of social agents – unlike its simpler version 'heritage', much more diffused and used among all categories and classes of people. The term itself, 'heritage', has slowly but continuously made its way into different social niches, transcending its etic connotation and becoming not only a label but also a tool used by social actors for social negotiations, political recognition, identity claims, religious agendas, economic interests and other motives. As one of the symbolic mechanics in the functioning of the politics of culture in a given context, heritage can also be used as a political tool, contributing to the establishment of hierarchies and authorities. In the carnival of Castelnuovo al Volturno, the management and promotion of the event and other correlated dynamics have intersected or collided with political authorities and with individual ambitions, whereas in Hlinsko v Čechách an evident continuity – or even synergy – of intentions could be observed between the public administration, UNESCO personnel, native functionaries and other prominent figures of local public life (Testa 2014c, 2017b). In Solsona's festival, likewise, the level of entanglement between the administrative exercise of power, cultural politics and policies, and the political positioning of certain individuals and groups has also assumed rather interesting forms. All these examples demonstrate that, if on the one hand the symbolic capital of the heritagised festival is expressed differently and used for a variety of purposes, on the other it is also easily and often converted into political or social capital, or even, as will be shown in the following section, into economic capital (Testa 2014a), structuring a wide range of social dynamics that transcend the time/space framework of the events themselves.

One way of looking at the vernacularisation of the heritage discourse and practices is to consider the general transformations that have been observed comparatively and theorised/named in the last few decades in the literature. These general processes of change and adjustment constitute now a rich collection of 'ations', among which are revitalisation, refunctionalisation, restoration, ritualisation, folklorisation, institutionalisation, bureaucratisation, petrification, falsification, ossification, touristification, massification, homogenisation, contamination, mediatisation, commodification, commercialisation, sacralisation, fetishisation, musealisation – and the list could go on. These are some of the transformations that are at the base – and are the object – of vernacularly inflected expressions of macro-processes of societal (economic, political, religious, etc.) changes at the micro-level of localities and communities. These locally observable processes have in fact been happening in Europe and globally, albeit unevenly, during the last few decades (the late modern times). They have triggered, among other things, a general ontological as well as a practical reconfiguration of local traditions and of the very notion of 'tradition' (Testa 2017b), which is also constitutional of the very idea of ICH (Testa 2016a). They have also triggered a deeper restructuring of the symbolic order of local communities, as demonstrated clearly in my case studies. This symbolic restructuring has, in turn, determined a certain taxonomic polarisation, rather widespread throughout Europe, centred around a few conceptual oppositions, such as tradition versus modernity, authenticity versus inauthenticity, genuine versus commercialised or touristified, local (typical and different) versus global (massified and homogenised). In my publications about the previously presented case studies, most of those 'ations' and subsequent polarisations are analysed and critically discussed with reference to historical and ethnographic evidence, whereas, for obvious reasons of space, in the following pages I will focus on only some of them.

## 6.3 Commodification, touristification and musealisation

If there is a problematic notion associated with all the phenomena mentioned in the previous paragraph, that notion is 'authenticity' (and therefore 'inauthenticity'), one of the conceptual black diamonds in the kin-disciplines of anthropology, folkloristics and heritage studies (Bendix 1997; Bortolotto 2013; Brumann 2014; Macdonald 2013: 109–136). In ICH-related issues, authenticity and inauthenticity have been problematised especially with respect to the interrelated processes of commodification and touristification, which have both featured in my case studies, especially in Castelnuovo and Hlinsko, and are actually often observable in many other European public rituals. The UNESCO ICH itself, in spite of its having taken a dislike to the term 'authenticity', continues to be based upon and foster social poetics of authenticity: '[although] rules about inappropriate vocabulary may eventually expunge the term "authenticity" from UNESCO documents, the values conveyed by this word are not likely to be eradicated from heritage discourse since the two are closely interrelated' (Bortolotto 2013: 78). In the case of 'traditional' public rituals like carnivals, which are very often either old festivals or so considered, this critical observation is particularly piercing, because in these cases '"traditional" means not only old, but also original and authentic' (Istenič 2012: 79); moreover, 'what is historical and typical is authentic, and it is assumed that authenticity is objectively ascertainable' (Handler 1988: 200). Very often, for this kind of festivals, the best 'historicity' or 'type of past', in a manner of speaking, is the antique time of pagan festivals. The locals engage in 'popular Frazerism' (Testa 2017b), that is, an operation of 'cultural bricolage' and symbolic manipulation, circulation and diffusion of a popularised version of Frazer's theses on European agrarian festivities and folk rituals. These include, for instance, those concerning the notion of ritually fostered fertility, agrarian magic, the supposed pagan origins of carnival and other European festivals and their being a 'survival' of ancient rituals, at times considered to be of presumed unfathomable antiquity. This 'sense of the antique', more than any possible and actual antique feature, which can be easily altered or even invented, is one of the factors that permit binding a tradition and the people who practise it to a past that can be used to enhance collective sentiments of belonging and identity, as has emerged clearly in the ethnographies I undertook in Castelnuovo and Hlinsko. These poetics and practices of time and 'past presencing' produce in turn symbolic depth, which fuels social memory and usually translates into sentiments of typicity, originality and authenticity. Thus can be explained the emic usage of adjectives like 'very ancient', 'Dionysian' and 'pagan', often associated with these rituals: the equation at work is that the more remote the evoked past is, the more 'authentic' the tradition. Hence, once the oblivion endangering the local tradition is 'defeated' through revitalisation (Macdonald 2013: 152), and authenticity is so 'ascertained' and felt, it can then be itself commodified: it becomes the additional value needed by the local tradition/event/heritage to be 'offered', 'sold' and 'consumed'.

The commodification of 'authentic' festive or ritual forms of ICH, like those of my three ethnographic examples, shows three distinct but correlated aspects:

1. the juridical and institutional framework comprising conceptual as well as factual matters of cultural property and ownership (Hafstein 2007; Tauschek 2010);
2. the somewhat spontaneous emergence of a micro-economy (a 'market') around the festival;
3. the actual will of 'selling' one's heritage for economic reasons (for a profit).

These widespread aspects have been associated with reconfiguration and/or loss of the social meaning of the events (Macdonald 2013: 110–112; Noyes 2003: 215–236). The second aspect among the aforementioned should be duly acknowledged: in Solsona, I have observed the development of an extremely complex economic dimension, madeup of the production and circulation of equipment, gadgets and carnival-related promotional materials, publications and audio-visual products, public subventions, private sponsorships, financial transactions of different kinds, lotteries, trades and purchases, accommodation, restoration and other services being offered and demanded; not circumscribed in the time-space brackets of the festival, this ritual micro-economy actually goes beyond them, manifesting itself throughout the year and transcending the locality of the event, but yet being deeply rooted in it.

The last of those three aspects also raises the question of why certain traditions and not others have actually been revitalised and heritagised: the answer is that, sometimes, it certainly happened due to their potential marketability, even though, as has been affirmed by Gerald Creed, in the same vein as in the citation by Dorothy Noyes that opens this chapter, 'commodifying the ritual for a tourist market is not simply a case of capitalism's well-known co-optation of critical practices into marketable goods but as equally the grassroots product of ritual aficionados trying to ensure the perpetuation of the practices in a radically changing context' (Creed 2011: 27). In Hlinsko, for instance, the revitalisation and heritagisation of the *Masopust* have followed the evident degradation of the material living conditions of the local communities during the post-socialist transition, which led to a generalised situation of social stress, characterised by the diminishing or dismissal of rural and industrial productive activities, economic impoverishment, emigration towards bigger cities and consequential depopulation. A similar situation of social stress and degradation has been happening in Castelnuovo for several decades now, and here again the revitalisation of the Carnival emerged in the years when the crisis became manifest. I am not making an argument for a cause–effect relation (revitalisation/heritagisation and an increase in symbolic value as a direct consequence of material deterioration or loss) but a correlation can certainly be hypothesised.

Commodification is also strongly associated with internal or external visitors ('tourists') who may be willing to pay to participate in or just witness the rituals, or be differently involved in the events or buy something connected with them. Unlike the case of Solsona, where the entire town seems to enjoy the presence of masses of tourists (probably because of the tradition being younger and consequentially its sense of historicity and authenticity thinner), in Hlinsko and Castelnuovo the presence of tourists is usually met with mixed feelings by the locals participating in the rituals. Unsurprisingly, the literature about rituals, festivals and tourism has dwelled on the ambiguities and inconsistencies in the local perception of tourism and the tourists (Isnart 2014; Macdonald 2013; Picard and Robinson 2006). This perception can sometimes be 'detrimental of the local people's sense of the meaningfulness of the ritual' (Macdonald 2013: 111). This usually results in implicit or explicit emic positioning and the emergence of a certain polarisation among the locals, with attitudes oscillating between the hardcore purists who utterly dislike or despise the presence of tourists, considering it a symptom of massification and trivialisation, and those who contrariwise show appreciation and even support for the visits. Many gradations subsist between these two poles, and sometimes different postures can even be incorporated, seemingly contradictorily, by the same individual, according to the circumstances.

Institutions, among which is UNESCO, usually openly support 'cultural' and 'sustainable' tourism, considered a possible source of local development. This motivation can also subsist at the grassroots level, when communities or some groups within them think of tourism also in terms of indirect 'proof' that the local traditions (whether or not officially recognised as cultural heritage) are worthy of preservation and promotion. It is precisely in this conceptual segment that the paradox of tourism emerges clearly: on the one hand, tourism is desired as a source of cultural recognition and/or for economic reasons; on the other, however, the more a tradition becomes the object of popular interest and tourists' presence and participation, the less 'authentic' it might be considered, for tourism also brings sentiments of dispossession and 'cultural contamination' (Meethan 2001: 90).

The point of view of tourists is worth mentioning because it also seems to stand on a rather paradoxical association: tourists are often in search of authenticity – this is why ICH can very often be the object of genuine touristic interest; however, it is precisely the presence of tourists that make a certain piece of heritage less authentic. Tourists become the very source of their own disappointment: another apparently inescapable paradox.

In Castelnuovo, most of the people involved in the local public ritual are longing for more official recognition; in Hlinsko, in spite of several discordant voices, the enlisting on the UNESCO ICH was met with enthusiasm precisely on the grounds of the potential incorporation of that sleepy region into the network of cultural tourism in Czechia. Furthermore, the appointment of a heritage label is associated with prestige and with the prospect of augmented visibility in the growing but also competitive market of tourism, and therefore with consequential economic advantage, in order to reinvigorate economies that are, especially in the rural, marginal, and 'provincial' (Noyes 2003) areas of Europe, often anaemic.

The coexistent, complementary and interconnected processes of heritagisation, commodification and touristification are related to an emic desire for external recognition, social prestige as well as pride and for the idea of 'local development', at times (in rural and peripheral contexts) motivated more by the necessity of economic survival than by a will for profit. This does not mean that heritagisation should always be considered as an instrumental strategy for self-marketability. Nor, however, can this be utterly excluded (Tauschek 2010), for several social agents, in neo-liberal Europe, also affirm the economic rationale of their actions in the sphere of all things cultural. Heritage is but one thread in the tightly woven fabric of the politics and the economics of culture in Europe today. Those are some of the reasons why certain events may want to become heritage.

Strictly connected with social representations of authenticity and with tourism is the process of ICH musealisation. In a sense, it is actually impossible to disentangle heritagisation from musealisation, for they are strictly interconnected and rely upon the same sensibility for the safeguarding, protection and transmission of what is considered not only authentic and aesthetically or socially valuable but also potentially 'endangered' and therefore in need of being preserved. Heritagisation could be considered a cultural variant of musealisation or vice versa. They are both practices of 'saving' as well as 'institutionalising' the past (Macdonald 2013: 138), detaching certain things or categories of things from their normal 'social life' and resulting sometimes in forms of cultural fetishisation, glorification of authenticity and historicity and even material 'sacralisation' (Macdonald 2013: 138).

Musealisation of folklore and ICH have escalated in Europe since the 1970s. It occurred in Castelnuovo, Hlinsko and Solsona, where museums or exhibition sites devoted to masks, memorabilia, pictures and gadgets (often for sale) connected with the local ritual events were established, at different moments, during the last three decades. Castelnuovo has (unsuccessfully) been trying to found a museum of the local carnival for fifteen years now; in the meantime, a permanent exhibition of carnival-related memorabilia and other objects is hosted at the local organisation's venue. Solsona has several sites (a tourist centre with a small exhibition gallery, the places where the masks and the giants are kept, and others) that serve as ethnographic galleries. Hlinsko saw the birth of a museum of the *Masopust* in conjunction with the UNESCO recognition. These sites and institutions have acquired a great importance and contribute today to the structuring, the reproduction, the circulation and the normativisation of narratives of typicity and locality, crystallising the local festive imaginaries but also instructing the locals as well as the outsiders to distinguish what is old and traditional, and therefore (in their view) authentic, and what is not.

But musealisation is also strongly connected with commodification, for at least two reasons. First, it very often depends on private or public funding (through sponsorships, subventions and subscriptions); second, the creation of a museum is also the creation of a space where cultural commerce can be regulated and legitimately undertaken. Through museums, galleries and the like, the 'material' dimension of heritage emerges clearly, not only by means of financialisation and commodification proper (Bendix 2009: 263; Tauschek 2010) but also in the sense of making tangible what is (supposed to be) intangible: the ICH and the social practices and representations that it embodies and triggers 'embed' themselves in these objects; in this way, ICH 'materialises'. However, this dynamic makes it clear that the material dimension alone cannot acquire, keep or transmit meaning without its 'intangible' counterpart, formed of the discourses, narratives and representations that make the tangible (whether a monument, a piece of art, artefact, picture, etc.) socially recognisable, relevant and desirable: the integrated or symbiotic nature of heritage (Nic Craith and Kockel 2015). The foundation of a museum or a similar institution is another reason why certain events may want to become heritage.

## 6.4 ... and identity, of course

If, on the one hand, representations of authenticity are widely at work in phenomena like commodification, touristification and musealisation, on the other, collective identity as a relational and structural social dimension encompasses, or rather implies, all of the previously mentioned aspects and processes. It is at the core of the design, functioning and reproduction of public rituals and/as ICH. No wonder that in an era dominated by the markets and other expressions of global capitalism, identity itself, that is, a specific, culturally oriented way of defining a group's sense and modality of belonging, whether or not ritualised, can become touristified and commodified (Comaroff and Comaroff 2009).

Identity-related issues (especially identity construction and expression) in connection with ICH and heritagisation have been the object of a rich anthropological scholarship (abundant references can be found in Macdonald 2013 and Nic Craith 2008). It has actually been argued that the very process of 'filing' heritage (for example, in the form of an application for the UNESCO ICH or the registration on a national list) can be a powerful act of self- or external representation, triggering feelings of social belonging and therefore shaping a sense of community (Kuutma 2007). I have myself observed this process. In fact, in all of my ethnographic cases, the festivals and the performances embedded within them operate as platforms for identity construction, mostly enhancing feelings of local, regional and/or national belonging. However, tensions and even forms of cultural 'dissidence' (for example, in the form of openly criticising the heritagisation process or not participating in the public ritual) do subsist. It is important to stress this aspect here in order not to fall into the trap of an implicit and uncritical neo-functionalism. Identity is not a monolithic social configuration, nor are its processual dynamics linear and predictive. Besides, as I have tried to explain in the previous pages, the process through which European public rituals have become heritage is far from being unidirectional, homogeneous or free of ruptures and tensions.

Different worldviews, political positioning based on local frictions or ideological frameworks, as well as discrepancies in the vision of the past, or even open rivalries between close communities or within the same community can emerge around the 'heritage discourse' and the process of festive heritagisation. In my three ethnographic cases, tensions were frequent especially between members of local NGOs and politicians (for example, for organisational issues), and dissidence open among heritage 'discontents' or 'sceptics'. In Castelnuovo, heated debates and intellectual disagreements have characterised the local construction of traditional meaning, leading to veritable 'conflicts of interpretation' about the local heritagised carnival pantomime (Testa 2017b). Contrapositions and dissidence lead to more or less structured modalities of open or implicit negotiations among social agents, as in the case of Solsona, for example, where the political establishment sitting in the local government – the ultimate authority concerning public order but also the object of overt mocking during the carnival – has had to come to terms with the carnival leaders and figure out viable ways of mutual tolerance. The aforementioned, and many other 'heritage problems', have been observed and analysed in the anthropological literature about ICH (Adell et al. 2015; Bendix 2009; Berliner 2012; Bortolotto 2011; Knecht and Niedermüller 2003; Kuutma 2007; Logan, Kochel and Nic Craith 2015). Likewise, minority views and practices should also be taken into consideration, for they always subsist and are, in one way or another, significant. True is that, in the end, a certain level of generalisation flattening down differences and nuances becomes inevitable: as all sciences, anthropology, too, rests on attempts of generalisation, in order to be able to handle the complexity of reality and 'reduce' it to models and patterns (map is not territory). And in fact, minority issues, minor inclinations, occasional dissidences or frictions, and exceptional examples should not overshadow the general trend, which regards heritagisation as a resource useful for a variety of purposes for a variety of social agents and institutions. This general trend, consisting of all the transformations and processes described in the previous sections, remains solidly anchored in patterns of communitarian and identitarian significance – locals are very often unbeknown functionalists.

To conclude with a few last reflections about the interplay of identity with other representational dimensions, I would like to stress once again how deeply influential the sense of 'typiqueness' and 'uniqueness' of the local festive heritage is in the construction of locality and of local identities. This conclusion can again be easily deduced from my own cases as well as from plenty of other examples in the anthropological literature. The symbolic interaction between ritual structure, festive behaviour, the tangible features of the festival (decorations and other paraphernalia, masks and figures, the equipment used during the performances, etc.) and the location can lead to an emergence of a rather new, and specific, 'sense of place', a veritable heritagised and heritagising *genius loci*, as has already been observed (Lähdesmäki 2016; Nic Craith and Kockel 2015), which is literally the soil in which identity can root and grow.

Regional and national identities, as well as the social construction of space and of the sense of locality (and of the fact of belonging to it), are not the only stakes, though. European identity is another one: 'the contemporary concepts of cultural heritage must be seen as symbolic constructions which territorialise cultural differences and which play an important role in the symbolic formation of regions, nations, and supernational entities like the EU' (Knecht and Niedermüller 2003: 90). The sense of belonging to a locality and community and processes of emergence of European symbolic spaces and broader, transregional and transnational identities intersect with each other on many levels (Johler 2003; Lähdesmäki 2016), among others, in the field of festive heritagisation. This appearance of local(ised) variations of European identities is something I have also observed and recorded during my investigations: different social agents articulate their ethnic, political or more generically cultural identities also referring explicitly to Europe and to 'being Europeans'. Often, in spite of the emic claims of these festivals being 'unique', their being actually variations of a historical 'pan-European' type of public event (carnival) is more or less acknowledged and variably taken into account, leading to an equation between festive culture and belonging (having similar festivals throughout Europe = being part of the same 'culture'). This aspect of cultural recognition and folkloric narrative also plainly exemplifies the typically 'European' identity interplay between the local micro-level and the transregional and transnational macro-sphere (Delanty 1994; Macdonald 2013; Wilken 2012). It is in the cultural interstices of this dimension that variations of European identity acquire their actual collective configurations and emerge from within and in the light of the social fabric.

Last but not least, a local public ritual becoming heritage allows a 'reflexive' kind of identity construction: being collective identity a differential and relational social dimension (albeit ultimately rooted in individual psychology), it cannot but be grounded on an 'us ≠ them' logic (Delanty 1999): 'we' can only exist insofar as there is a 'you' or a 'they'. Therefore, external cultural feedback in the form of an official recognition (e.g. by UNESCO) or the presence and interest of visitors become symbolically relevant and mostly – though not always – socially desirable: in a way, institutions and tourists embody the best type of 'them' (also, as already stressed, for reasons of prestige and economic benefit). Therefore, even though a theoretically simplistic functionalism should be avoided when analysing and interpreting these phenomena, due to the fact that tensions within communities and groups might and actually do arise or are even triggered by the heritagisation process, the prevalent general function of heritagised public rituals in Europe should be considered as fundamentally prosocial – especially in times of crisis. This is yet another reason why certain events may want to become heritage.

## References

Adell, N., R. Bendix, C. Bortolotto and M. Tauschek eds (2015), *Between imagined communities and communities of practice: participation, territory and the making of heritage* (Göttingen: Universitätsverlag Göttingen).

Bendix, R. (2009), 'Heritage between economy and politics: an assessment from the perspective of cultural anthropology', in L. Smith and N. Akagawa (eds), *Intangible heritage* (London: Routledge), 253–269.

Bendix, R. (1997), *In search of authenticity: the formation of folklore studies* (Madison: University of Wisconsin Press).

Berliner, D. (2012), 'Multiple nostalgias: the fabric of heritage in Luang Prabang (Lao PDR)', *Journal of the Royal Anthropological Institute* 18(4), 769–786.

Blahůšek, J. and I. Vojancová (2011), *Vesnické masopustní obchůzky a masky na Hlinecku* (Strážnice: Národní ústav lidové kultury).

Boissevain, J. ed. (1992), *Revitalizing European rituals* (London: Routledge).

Bondaz J., F. Graezer Bideau, C. Isnart and A. Leblon (2014), 'Relocaliser les discours sur le "patrimoine"', in J. Bondaz, F. Graezer Bideau, C. Isnart and A. Leblon (eds), *Les vocabulaires locaux du 'Patrimoine'* (Münster: LIT), 9–30.

Bortolotto, C. (2013), 'Authenticity: a non-criterion for inscription on the lists of UNESCO's Intangible Cultural Heritage Convention ', in *2013 IRCI Meeting on ICH – The 10th Anniversary of the 2003 Convention. Final Report* (Sakai City: International Research Centre for Intangible Cultural Heritage), 73–78.

Bortolotto C. (2011), 'Introduction: le trouble du patrimoine culturel immatériel ', in C. Bortolotto (ed.), *Le patrimoine culturel immatériel: enjeux d'une nouvelle catégorie* (Paris: Maison des sciences de l'homme), 21–43.

Brumann, C. (2014), 'Heritage agnosticism a third path for the study of cultural heritage ', *Social Anthropology* 22(2): 173–188.

Comaroff J., and J. Comaroff (2009), *Ethnicity, Inc.* (Chicago: University of Chicago Press).

Creed, G. (2011), *Masquerade and postsocialism. Ritual and cultural dispossession in Bulgaria* (Bloomington: Indiana University Press).

Delanty, G. (1999), 'Die Transformation nationaler Identität und die kulturelle Ambivalenz europäischer Identität. Demokratische Identifikation in einem post-nationalen Europa', in R. Viehoff and R. Segers (eds), *Kultur. Identität. Europa. Über die Schwierigkeiten und die Möglichkeiten einer Konstruktion* (Frankfurt am Main: Suhrkamp), 267–288.

Delanty G. (1994), *Inventing Europe: idea, identity, reality* (London: Macmillan).

Faeta, F. (2005), *Questioni italiane. Demologia, antropologia, critica culturale* (Torino: Bollati Boringhieri), 151–170.

Hafstein, V. (2012), 'Cultural heritage', in R. Bendix and G. Hasan-Rokem (eds), *A companion to folklore* (Malden, MA: Wiley), 500–519.

Hafstein, V. (2007), 'Claiming culture: intangible heritage inc., folklore©, traditional knowledge™', in D. Hemme, M. Tauschek and R. Bendix (eds), *Prädikat 'Heritage': Wertschöpfungen aus kulturellen Ressourcen* (Münster: LIT), 81–119.

Handelman, D. (1999), *Models and mirrors: towards an anthropology of public events*, 2nd ed. (New York: Berghahn).

Handler, R. (1988), *Nationalism and the politics of culture in Quebec* (Madison: University of Wisconsin Press).

Hemme, D., M. Tauschek and R. Bendix eds (2007), *Prädikat 'Heritage': Wertschöpfungen aus kulturellen Ressourcen* (Münster: LIT).

Herb, G. and D. Kaplan (1999), *Nested identities: nationalism, territory, and scale* (Lanham: Rowman & Littlefield).

Hodges, M. (2011), 'Disciplinary anthropology?: Amateur ethnography and the production of "heritage" in rural France', *Ethnos* 76(3): 348–374.

Isnart, C. (2014), 'Changing the face of Catholicism in a tourist context. Ritual dynamic, heritage care and the rhetoric of tourism transformation in a religious minority', *Journal of Tourism and Cultural Change* 12(2): 133–149.

Istenič, S. (2012), 'Aspects of tradition', *Traditiones* 41(2), 77–89.

Johler, R. (2003), 'Local Europe. The production of cultural heritage and the Europeanisation of places', in J. Frykman and P. Niedermüller (eds), *Articulating Europe. Local perspectives* (Copenhagen: Museum Tusculanum), 7–18.

Knecht M., and P. Niedermüller (2003), 'The politics of cultural heritage. An urban approach', *Ethnologia Europaea* 32, 89–104.

Kuutma, K. (2007), 'The politics of contested representation: UNESCO and the masterpieces of intangible cultural heritage', in D. Hemme, M. Tauschek and R. Bendix (eds), *Prädikat: 'Heritage': Wertschöpfungen aus kulturellen Ressourcen* (Münster: LIT), 177–196.

Lähdesmäki, T. (2016), 'Politics of tangibility, intangibility, and place in the making of a European cultural heritage in EU heritage policy', *International Journal of Heritage Studies* 22(10): 766–780.

Logan, W., U. Kockel and M. Nic Craith (2015), 'The new heritage studies: origins and evolution, problems and prospects', in W. Logan, M. Nic Craith and U. Kockel (eds), *A companion to heritage studies* (Malden, MA: Wiley), 1–25.

Macdonald, S. (2013), *Memorylands: heritage and identity in Europe today* (London: Routledge).

Meethan, K. (2001), *Tourism in a global society* (Basingstoke: Palgrave Macmillan).

Nic Craith, M. (2008), 'Intangible cultural heritages: the challenges for Europe', *Anthropological Journal of European Cultures* 17(1): 54–73.

Nic Craith, M. and U. Kockel (2015), '(Re-)building heritage: integrating tangible and intangible', in W. Logan, M. Nic Craith and U. Kockel (eds), *A companion to heritage studies* (Malden, MA: Wiley), 426–442.

Niedermüller, P. and B. Stoklund eds (2001), *Europe: cultural construction and reality* (Copenhagen: Museum Tusculanum).

Noyes, D. (2003), *Fire in the Plaça: Catalan festival politics After Franco* (Philadelphia: University of Pennsylvania Press).

Picard, D. and M. Robinson eds (2006), *Festivals, tourism and social change. Remaking worlds* (Clevedon: Channel View).

Shore, C. (2000), *Building Europe: the cultural politics of European integration* (London: Routledge).

Smith, L. (2006), *Uses of heritage* (London: Routledge).

Smith, L. and N. Akagawa eds (2009) *Intangible heritage* (London: Routledge).

Tauschek, M. (2011), 'Reflections on the metacultural nature of intangible cultural heritage', *Journal of Ethnology and Folkloristics* 5(2): 49–64.

Tauschek, M. (2010), 'Cultural property as a strategy: The Carnival of Binche, the creation of cultural heritage and cultural property', *Ethnologia Europaea* 39(2): 67–80.

Taylor, D. (2016), 'Saving the "live"? Re-performance and intangible cultural heritage', *Études Anglaises* 69(2): 149–161.

Testa, A. (forthcoming), 'L'impact de la création du patrimoine immatériel dans les différents domaines de la vie sociale: le cas des carnavals et les "fêtes de transition" en Europe', forthcoming in the proceedings of the Association of Critical Heritage Studies Biennial Conference, 2–10 June 2016, Montréal, Canada.

Testa, A. (2017a), '"Fertility" and the carnival 1: symbolic effectiveness, emic beliefs, and the re-enchantment of Europe', *Folklore* 128(1): 16–36.

Testa, A. (2017b), '"Fertility" and the carnival 2: popular frazerism and the reconfiguration of tradition in Europe today', *Folklore* 128(2), 111–132.

Testa, A. (2016a), 'From folklore to intangible cultural heritage. Observations about a problematic filiation', *Österreichische Zeitschrift für Volkskunde* 119(3–4): 183–204.

Testa, A. (2016b), 'Problemi e prospettive della ricerca demo-etno-antropologica su memoria sociale, (n)ostalgia, ritualità pubblica e patrimonio culturale immateriale nell'Europa post-socialista', *Lares* 82(2): 237–276.

Testa, A. (2014a), 'Rethinking the festival: power and politics', *Method & Theory in the Study of Religion* 26(1): 44–73.

Testa, A. (2014b), *Il carnevale dell'uomo-animale. Le dimensioni storiche e socio-culturali di una festa appenninica* (Napoli: Loffredo).

Testa, A. (2014c), 'L'homme-cerf, l'ethnologue et le maire. Les politiques du folklore dans un contexte rural italien', in S. Fiszer, D. Francfort, A. Nivière and J.-S. Noël (eds), *Folklores et politique. Approches comparées et réflexions critiques (Europe – Amériques)* (Paris: Le Manuscrit).

Vilaseca, N. and M. Trilla (2011), *El Carnaval de Solsona* (Solsona: L'Associació de Festes del Carnaval).

Wilken, L. (2012), 'Anthropological studies of European identity construction', in J. Frykman, M. Nic Craith and U. Kockel (eds), *A companion the anthropology of Europe* (Chichester: Wiley-Blackwell), 125–144.

# 7 Performing identities and communicating ICH: from local to international strategies

*Laurent Sébastien Fournier*

In order to document some of the strategies used today in Europe to perform identities and to communicate intangible cultural heritage (ICH), this chapter will focus on the case of traditional festivals and on some of their recent transformations. Festivals in traditional societies have interested ethnologists and cultural anthropologists for a long time. In the second half of the nineteenth century already, traditional festivals were considered as a most valuable lens to reflect on some major social and cultural phenomena (Mannhardt 1877; Frazer 1911). The French school of sociology (Durkheim 1912; Mauss 1950) then suggested that festivals in traditional societies could be considered as 'total social facts' within which aspects such as local politics, customary laws, economy, aesthetics, kinship relations and technology would coexist. The study of traditional festivals was also connected with the study of rituals and with the anthropology of religion (Cazeneuve 1971; Rivière 1995). More recently, scholars have focussed on the new connections between festivals, performances, spectacles and public events (Handelman 1990; Santino 2017). In this perspective festivals have been studied through innumerable monographs and articles during the last century and have given birth to an interdisciplinary field of studies mixing ethnology, folklore, cultural anthropology, sociology, history and economy, just to mention a few disciplines (Fournier et al. 2009; Santino 2017). Due to this long-lasting scholarly interest, traditional festivals progressively appeared as 'serious' matters, and the critiques aiming at them faded out when they came to be considered as symptoms of deeper cultural patterns. Once condemned as places for disorder, immorality, excess and unproductive behaviours, the festivals were eventually transformed into cultural resources.

This shift was encouraged by some major changes in the post–World War II context. Industrialisation and urbanisation led modern societies to question their past and to remember the traditional cultures they had left behind. From the 1970s onwards, at the same time when ethnological museums knew a great fad, a lot of local actors tried to revive village festivals, especially in the Mediterranean areas of Europe where tourism could serve as a resource for economic development (Boissevain 2013). This tendency was confirmed with the oil crisis and the need to find some alternatives to global industrial growth. Forty years later, the ways traditional festivals are considered have dramatically changed. In some cases the traditional way of performing the rituals has survived, but in most of the cases the festivals have also become a new means to attract a large audience and to feed the local economy while building up a valorising image of the place. Besides the traditional festivals, 'old style festivals' have also been created to enhance local historical resources or specific agricultural products (Champagne 1977). In such a context, traditional festivals don't keep the meanings they used to have. They have shifted from 'organic' to 'organised' tradition (Keszeg 2018), therefore being connected with new issues of cultural management and regional planning. In a world where culture has become an important economic resource, the traditional festivals are part and parcel of the local strategies to sell the best possible image of given territories.

In this context, the 2003 UNESCO Convention on the Safeguarding of Intangible Cultural Heritage appears as a meaningful tool to accompany the new valorisation strategies of a lot of revitalised local festivals. If cultural heritage was first limited to the fine arts and the historical monuments, its field opened up to ethnological matters long before UNESCO appeared. Folklorists in the nineteenth century were already aware of the importance of popular cultures and beliefs, and ethnological museums in the beginning of the twentieth century presented ethnological data as genuine cultural heritage (Dias 1991). However, with the notion of ICH, the whole field of ethnological heritage finds a new place in an official international organisation. Once frowned upon as a minor heritage field, it now becomes legitimised and institutionalised (Bortolotto 2011). Traditional festivals then earn a new status: they are not only turned towards the past and the traditional societies where they were born; they become a key feature in the recognition of ICH. From there on, the study of traditional festival opens on new fields of studies such as the performance of local identities or communication matters. How do the local actors manage to change the image of the traditional festivals into new strategic resources? How do they use these festivals to perform their identities? How do they use the new heritage categories for modern communication purposes? And what does all this say about new identity claims in Europe?

To answer these questions and to reflect on the changes met by traditional festivals in Europe today, this article will concentrate on two different case studies set in the frame of 'official' ICH. Indeed, I will suggest that the most productive analyses concerning the new category of ICH are the ones focussing on the action of UNESCO itself. Instead of taking ICH as a wide 'potential' category within which any given festival could stand, I contend that the best way to study ICH is to work out the local consequences of the institutional work of UNESCO. This is the reason why I will use two precise examples taken out of the UNESCO representative list: the 'Processional Giants and Dragons in Belgium and France', on the one hand, and the 'Fest-Noz, festive gathering based on the collective practice of international dances of Brittany', on the other. The first example shows a multinational candidature including several local town festivals, while the second deals with a French regional festive practice. Comparing them is interesting because they both concern Western

Europe and because they shed light on different strategies used to perform and to communicate ICH, on two different geographical scales. Hopefully, the comparison will help to understand better the ways of performing local identities and communicating them in contemporary Europe.

## 7.1 Processional Giants and Dragons

The first case study I would like to present concerns Processional Giants and Dragons in Belgium and France, a case I have already presented elsewhere (Fournier 2012). The UNESCO official website presentation identifies under this label a set of traditional processions of huge effigies of giants, animals or dragons encompassing an original ensemble of festive popular manifestations and ritual representations.

> These effigies, reads the official presentation, first appeared in urban religious processions at the end of the fourteenth century in many European towns and continue to serve as emblems of identity for certain Belgian (Ath, Brussels, Dendermonde, Mechelen and Mons) and French towns (Cassel, Douai, Pézenas and Tarascon), where they remain living traditions. The giants and dragons are large-scale models measuring up to nine metres in height and weighing as much as 350 kilos. They represent mythical heroes or animals, contemporary local figures, historical, biblical or legendary characters or trades.
>
> (UNESCO n.d. a)

The performances, often mixing secular procession and religious ceremony, vary from town to town, but always follow a precise ritual in which the giants relate to the history, legend or life of the town. Although these expressions are not threatened with immediate disappearance, UNESCO suggests that they do suffer from a number of pressures, such as major changes to town centres and increasing tourism, leading to the detriment of the popular, spontaneous nature of the festival. The Processional Giants and Dragons in Belgium and France were first introduced as a Masterpiece of the Oral and Intangible Heritage of Humanity in 2005. The ninety Masterpieces proclaimed before the 2003 Convention entered into force were incorporated in 2008 in the representative list of the Intangible Cultural Heritage of Humanity. The Processional Giants and Dragons (Figure 7.1) then remain among the oldest elements on the lists. They have now been on the list for ten years, which means that the people organising or simply attending the processions may have had some time to learn about the convention and its general scopes in order to adapt their strategies accordingly.

As a matter of fact, ethnographic fieldwork in the different towns concerned by this label showed that the actors organising the festivals often tried to transform them into new commodities. However, the idea was not only to transform the festivals into valuable economic features but also to change the image of

*Figure 7.1* Processional Giants in Douai, France (Photo: L. S. Fournier 2009)

the places through the festivals. During the process, entertainment progressively replaced tradition. Interviews among the audience and the local organisers of the festivals showed that there was no real opposition between the local and the global scale, because the locals often meet the people in charge of the nomination process at a global level. For instance, the people from the city of Tarascon remember very well when their Tarasque dragon had been invited to India at the end of the 1980s. The Indian show was organised by Charif Khaznadar, who then became an important UNESCO representative and helped a lot in the acknowledgment of the Processional Giants and Dragons as ICH. In the same way, the people in the cities of Douai and Cassel have been connected very early with Jean-Pierre Ducastelle, the director of the 'House of the Giants' in Ath, Belgium, who was one of the main Belgian experts in the nomination process prior to 2005. Opposing the local and the global, therefore, is not relevant when investigating ICH, as the use of such a label already implies strong connections between these two dimensions.

The results of fieldwork were manifold. One of them was to bring together the views of the different actors involved in the festivals and to compare their positions. In the different towns concerned by the nominations, activists willingly take part in the process, mainly through associations and other local networks. They use the new label to experiment strategies regarding the local implementation of cultural policies in general. In this respect, UNESCO matters are often only a pretext to discuss other local issues. As in each innovative process, there is a local polarisation between the ones who strongly believe in the benefits the label will bring in and the ones who criticise it and think of the new policies as a new means of domination used by the local elites against the people. Another result of fieldwork consisted in comparing the impacts of the UNESCO policies in the different towns where the 'Processional Giants and Dragons' appear. Some differences between the different towns can be emphasised. In Tarascon in the South-East of France, for instance, the general impact regards the visibility of the processional dragon. The Tarasque dragon was traditionally hidden out of the time of the procession; it is now exhibited in a special showcase in the centre of the medieval town. Moreover, a monumental stone sculpture is now on display in front of the local castle. The local actors also feel they have to become more professional in performing their traditions, and as such they have launched several exhibitions on the topics of dragons, medieval times and the imaginary. In other French towns, like in Pézenas in the South-West or in Douai in the North, the traditions rely on partnerships with local cultural associations. In Mons, in Belgium, a huge museum project followed the UNESCO nomination (Musée du Doudou n.d.). A last result of fieldwork came from comparing the initial project and its gradual transformations. Before the nomination a lot of actions were envisioned, but ten years later it happens that most of them did not occur. Sometimes this was due to the lack of financial resources. Sometimes, the people in charge of the implementation of the convention were transferred in other places; some of them died; new people were elected, etc. Such a situation shows that the UNESCO policies are more indicative than prescriptive. They strongly depend on the context, which legitimates a careful study of the different ways they are concretely implemented in the different places concerned by the convention.

The case of the Processional Giants and Dragons eventually enables us to reach a first series of conclusions regarding the performance and the communication of identities in today's Europe. Although the label was quite easily accessed by the communities because it represented the first generation of cultural elements to be put on the UNESCO list, it changed a lot in the self-perception of local identities on the field. With the UNESCO label in hand, the local town councils and the different actors involved in the performance of the festivals had suddenly a lot to do. Being on a UNESCO list was a great surprise for most of them and everything was still to invent. First the local actors just didn't know what to do with the label, and in this situation, they began elaborating strategies only afterwards. As in many cases, these strategies were used to face several structural difficulties, like working at a multinational level without having much initial contacts with the other partners. Meetings were programmed leading to gatherings of processional animals. Surprisingly however, not all the 'official' UNESCO giants and dragons came, whereas other effigies were present and claimed they should be added to the list. In the North of France, new giants are created every year, while in the Languedoc area in Mediterranean France, a lot of animal figures are also invented and take part in the local carnivals (see La Ronde des Géants 2010, concerning the giants in Northern France, and L'Occitanie au quotidien 2019, concerning the 'totem' animals in Southern France). Although the UNESCO list only mentions a dozen of examples, several hundreds of giants and dragons can be counted in the different countries concerned by the label. According to the UNESCO representatives this is not a problem because the list protects all the existing giants and dragons. But in the eyes of the locals, the vision is different, and every little village would like to see his own name on the list. A special question was raised by the Catalan giants as their region was not mentioned in the candidature file: were they supposed to join the label with the French and the Belgians or were they excluded from the UNESCO policies because they belonged to another country? The new UNESCO procedure, as a matter of fact, raised the question of cultural boundaries in Europe. While most of the cultural facts are transnational, the UNESCO ordered cultural safeguarding around the administrative notion of 'States Parties' (i.e., the countries who had officially adhered to the 2003 convention). From there on, the strategies had to be built on a double basis which could also easily become a double-bind: they had to be at once cultural and national.

### 7.2 Fest-Noz, a festive gathering in Brittany

The second case-study I will present in this article is the 'Fest-Noz, festive gathering based on the collective practice of international dances of Brittany' (Figure 7.2). Unlike the previous example, this one is limited to a region of France and has been put on the representative list of UNESCO ICH through the candidature of one country only. I will use this example to show the problems which can occur according to the variable relations a nation or a 'State Party' can have with its different regions.

On the official UNESCO website, Fest-Noz is presented as following:

> Fest-Noz is a festive gathering based on the collective practice of traditional Breton dances, accompanied by singing or instrumental music. The strong Breton cultural movement has preserved this expression of a living and constantly renewed practice of inherited dance repertoires with several

*Figure 7.2* A Breton Fest-Noz (Photo: Myriam Jégat, 2009, with the permission of UNESCO)

hundred variations, and thousands of tunes. About a thousand Fest-Noz take place every year with participants varying from a hundred to several thousand people, thousands of musicians and singers and tens of thousands of regular dancers. Beyond the practice of the dance, the Fest-Noz is characterised by an intense camaraderie among the singers, musicians and dancers, significant social and intergenerational diversity, and openness to others. Traditionally, transmission occurs through immersion, observation and imitation, although hundreds of devotees have worked with tradition bearers to compile the repertoires and lay the groundwork for new modes of transmission. Today, the Fest-Noz is at the centre of an intense ferment of musical experiences and has spawned a veritable cultural economy. Many meetings are held between singers, musicians and dancers from Brittany and different cultures. Moreover, many new inhabitants of Breton villages use Fest-Noz as a means of integration, as it is heavily implicated in the sense of identity and continuity of the people of Brittany.

(UNESCO n.d. b)

Fest-Noz was inscribed in 2012 on the UNESCO representative list, at a time when the convention had already entered into force and when the competition was getting sharper and sharper between all the different communities to access the lists. Soon afterwards, in 2014, UNESCO would ask France to limit its number of national candidatures and to propose multinational files in priority. Because UNESCO is in favour of more candidature coming from southern countries, France was asked to limit the national French candidatures to only one every other year, which intensified the competition and ended in intense lobbying among the national candidates in order to draw the attention of the Ministry of Culture. From 2014 onwards, it became extremely difficult for French tradition bearers to get on the lists without strong political support or international partnerships. Fest-Noz, however, had managed to get onboard the representative list, to the surprise of many specialists as it is considered as a rather usual form of festive event in Brittany. The main argument in favour of the nomination of the Fest-Noz, however, was that it was not endangered. As such it would fit on the representative list more than on the urgent safeguarding list. But the backstage context of the process is interesting to look at, as it highlighted different interesting communication strategies.

As a matter of fact, Bretons have always paid great attention to their regional traditional culture. In the nineteenth century already, when France emerged as a modern nation, the regional Breton elites founded the Celtic Academy to collect local and regional dialects, beliefs, customs, crafts and popular traditions (Belmont 1995). Under the threat of centralism and cultural homogenisation, the Bretons took care since then of their language, their folklore, their traditional festivals, their traditional sports and games etc. Unlike a lot of other French regions, the Bretons claimed their independence and often organised political protests against different national decisions. This regionalism was paradoxically reinforced by Breton activists settled in Paris and led to fix the reputation of Brittany as one of the French regions having the highest conscience of its local specificity. In the 1970s Breton activism was fuelled by the counter-culture movements, and regional folklore was still thoroughly collected. It was then no surprise when Brittany became a leader region in the promotion of ICH after the signature of the UNESCO convention by France in 2006.

The Breton strategy first consisted in creating a regional working group on ICH. This group was active in 2010 and gathered several cultural associations among which were folk singers, musicians, people playing traditional games and sports, some regional intellectuals, local politicians and regional activists. The non-governmental organisation '*Dastum*', meaning 'to collect' in Breton and which specialised in collecting oral and musical folklore since 1972, was at the heart of this working group and began intense networking to raise the claims of the Breton community in the new field of ICH (Dastum n.d.). Outside Brittany the aim was to raise awareness among influent political actors such as Jean-Yves Le Drian, who by this time was the president of the Breton regional council and who would in 2012 become the French Minister of Defence. Inside the region the work consisted in obtaining the consent of the community through petitions and in mediating between the different possible candidates. The strength of the Bretons was then to propose several candidates, in order to get at least one on the list. Three different proposals were in the running: the Breton traditional sports and games, the '*gwerz*' folk-singing art and the Fest-Noz. The Breton working group discussions in 2010 and 2011 ended in selecting and proposing the least discriminating cultural element. When traditional sports and games and folk-singing were limited to a small number of specialists and practitioners in the local communities, the Fest-Noz was largely known in the middle-classes, in the cities and even in the Breton diaspora abroad. It could be organised anywhere, in modern folk-music festivals and even in connection with huge concert halls in Paris. It had the favour of the urban elites and could easily be related to the art scene in places like Lorient, Quimper, Rennes or Brest. Moreover, it complied with the UNESCO requirements concerning gender-balance and integration. Even if it was not considered as something really exceptional, the Fest-Noz had many strategic assets.

The Fest-Noz candidature was submitted in March 2012 to the French Ministry of Culture and nominated for the representative list of the UNESCO ICH in December of the same year. The nomination file insists on the fact that tens of thousands of people participate. Dancing in the round during the Fest-Noz would embody the values of conviviality, warmth, socialising, openness to others and welcoming. It would help to resist to the standardisation of Western culture. Accordingly, the Fest-Noz is presented as a symbol for regional identity and continuity and deserves a UNESCO label. Looking carefully at the Breton strategy is interesting because it shows well how UNESCO matters can be driven by local interests. Another interesting thing is to consider how the nomination of the Fest-Noz led to considerably reinforce the heritage apparatus in Brittany. Since 2012, two important institutions connected with ICH have appeared in Brittany. The first one is the non-governmental organisation (NGO) BCD, meaning '*Bretagne Culture Diversité*' and founded under the aegis of the Breton regional council. This new NGO deals with the promotion and the diffusion of Breton cultural matters and works at a 'permanent inventory of Britton Intangible Cultural Heritage' (BCD n.d.). Interestingly, the direction of this new institution was entrusted to Charles Quimbert, a folk singer and collector, former manager in the NGO *Dastum*. The second one is another NGO, the CFPCI, or '*Centre Français du Patrimoine Culturel Immatériel*', which has been certified by the French Ministry of Culture as the national centre for ICH and works in networking and promoting this category of cultural heritage (CFPCI n.d.). The president of this NGO is Charif Khaznadar, a writer and stage director we've already mentioned above, who worked several years in the 1970s in Brittany before playing an important part in the elaboration of the UNESCO 2003 Convention and who had the opportunity in the meanwhile to build up solid bridges between the Breton and the world cultural scenes.

## 7.3 Comparing different strategies

The two case studies I have referred to in this article are interesting because they show two very different strategies in the valorisation of ICH and of local identities. In this section I will compare them, and I will try to discuss the diverse ways of performing identities and communicating ICH in Western Europe today. The discussion will lead to assess different strategies and will suggest that such strategies suppose as much creativity as planning, which is coherent with the findings of the best specialists in strategic management who have since a long time put the emphasis on the importance creative tasks have for managers (Mintzberg 1980).

If management, according to management specialists, is more a matter of grasping opportunities than a matter of rational planning, then I would contend that the field of ICH offers a fine example to illustrate this view. In the two case studies documented above, the local actors take the advantage of a new situation resulting from the existence of the new 2003 UNESCO convention framework. However, the way they envision this new situation is very different in the two cases. In the Processional Giants and Dragons case, the impetus clearly comes from the outside, the local actors suddenly being asked to join the new convention and to build up a common candidature file even without knowing each other very well. This way of working out the candidature 'in the making' and in a 'top-down' perspective clearly appears in the letters of consent accompanying the 2005 candidature file. The mayors of the different cities or the civil servants locally in charge of cultural development simply join short letters testifying that they 'accept' their processional effigies to be put on the UNESCO list. A few years later, the situation has become very different in the Fest-Noz case. Here, the actors work together within a specific working group and they explicitly decide which cultural element they want to promote. The perspective is a 'bottom-up' one and supposes a lot of lobbying and a lot of discussion among the different partners to push forward the element which they think will comply better with UNESCO requirements. As a result, several thousand people sign petitions, children's drawings are collected all over Brittany, websites are set up, new organisations appear and a whole communication strategy is created, leading to the nomination of the most shared element, which might also be the lowest common denominator.

Of course, it is difficult to compare the two cases on identical bases, as the case of the Processional Giants and Dragons belonged to the first generation of UNESCO nominees, whereas the Fest-Noz was acknowledged at a time when the competition had become much sharper to get on the lists. In less than a decade, a lot of things had changed. However, some objective features can help such a comparison. If both cases concern Western Europe, the Giants and Dragons are multinational whereas the Fest-Noz is regional. In this context, networking doesn't have the same value in the two cases. In the case of an international partnership, the ties are relatively loose between the partners and the network relies on the action of the UNESCO above all. The different cities discover each other through the candidature process and learn about their own identity on the way. Before the candidature they were sure about the uniqueness of their local folklore and didn't even know about the existence of comparable festive forms existing elsewhere. Different monographs clearly document this feeling of uniqueness (Dumont 1951; Gueusquin 2000; Ducastelle and Dubuisson 2014; Baroiller 2015). Comparing the Doudou dragon in Mons, Belgium, and the Tarasque in Tarascon, France, speaks for itself because the two effigies look similar from an aesthetic point of view, but they have developed separately and have no certified historical relations. In the case of the Giants and Dragons, the candidature created something new because it helped the local actors to become conscious of their own specificities but also of the existence of very close forms of culture in distant towns or countries. It is then possible to conceive the candidature as a performative action creating a new form of identity. The case of the Fest-Noz is very different because it is caught in a much smaller and homogeneous regional context where networking ties were much stronger between the different actors already before the beginning of the candidature process. Here, the Fest-Noz was unanimously conceived as a Breton label and as a major sign of regional identity (Guilcher 1972). The candidature process then only came to consolidate an existing feeling. It gave an official international recognition to an accepted element of the Breton regional culture but didn't really create something new, even if it undoubtedly boosted the dynamism of this regional form of festival.

In any case, the UNESCO lists proceed to inclusions and exclusions, even if the philosophy of the convention is to be potentially open to any cultural element in the different signatory States Parties. Getting on the lists supposes for the actors to build up networks and sometimes to compete against each other. As I have already mentioned, working out the candidature process can have different implications according to the scales within which it is applied. Multinational files suppose other strategies than local or regional files. Even if the comparisons are biased by the evolution of the global heritage market and the progressive limitation of the number of candidatures admissible for each States Party, I would suggest that the examination of the local strategies of heritage-building tells us a lot concerning the ways of performing identities in Western Europe today. With the UNESCO convention on ICH, a new track is open for European local communities to valorise their identities regardless of the older layers of national or regional cultural references. However, the communities don't always use this new track. In some cases, like in the Processional Giants and Dragons, a new geography is invented connecting places which wouldn't have imagined their affinities before. In other cases, like the Fest-Noz, the situation is different because the nomination only confirms the existing identity value of a given cultural element. But the interesting thing is that ICH, as a new institutional tool, regulates the building up and the performance of European identities. In the next section, I then propose to examine some of the changes in the self-perception of European identities as a consequence of ICH communication strategies.

## 7.4 European identities and UNESCO

Traditional festivals offer interesting case studies for identity matters because they are at once stable and flexible. They are stable because they have been organised during decades and sometimes centuries in local towns and villages, and they are flexible because they are permeable to outside influences and contextual changes. In a paper, I have suggested that the UNESCO convention for ICH represented the birth of international festival politics, because it created a new arena where festivals could be discussed both by the researchers, the communities and the political institutions (Fournier 2014). Using adapted instruments like the general assembly of States Parties, the lists, the national commissions, UNESCO selects specific festivals, while other ones remain in the background. In order to answer the criteria of UNESCO and to go through the selection process, the communities develop specific strategies. A new implicit social contract appears, in which the festivals are not determined anymore by their relations with the beliefs of the local communities organising them but by their ability to meet the UNESCO requirements. In this new deal, external determinations replace the internal reasons of the festivals. As a consequence, new actors appear, as well as new ethics, new codes, new standards, new institutions, new stakes, new scales and new identities.

Assuming that cultural identities are always a social construction and that traditions can often be 'invented' (Hobsbawm and Ranger 1983), I contend that the analysis of the ways the UNESCO policies reframe traditional festivals today can be extremely useful to understand contemporary processes of building up new identities in Europe. In this respect, the actual 'heritage boom' (Logan, Kockel and Nic Craith 2015) in Europe is not only a symptom to interpret but also a very productive field to study. Different scholars have criticised the modern taste for cultural heritage as a way to escape the present in troubled times (Lowenthal 1998, Jeudy 2001). I consider that this sort of critical statement stops the reflection in mid-stream. In order to go further, I propose to study the consequences and the impacts of the new heritage policies. How do they lead to original ways of performing identities? I find it interesting to look carefully at the different answers the actors elaborate to answer the new heritage context, and I suggest that these answers play a great part in the building of the new heritage categories themselves. In short, there would be a circulation between the communities and the institutional incentives, resulting in a twofold movement in which cultural heritage policies encourage the actors' strategic creativity and this creativity leads to a better recognition of cultural heritage. Heritage in the making would then work as a virtuous circle fuelled by the communities' beliefs in its efficiency.

From there on, one of the most important tasks for the researcher is to describe the concrete consequences of the new categories of cultural heritage on local practices. How are identities performed in heritage times? And how do the performances, in turn, contribute to build up cultural heritage? Answering these questions through the perspective of ethnographic fieldwork leads to underline some common features as well as some differences. In most of the cases, the existence of an institutional frame for the recognition of traditional festive events as cultural heritage encourages some kind of standardisation. Indeed, there is a risk to confuse 'live performance' and 'archive' when trying to safeguard a living cultural form (Taylor, 2016). The transformation of a traditional festival into cultural heritage, then, raises the problem of its canonical definition and one can wonder about the possibility for a given festival to be kept alive outside its own initial temporality and context. However, there are different manners in transforming a traditional festival. Accepted researches on Mediterranean tourism note some differences between 'revitalising' and 'recreating' traditional rituals (Boissevain 2013). Following this perspective, I would suggest that there is a whole range of possible transformations going from moderate adaptations to more drastic changes. On the field, the transformations vary according to the positions of the tradition bearers and to their approaches of communication. When the stakeholders are local amateurs, the consequences of a UNESCO nomination can remain relatively limited. More important transformations generally occur when professional experts use the nomination in an openly strategic way. The risk is then to melt the initial cultural form in a wholly modern communication project. As long as communication is used as a simple tool to help the local culture to be revitalised, the transformations have a chance to remain limited. But when the local culture becomes a new resource for communication and when communication becomes valued for its own sake, then the impacts may be stronger.

As a conclusion, a few supplementary points may be stressed. The apparition of ICH as a new heritage category has pushed forwards new actors, new valorisation strategies and eventually new identities in Europe as in other parts of the world. Europe, however, has a specific place in the UNESCO puzzle because it has been confronted in the meanwhile with the challenge of its political unification. At the same time when UNESCO was elaborating its convention on ICH, European institutions have reinforced the concept of a common heritage (Nic Craith 2012) and new political myths have appeared (Kølvraa 2016). The category of ICH has then become especially relevant in Europe as a new means of building up identities, while the UNESCO claims that the convention is first and foremost devoted to developing countries. Considering this shift between the initial aims of the convention and the ways it is used in Europe to promote new identity performances is important to study the transformations of identity claims in Europe today.

## References

Baroiller, A. (2015), *Faire vivre le folklore. Dynamiques de transformation de la Ducasse de Mons* (Bruxelles: Fédération Wallonie-Bruxelles).
BCD (n.d.), Bretagne Culture Diversité website. Available at: www.bcd.bzh/fr/ (accessed 10 January 2019).
Belmont, N. ed. (1995), *Aux sources de l'ethnologie française, l'Académie Celtique* (Paris: CTHS).
Boissevain, J. (2013), *Factions, friends and feasts. anthropological perspectives on the Mediterranean* (Oxford: Berghahn).
Bortolotto, C. ed. (2011), *Le patrimoine culturel immatériel. Enjeux d'une nouvelle catégorie* (Paris: Editions de la MSH).
Cazeneuve, J. (1971), *Sociologie du rite* (Paris: PUF).
CFPCI (n.d.), Centre français du patrimoine culturel immatériel website. Available at: www.cfpci.fr/ (accessed 10 January 2019).

Champagne, P. (1977), 'La fête au village', *Actes de la Recherche en Sciences Sociales* 17–18: 73–84.
Dastum (n.d.), Dastum website. Available at: www.dastum.bzh/ (accessed 10 January 2019).
Dias, N. (1991), *Le musée d'ethnographie du Trocadéro (1878–1908). Anthropologie et muséologie en France* (Paris: Editions du CNRS).
Ducastelle, J.-P. and L. Dubuisson (2014), *La Ducasse d'Ath, passé et présent* (Ath: Maison des Géants).
Dumont, L. (1951), *La Tarasque* (Paris: Gallimard).
Durkheim, E. (1912), *Les formes élémentaires de la vie religieuse* (Paris: Alcan).
Fournier, L. (2014), 'Intangible cultural heritage and the birth of international festival politics', in G. Barna and I. Povedak (eds), *Politics, feasts, festivals* (Szeged: Department of Ethnology and Cultural Anthropology), 111–120.
Fournier, L. (2012), 'Intangible cultural heritage in France: from state culture to local development', in R. Bendix, A. Eggert and A. Peselmann (eds), *Heritage regimes and the state* (Göttingen: Universitätsverlag Göttingen), 327–340.
Fournier, L., D. Crozat, C. Bernié-Boissard and C. Chastagner eds (2009), *La fête au présent. Mutations des fêtes au sein des loisirs* (Paris: L'Harmattan).
Frazer, J. (1911), *The golden bough*, 3rd ed. (London: Macmillan).
Gueusquin, M-F. (2000), *La Provence arlésienne, traditions et avatars* (Arles: Actes Sud).
Guilcher, J-M. (1972), *La tradition populaire de danse en Basse-Bretagne* (Paris/La Haye: Mouton).
Handelman, D. (1990), *Models and mirrors. towards an anthropology of public events* (Cambridge: Cambridge University Press).
Hobsbawm, E. and T. Ranger eds (1983), *the invention of tradition* (Cambridge: Cambridge University Press).
Jeudy, H-P. (2001), *La machinerie patrimoniale* (Belval: Circé poche).
Keszeg, V. (2018), 'Introduction: culture and cultural researches', in A. Töhötöm Szabo and M. Szikszai (eds), *Cultural heritage and cultural politics in minority conditions* (Cluj-Napoca/Aarhus: Kriza Janos Ethnographic Society, Intervention Press), 11–40.
Kølvraa, C. (2016), 'European Fantasies: On the EU's Political Myths and the Affective Potential of Utopian Imaginaries for European Identity', *Journal of Common Market Studies* 54(1): 169–184.
L'Occitanie au quotidien (2019), La Ronde européenne des Géants et Totems programme. Available at: www.loccitanieauquotidien.com/attachment/864579/ (accessed 10 January 2019).
La Ronde des Géants (2010), La Ronde des Géants Association website. Available at: www.geants-carnaval.org/ (accessed 10 January 2019).
Logan, W., U. Kockel and M. Nic Craith (2015), 'The New Heritage Studies: Origins and Evolution, Problems and Prospects', in W. Logan, M. Nic Craith and U. Kockel (eds), *A companion to heritage studies* (Malden, MA: Wiley), 1–25.
Lowenthal, D. (1998), *The heritage crusade and the spoils of history* (Cambridge: Cambridge University Press).
Mannhardt, W. (1877), *Wald- und FeldKulte* (Berlin: Borntraeger).
Mauss, M. (1950), *Sociologie et anthropologie* (Paris: PUF).
Mintzberg, H. (1980), *The nature of managerial work* (Englewood Cliffs: Prentice Hall).
Musée du Doudou (n.d.), Musée du Doudou website. Available at: www.museedudoudou.mons.be/ (accessed 10 January 2019).
Nic Craith, M. (2012), 'Europe's uncommon heritages', *Traditiones* 41(2): 11–28.
Rivière, C. (1995), *Les rites profanes* (Paris: PUF).
Santino, J. ed. (2017), *Public performances. Studies in the carnivalesque and the ritualesque* (Logan: Utah State University Press).

Taylor, D. (2016), 'Saving the "live"? Re-Performance and intangible cultural heritage', *Études Anglaises* 69(2): 149–161.

UNESCO (n.d. a), Processional giants and dragons in Belgium and France. Available at: https://ich.unesco.org/en/RL/processional-giants-and-dragons-in-belgium-and-france-00153 (accessed 10 January 2019).

UNESCO (n.d. b), Fest-Noz, festive gathering based on the collective practice of traditional dances of Brittany. Available at: https://ich.unesco.org/en/RL/fest-noz-festive-gathering-based-on-the-collective-practice-of-traditional-dances-of-brittany-00707 (accessed 10 January 2019).

# 8 Memory, pride and politics on parade

## The Durham Miners' Gala

*Andreas Pantazatos and Helaine Silverman*

On coal mining maps of England, the north-east is appropriately coloured pitch black, indicating the density and richness of the underground resource. Within that patch is County Durham (Northern Mine Research Society n.d.). Archaeological and documentary evidence attest to coal mining in County Durham for almost a thousand years (Hair 1839: 3–4, 1844: 3–5; Emery 2009: 4). But it was the technological breakthroughs of the Industrial Revolution that permitted exploitation of deep lying seams and greatly expanded coal mining (Pocock 2013). The peak of coal production was 1913 when County Durham alone produced 41 million tons from the region's 304 pits; 164,256 men were employed (Emery 2009: 11).

Coal mining was a horrific occupation, rife with physical danger because of mine accidents (disaster records are at least as early as 1785; see Hair 1844; Sykes 1835; Emery 2009: 81–106), occupational disease (pneumoconiosis, bronchitis, emphysema, hand-arm vibration syndrome, etc.) and heartless labour exploitation by the mine owners (see, e.g., Emery 2009; Frankeleyn 1775; Temple 2011 *inter alia*). Yet for the miners, this was a profession that generated close-knit communities, tremendous male camaraderie and pride in work, strong families, deep faith and perseverance and political action in the face of harsh conditions.

The Durham Miners' Association (henceforth, DMA) was formed in 1869 out of this mix, and two years later (1871), it celebrated its birth with a 'Big Meeting', organised by delegates of the recently formed union, with the intent that it be an annual 'general meeting of miners' (Beynon and Austrin 1994: 206). All of the pit villages were invited to Wharton Park, overlooking the dramatic peninsula where the elite of the region had their ecclesiastical, political, social and economic base. The *Sunderland Times* stated at the time that the miners used the day 'to bond themselves more closely … and to show the country at large that the Durham Miners' Association was not a myth or a creation of the imagination, but a stupendous fact' (20 July 1871, cited in Beynon and Austrin 1994: 207). The Big Meeting also was recreational, a day of food, relaxation and conversation with people from beyond one's colliery village, which in itself supported the goal of making miners aware of their shared problems and thus facilitated political solidarity.

The 1871 event was so successful that the next year it moved onto the racecourse inside the peninsula itself. The pit villages paraded into town carrying beautiful, large, inspirational, painted silk banners, representing their local union lodges, for a day of fun and political speeches. That 1872 Big Meeting sealed the establishment of the DMA (Beynon and Austrin 1994: 211) and the 'Gala' – as the Big Meeting came to be known. The Gala has taken place almost uninterruptedly, on the second Saturday of July, since then, withstanding two world wars, strikes, successive pit closures over the course of the twentieth century (and as early as the late nineteenth century) and, ultimately, Prime Minister Margaret Thatcher's final elimination of the coal industry in 1993 following her government's brutal response to the 1984–1985 miners' strike.

The long death of Britain's coal mining industry severely impacted County Durham. Only 127 collieries remained in 1947 when nationalisation was enacted (Emery 2009: 14). Almost half (fifty-four) of the remaining mines were closed between 1958 and 1967 (Temple 2011: 139). Twenty-five thousand mining jobs in Durham were lost between 1958 and 1963 (Temple 2011: 136). By 1960, only 87,200 miners had jobs, and by the end of the 1960s there were only thirty-four working pits in Durham (Emery 2009: 15). Sixty per cent of the Durham coalfield had been closed by 1970 (Temple 2011:141). In 1975–1976, only 25,500 miners were employed (see Bulmer 1978: table 11.1). Indeed, whereas coal accounted for 66.2% of UK fuel consumption in 1964, it was only 37.1% in 1976 (Bulmer 1978: table 11.4) because Britain was developing oil and nuclear power for energy.

Understandably, then, the Gala's survival was seriously threatened as many mines already had closed and were closing. Participation in the Gala plunged in the 1970s, 1980s and early 1990s (see Gillum 2009; Temple 2011). With the final closing of the mines, wasn't the Gala irrelevant on a pit-less landscape? With the miners so utterly defeated after the great strike, wasn't their enthusiasm for it gone? How could the Gala continue in the face of obvious cognitive dissonance since the logic of the union lodge, featured on every banner, was inconsistent with the new reality? Indeed, Gorman observed that after the 1951 defeat of the Labour Party, many mining lodge banners – themselves the maximal expression of and in the Gala – 'lay neglected in damp basements, beneath the stages of dusty Labour halls, crumpled beneath cardboard fileboxes of ancient minutes in cramped cupboards. The colourful pride of generations left to crumble' (1986: 10). Wozhere (2017) similarly observed that 'about 40 years ago you could count those [villages] who maintained them [the banners].' And how could the cost of Gala participation – notably the expense of the banners, without which there is no Gala (see Wray 2011) – be borne by the displaced miners in economically devastated villages?

But the Gala did not die. By 1998, 'crowds at the 114th Miners' Gala were the biggest in 20 years' (newspaper cited in Temple 2011:172). In 2006, there were 50,000 participants (newspaper cited in Temple 2011: 174). And in 2016 and 2017, when the authors began to research the Gala, there were 150,000 and

*Figure 8.1* The Gala, July 2018. Banner groups with their bands, accompanied by members of their pit villages, parade through Durham. All march past the Royal County on whose hotel balcony stand officials of the Durham Miners' Association and invited members of the Labour Party, greeting them. They are watched by tens of thousands of spectators (Photo: Helaine Silverman 2018)

200,000 participants, respectively (*Durham Times*, 22 July 2016; *Durham Times*, 14 July 2017). In 2018, we observed participation to be 'huge' (no statistical data available) (Figure 8.1).

What changed? What made pit villagers recall and revive their banners and their Gala? What made the banners become, in essence, sacred heirlooms (or icons: see Wray 2011) and now objects and animators of heritage? In this chapter, we explore the rich phenomenology of the Gala, focussing on its struggle for survival, its heritagisation process, the seemingly incongruous character of mining heritage and the associated epistemic implications for the Gala.

## 8.1 Why didn't the Gala disappear?

The Gala is the largest, single-day trade union festival in Europe, attracting tens of thousands of participants from the former coal mining villages of County Durham to the city. The Gala was saved by the interaction of three factors, which can be summarized as *politics not passivity*, *community not place* and *object not industry*. We explain below.

First, the 'mourning period' (Wray 2011: 111) for the unsuccessful 1984–1985 strike and the final loss of coal mining has come to an end. Whereas the previous hundred years of political discourse at the racecourse had focussed on amelioration of miners' unsafe and unhealthy working conditions and their labour rights, post-strike/post-pit closure political discourse under then DMA General Secretary David Hopper and then DMA President David Guy was imbued with an expansive socialist rhetoric encompassing causes relevant to all members of the labour class: social justice, economic equity, affordable housing, guaranteed health care, pension protection, government investment in the region and so forth.

In the absence of their industry, the former miners were exhorted to stay with the union as a political action group and to oppose 'the selfish and antisocial politics of the Tories … the Tories' legacy of unemployment and low pay' (David Hopper 1997 speech, cited in Temple 2011: 171). The relevance of the political speeches on the racecourse at each Gala became a rallying cry, drawing more and more pit villages back to the Gala, encouraging the care and display of historic banners and, if necessary, production of new banners and motivating County Durham to be a 'people's opposition' (Temple 2011: 177). The popularity of the Gala's political message has been a major contributor to its survival and its subsequent growth, aided by Hopper and Guy's opening of the Gala to participation by all trade unions (carrying their own banners).

The near bankruptcy of the National Union of Mineworkers (NUM, to which the DMA is an affiliated member) at the end of the 1984–1985 strike had negative repercussions for the perpetuation of the Gala for it is a very expensive event to produce and coordinate. Police must be hired for security. Streets must be closed, and traffic diverted. In the villages, the banners may need to be restored and/or remade, and brass bands must be hired if there is no local one. Transportation into Durham must be contracted. So the second factor that saved the Gala was a fortuitous six-year financial contribution to the DMA from a New Zealand entrepreneur and philanthropist, Michael Watt (*Northern Echo,* 7 July 2017), combined with a creative new financing scheme for the NUM (see Temple 2011: 201–202). This enabled the DMA to assist pit villages to participate along with the creation of the 'Marra' ('buddy') campaign whose subscription is a contribution to the DMA (see below). Also, over the past decade banner groups have been successful in obtaining funding from the Heritage Lottery Fund and other sources for the costly manufacture of new banners.

While no amount of pride and revelry alone would have been able to remediate the social and economic devastation wrought on the pit villages by the mine closings, the heritagisation of mining is the third factor in the resurgence of the Gala. This heritagisation has promoted community well-being by affirming mining culture and renewing a sense of identity and belonging (see Stephenson and Wray 2005; Wray 2011). The very act of a community coming together to repair or replace a banner and to parade it is an act of social healing and social (re)production of the community, for each banner has its own history which is consonant with the narrative of the mining lodge and community to which it belongs. Banners are painted on both sides and carry elaborate iconography. These images and their texts communicate a range of messages about social progress, the power of union, education, equality, human rights, working conditions, solidarity, liberty and so forth (Figure 8.2); some present Christian themes of love and compassion (Emery 1998). The messages on banners

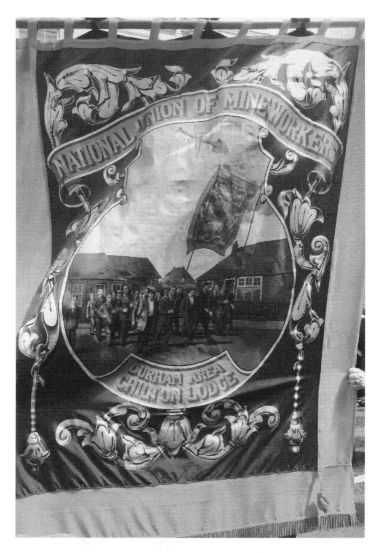

*Figure 8.2* The iconography on the Chilton Lodge banner depicts miners marching with their aspirational banner and clearly affirms the fundamental role of banners in mining communities. Chilton's banner professes one dramatic sentiment in a single profound word: liberty (Photo: Andreas Pantazatos 2018)

indicate what a mining community has selected to prioritise from their past so as to focus on the present and future (Figures 8.3 and 8.4).

In addition to the banners that are paraded in the Gala, we have observed curated old banners and other mining memorabilia displayed in miners halls/clubs/institutes and in schools (also see Wray 2009); we also note the varied collections exhibited in the small Durham Mining Museum in Spennymoor, which has been created by former miners. All are working against the loss of memory in the absence of a mining landscape, against the loss of employment

*Figure 8.3* At the time of manufacture, the Harton and Westoe banner of South Shields stated this community's hopes, too soon dashed, that the 1947 nationalization of the coal industry would bring security to mining families. The banner's saying, 'Our Heritage', expresses the deep sense of identity of families with the industry that employed them (Photo: Andreas Pantazatos 2018)

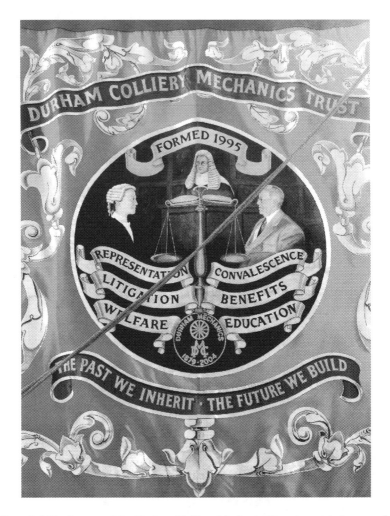

*Figure 8.4* The banner of the Durham Colliery Mechanics Trust is post-industry as the trust was formed two years after the last mine was closed. It asserts six new goals in the post-mining era and iconographically argues for resolution of the displaced miners' demands through legal means. Of particular note is its heritage message. It cogently expresses in words the epistemic resistance of miners to the establishment's portrayal of them and how their incongruous heritage is deployed: 'The past we inherit. The future we build' (Photo: Andreas Pantazatos 2018)

and against the loss of attendant social life. In addition, children and grandchildren of miners have become local activists in their communities, creating banner groups and respecting and remembering their relatives and the mining past as a totalising community experience of great social value: when a village was a self-contained, socially healthy community of mutual support and respect.

A strong male narrative of marras – the word used by miners for their buddy in the mine, the person on whom they could depend for their lives – continues, reinforced by the DMA's funding campaign – Friends of the Durham Miners' Gala – whose subscribers are called marras. And, at long last, the vital, multifaceted role that women played on the home front through that terrible year of the great strike – and had always played in the pit villages – is recognised. In 2018 a group of former miners' wives formed to celebrate and recall their heritage. In July 2018, they became part of the script of the Gala by carrying their homemade banner in the parade through Durham and having it blessed in Durham Cathedral along with the new banners of three pit villages. The DMA also hosted the women's group for a series of educational events in their building in Durham.

Together, these three factors have generated a widespread commitment to the continuation of the Gala.

## 8.2 Heritagisation and the incongruous

Outside observers (such as ourselves) might consider the Gala a celebration of an 'incongruous' heritage given the physical, economic, social and emotional suffering caused by the mining industry to its labourers and the cataclysmic loss of that industry (Figure 8.5). Incongruous heritage refers to inconsistencies that occur when stakeholders focus on those parts of what was inherited from the past that reasonably would not be considered positive, such as a disease-causing occupation, backbreaking labour and exploitation by the bosses. By saying 'incongruous heritage', we signal the inconsistencies of the selective process of heritage-making, of which the Gala would be an example. We suggest that this sense of incongruous heritage is a worthwhile addition to the well-known concepts of 'negative' heritage (Meskell 2002) and 'dissonant' heritage (Tunbridge and Ashworth 1996).

But the Gala's celebration of mining is and always has been quite the opposite for its participants. Thus, when we used the term 'incongruous heritage' in speaking with Ross Forbes (July 2017), the press and heritage officer for the Durham Miners' Association, he cautioned us that 'mining heritage is not incongruous from the miners' point of view'. He is correct as we know from many interviews with former miners. They emphasise their marras and the intense male bonding and friendships generated in the mines, pride in their jobs, mining as appropriate and esteemed masculine work, pit village unity and mutual support above ground, determination of the pit villagers to overcome their harsh lives and a historically enduring unjust relationship with the mine owners – be they private individuals or, following the 1947 nationalisation of the industry, the State.

The incongruous character of mining heritage entails epistemic implications. The incongruous character here is related to questions of focus and priority. Miners selectively focus and prioritise aspects of industrial heritage that they understand as unique to their identity, which we have indicated above. These

*Figure 8.5* The banner of the Boldon lodge being paraded in the 2017 Gala. Note the pathos of its textual message, 'Sunset on an industry', and the image of miners departing their work shift for the last time. Soon that surface infrastructure would be demolished, leaving a landscape devoid of the evidence of a once thriving coal industry (Photo: Helaine Silverman 2017)

aspects of mining are not diminished, in their minds, by all the indisputably negative aspects of mining.

The fact that miners choose to focus on and prioritise that which appears to be distressing, dangerous and painful – and feel pride in this – reveals the incongruous character of their heritage. Which part of the narrative of a shared past is communicated to the present communities and how these communities want to be remembered in the future is an exercise of their own epistemic powers. Their epistemic exercise does not seek to include all or exclude any parts of the mining past, they simply aim to reveal, remind and sustain the significance of the mining identity so that it is not forgotten or compromised as part of the larger assemblage of industrial heritage and not a mere episode on the margins of industry.

These two differing interpretations of mining – positive and negative – remind us that within the fabric of heritage there may be narratives of pain and oppression as well as resilience, creativity and strength. And in the case of the miners, their punctuated labour successes enabled them to continue to envision better times and thus see positive aspects in their lives. Understanding the nuances of incongruous heritage helps us to recognise the distinct identity that former miners have tried to craft and communicate to the world – literally and metaphorically – through the Gala and its banners.

## 8.3 The landscape of the Gala

Cultural landscapes are created over time by human activities and have broad cultural contexts and particular ideologies and iconographies. Landscape is one of the domains generating, influencing and maintaining a person's/community's sense of identity and belonging. Memory inheres in landscape. This is why even voluntary migration (let alone refuge-seeking diasporas) can be so unsettling (*sensu strictu*) to their enactors. But movement on a landscape also can be an act of resistance. We would venture to characterise the Gala from its very beginning as a thumbing of the labour nose at the elite class of Durham and the British establishment, such as the favela Carnival groups of Río de Janeiro, which descend into the elite centre of that city in a massive assertion of identity, pride and temporary claiming of social and political space (see, e.g., da Matta 1991). The Gala and Carnival were and are a stage of resistance to the marginalisation of their performers. As with Carnival, when the Gala is over, the groups of these social and geographic peripheries of their society return to that margin.

The landscape of the formerly productive mines has disappeared. Upon closing, all of the collieries were demolished, and the sites quickly cleared of the debris (Emery 1998: 129). Writing of the destruction of the last operating pit in Durham, Temple says, 'the winding towers of Wearmouth Colliery were packed with explosive and blown up, erasing the last physical evidence in Durham of a once great industry' (2011: 170). The impact of this erasure has been summarised by Norman Emery as 'leaving blank spaces at the heart of each community' (1998: 129). Hareven and Langenbach are more explicit:

an entire community is subjected to what amounts to social amnesia as a result of massive clearance or alteration of the physical setting. The demolition of [...] factory buildings wipes out a significant chapter of the history of the place. Even if it does not erase them from local memory it tends to reduce or eliminate the recall of that memory, rendering less meaningful the communication of that heritage to a new generation. Such destruction deprives people of tangible manifestations of their identity.

(1981: 114–115)

As we have travelled to pit villages in County Durham, we, too, observe a landscape without even the ruins of coal mining (their recreation is to be seen at Beamish). Indeed, Tony Smith, formerly an urban designer in the Durham County Council, described his job of directing landscape remediation as an effort to turn scarred hills and dales into a physically appealing green scenery that would attract investment to the county (personal communication, 5 July 2018). En route from Durham to Easington – site of one of the last mines to close – energy-producing windmills dot the landscape that once was covered by collieries. But we argue that in the absence of the physical landscape of mining, the miners' banners have become a landscape of memory.

Moreover, it is important to recognise that the Gala did not and does not take place only in Durham City. It has a local choreography in the surrounding pit villages where 'it became patterned into village life' (Beynon and Austrin 1994: 213) through preparations for the Gala. Before departing with the banner for Durham, communities created a sacred landscape in their villages. Typically, the banner with its band would parade through town and stop (like the stations of the Cross) at significant local landmarks; a banner group will pick up a priest/ minister at a church; pay homage at the old-age miners home; and offer a prayer at the memorial for victims of a mining disaster (if such exists in a village), accompanied by the brass band playing *Gresford*, the moving miners hymn (Platt 2010). Then the buses to Durham are boarded. That local sacred landscape then disappears until the next year. The banner and its group arrive in Durham and perform in the Gala. Then the banner returns home where it is typically displayed in a school, community or welfare hall or miners' club. In some villages, the banner will be taken out during the year for use in particularly significant events. These activities support the current heritagisation of mining and enable the mining past to become a catalyst for the social activities of pit villages.

## 8.4 Heritage education

Like Emery (2009) and Wray (Stephenson and Wray 2005; Wray 2011), we, too, observe across County Durham keen community interest in curating banners and obtaining new banners, if needed, and other physical memorabilia of mining: framed photographs and paintings, miners' lamps, documents, maps and so forth. In the absence of the occupation itself on the landscape, these objects come to be the expression of the community – they re-establish the place of the community and reaffirm the pit villages' and villagers' identities. Stephenson and Wray (2005) describe this process as emotional regeneration through community action.

The banners play a critical role in visualising the memory of a community, in creating a community of memory (Nic Craith 2008) that is then performed at the Gala, which is especially important in 'socialising' the younger post-industrial generation (Stephenson and Wray 2005: 193). But mining families are not relying solely on the Gala and exhibitions to perpetuate the memory of mining, respect for it, and commitment to bettering the economically devastated pit villages through identification with their heritage. In Easington, for instance, virtually all students are the grandchildren of miners and have heard stories of the mines around the family table. They also have been taken by the school and their families to the memorial honouring the eighty-three miners who lost their lives in the 1951 Easington Colliery disaster, the victims still known personally in Easington. Moreover, all know that Easington is the town in which the most memorable scene of the 2000 movie, *Billy Elliott*, was filmed: Billy dancing on the roof and in the alleyway between the backs of the miners' homes. In the movie, Billy Elliott is the son of a miner during the great strike of 1984–1985, which is vividly portrayed. The real Easington was brutally occupied by the police for an entire year.

Recent school programs are educating young children about mining history in learning modules. The education program is also literally crafted as embodied performances of heritage whose goal is to generate a socially, politically and historically aware new generation. In Easington, primary school teachers enlisted the renowned banner maker, Emma Shankland, to help the children create their own banner. Then they held a mini Gala in town in which the children paraded their new banner. Mothers dressed up their children in miners' overalls, covered their faces in soot and put mining helmets and miners' lamps on them. Children pushed little tubs of papier-maché coal and carried protest placards with slogans of the 1984–1985 strike, such as 'Support the Miners', 'Coal Not Dole' and 'Stop the Scabs'. A song was created for the children, *I want to be a miner*, which they sang at intervals as they paraded through the town. However, the teaching module did not address the physical dangers of mining caused by this industry, even though various children told us about dead and injured mining relatives. Rather, the children's Gala presents a romantic and idealised vision of a time past. No longer expected by their fathers to work in the mines (the drama depicted in *Billy Elliott*) and with the mines no longer controlling pit village life, mining is now a safe past on which to draw.

## 8.5 Mining heritage and epistemic implications for the Gala

Heritage education aims to sustain the memory of mining heritage for future generations. This marks, to some extent, the long struggle of mining communities against epistemic oppression and hermeneutical marginalisation with regard to their heritage. Epistemic oppression occurs when there is no available space for voices to provide alternative interpretations of the past. Epistemic resistance occurs when an oppressed group's interpretation of the past refuses to accept the same events and ideologies in the same way as the dominant narrative. For instance, an oppressive account of the miners' past focusses on the negative aspects of the great strike of 1984–1985 and ignores the devastation wrought by the end of the mining era. Epistemic oppression in this sense is accompanied by hermeneutical marginalisation.

In contrast, epistemic resistance is social interaction and communication that aims to undermine and change oppressive structures and the function of those structures (Medina 2012). The Gala is a unique festival where struggle against marginalisation is transformed into epistemic resistance, vocally contesting oppressive structures. Miners are contesting their horrific denigration and demonisation during the great strike and that legacy, which contributes to the lack of government and private investment in the north-east. They are asserting pride about their status as miners with its associated values. This once and still cherished identity is enabling them to interpret their own past, and they therefore focus and prioritise the heroic, stoic and social aspects of that past. The pit village communities are thus involved in acts of epistemic resistance through their struggle against oppressive structures that have portrayed a picture of their past that is not compatible with their efforts to build a sustainable future.

Mining communities are struggling against marginalisation and seeking appropriate conceptual tools to interpret and engage with their past. Discourse is one such tool. Over many decades the Gala's organisers have been able to generate messaging that is responsive to each era. As David Guy, then President of the DMA, exclaimed in 2010, 'they [the British establishment] could not destroy that pride, community spirit and solidarity, which has been forged over centuries of adversity. That is why the Durham Miners' Gala did not die with the industry but has increased in strength and […] has become a beacon for the whole of the working class.' Then DMA Secretary General David Hopper said at the same time, 'This is our history and the Gala is all about remembering and celebrating our past – a past which not only tells us who we are but determines where we are going … the Durham Miners' Gala, the largest and most colourful working-class demonstration in the world, is once again the focus of the socialist and trade union movement'. The DMA is playing a critical role by offering both physical and discursive space as well as actual training. And the Gala itself, as Hopper inferred, is the key discursive and performative space where epistemic resistance takes place.

The social interaction and communication of epistemic resistance thrive in any available space where people from diverse backgrounds can meet, talk, exchange views and knowledge and contest different ideas. We distinguish between two kinds of social interaction during Gala: formal and informal. Formal interactions are those interactions that take place before and during the parade at the Gala. They are formal because they follow patterns that are central to the meaning and functioning of the Gala. Examples would be the processions that take place in pit villages before arriving in Durham and the tightly choreographed parade of banners in Durham that proceeds past the Royal County Hotel balcony and onto the racecourse, where each banner group is announced and contextualised. The obligatory playing of *Gresford* by each banner group's band is a ritual of remembrance that is integral to the meaning of the Gala. Children marching with their parents or grandparents learn the formal pattern of the Gala. Also formal is the blessing of new banners in Durham Cathedral. Eventually, each pit village with a banner will receive a blessing as three or four banners are blessed each year in the Miners' Memorial Service.

Informal interactions at the Gala are the expectable socialities that would take place at any large gathering. People from one village chat with villagers from other communities. They listen to the political speeches given at the racecourse by leaders of the Durham Miners' Association and members of the Parliament from the Labour Party and comment on them in avid conversations. Banner groups and music bands converse with each other while they wait to join the parade in the formal pattern, and once on the racecourse and finished, they relax with each other. There also are interactions between members of the public who attend and follow the parade. Anyone can engage with anybody. Any participant can wander around. The Gala's diverse public has different values, shares diverse experiences and manifests diverse communicative habits – but uniting everyone is progressive politics. The popularity of the Gala makes it the most effective platform for the DMA's political recruitment to the cause of labour unionism and its social and socialist agenda.

While social interactions and contestations of different forms are central to epistemic resistance, one should not forget that what underlies this kind of resistance is the use of epistemic resources (Medina 2012). These resources can be anything that can contribute to the production and interpretation of knowledge. The Gala is the primary epistemic resource for pursuing resistance and its main actor is the parade of mining lodge banners. Banners bring together the members of the mining communities, enabling multifaceted social interactions. Banners are the catalyst for epistemic resistance because they communicate the ideas that the mining communities stand for and they remind everyone of the struggles of the mining communities for these ideas.

The Gala is also an arena of epistemic friction. Although all publics drawn to the Gala are politically progressive, they are diverse and put forward their own discourses about some of the values mentioned earlier, resisting hegemonic standpoints and expressing their own accounts of equality and justice, communicating their own struggles and responding to the call for solidarity with those whose voices are not heard (Medina 2012). The Gala is a space where they can articulate alternative descriptions and interpretations of experiences and needs, a space for performance and a place for the meeting of diverse values and experiences.

## 8.6 The future of the Gala

Today, the one-day participation in the Gala by members of the pit villages is the embodied, substitutive memory of a life once lived around mining.

Participation generates intense feelings of community solidarity, village identity, personal identification with one's family history and collective memory of the pit village past (see, for example, Bailey and Popple 2011: 29–30; Beynon and Austrin 1994; Scott 2009). The banner is the incarnation of those sentiments and a significant epistemic resource that conveys values that sustained mining communities over many decades. Each banner is now a heritage object with its own distinct biography, cherished by its community, whether old and repaired or newly fabricated at significant expense and with community-selected iconography (Beynon and Austrin 1994). The banners are the representation of the pit villages' past as well as its aspirations for the future. The banners are the moving element that animates the celebration. The Gala has no meaning or appeal without the banners, which represent the history and are the heritage of the mining communities. They are the axis around which political discourse and epistemic resistance are grounded. Their illustrated values have sustained the pit villages in the past against terrible difficulties and oppressive structures. These values have led them to the present and will help them to move to the future.

As we indicated above, the Gala has survived for more than a century because of its discursive flexibility. Its organisers have been brilliant in maintaining the relevance of the Gala by being responsive to changing contexts. While the Gala respects, reveres and (re)collects the mining past, today's DMA leaders direct that sentiment toward a more inclusive Labour/socialist political agenda of workers' rights, social justice, health, housing, education and income fairness to which all can rally. The Gala also has been supported by and recursively prompted a heritagisation in the former mining communities, incarnated in the banner groups (see, especially, Wray 2011). The heritagisation of the mining past is how the mining communities interpret their own past and envision their future. Heritagisation of the mining past is engendering renewed enthusiasm for the Gala. Thus, politics and heritage are interlinked.

But one of the greatest challenges is for these village banner groups to engage younger members to carry on the Gala. Currently, tradition and innovation within the context of regional and national political relevance auger well for the Gala's future so long as – and this is a big condition – the miners' children, grandchildren and, eventually, their great-grandchildren will remain in the pit villages and identify with and perform as members of a community to whose sustainability they are committed. There must be critical mass in each pit village to form a banner group and obtain, maintain and parade a banner. Here enthusiasm, emotion and heritage hit reality because the North-East is significantly ignored by London. If jobs cannot redress the dire economic situation of Durham's pit villages, young people will move away or simply be so disaffected as to be uninterested in the Gala. And if the Gala's mining heritage becomes overwhelmed by the participation of other trade unions and the recent addition of international political concerns, then the Gala may cease to have its local relevance and, potentially, participation. The outcome could be a Gala that is heritage performance (Taylor 2016) but not heritage community.

This study thus has implications for the heritage field beyond the specific case of the Gala. Ultimately at issue is sustainability of a community's intangible cultural heritage when recontextualised in a dramatically altered social and economic landscape. While the performance of collective memory and its material culture may be traditional (*sensu strictu*) – visually, physically and audibly virtually identical to previous versions – it is possible that the intangible cultural heritage may become unmoored and ultimately a pseudo-event in Boorstin's (1962) sense, indeed a simulacrum (Baudrillard 1994). Whether the heritage – its communal and social value – is made newly 'authentic' and meaningful by its revised or expanded discourse or not is a conscious decision in the hands, literally, of its constituency.

Also at issue is remembering, which intuitively would mean not forgetting. But Harrison (2013) has argued that forgetting is integral to remembering, that some things must be forgotten so as to form new memories and attach value to them. Holtorf (2006) has more provocatively argued with specific reference to the tangible world that destruction and loss are part of the very substance of heritage. Certainly it is true, as Holtorf recognises, that cultural heritage functions and is understood differently in one period of time than another. Rather than destruction and forgetting, accretion – at least for an intangible cultural heritage – and evolution of meaning(s) may be the driver of sustainability if some form of continuance (rather than continuity) is what a community is seeking. As we have argued in this chapter, it is this flexibility and adaptation to new circumstances that enabled and is enabling the survival of the Gala – the performance. As to the heritage community, that remains to be seen.

## Acknowledgements

We are immensely grateful to many people in Durham for the insights they generously shared with us about mining history, mining communities and mining heritage. Conversations with David Wray were especially helpful. The DMA welcomed us, and we wish to thank Ross Forbes, Alan Cummings and Joe Whitworth for their time and knowledge. The role of women was opened to us by Heather Ward, Kath Connolly and Lynn Gibson. Norman Emery shared his professional as well as personal perspective on the Gala. James Coxton discussed his research, in progress. Emma Shankland explained banner-making to us as only she could. Mike Syer helped us to understand banner groups through his invitation to visit Bowburn. Philip Blakey explained the complex mechanics of producing a Gala. The dedicated and talented teachers at Easington's remarkable primary school – Georgina Lawrence and Steph Reddel – helped us to understand children's knowledge of mining. The Durham Mining Museum volunteers were always keen to talk with us. Any errors in this chapter are solely ours. Finally, we profusely thank University College at Durham University and Vice Master Richard Lawrie for help with accommodation and logistics.

## References

Bailey, M. and S. Popple (2011), 'The 1984/85 miners' strike', in L. Smith, P. Shackel and G. Campbell (eds), *Heritage, labour and the working classes* (London: Routledge), 19–33.

Baudrillard, J. (1994), *Simulacra and simulation*. (Ann Arbor: University of Michigan Press).

Beynon, H. and T. Austrin (1994), *Masters and servants. Class and patronage in the making of a labour organisation. The Durham miners and the English political tradition* (London: Rivers Oram).

Boorstin, D. J. (1962), *The image. A guide to pseudo-events in America* (New York: Vintage).

Bulmer, M. (1978), 'Employment and unemployment in mining 1920–1970', in M. Bulmer (ed.), *Mining and social change. Durham County in the twentieth century* (London: Droom Helm), 150–165.

da Matta, R. (1991), *Carnivals, rogues and heroes. an interpretation of the Brazilian dilemma* (Notre Dame, IN: University of Notre Dame Press).

Emery, N. (2009), *The coalminers of Durham* (Stroud: History).

Emery, N. (1998), *Banners of the Durham coalfield* (Stroud: Sutton).

Frankeleyn, W. (1775) (?) A letter from William Frankeleyn to Cardinal Wolsey Bishop of Durham, relating certain coal mines at Whickam and other rights and privileges of the bishoprick, and the cardinal mint there for the coinage of money (Darlington: George Allan).

Gillum, D. (2009), *Banners of pride. Memories of the Durham Miners' Gala* (South Shields: CVN).

Gorman, J. (1986), *Banner bright. An illustrated history of trade union banners* (London: Scorpion).

Hair, T. (1844), *A series of views of the collieries in the counties of Northumberland and Durham* (London: T.H. Hair)

Hair, T. (1839), *Sketches of the coal mines in Northumberland and Durham* (microfilm) (London: T.H. Hair).

Hareven, T. and R. Langenbach (1981), 'Living places, work places and historical identity', in D. Lowenthal and M. Binney (eds), *Our past before us. Why do we save it?* (London: Temple Smith), 109–123.

Harrison, R. (2013), 'Forgetting to remember, remembering to forget: late modern heritage practices, sustainability and the 'crisis' of accumulation of the past', *International Journal of Heritage Studies* 19(6): 579–595.

Holtorf, C. (2006), 'Can less be more? Heritage in the age of terrorism', *Public Archaeology* 5: 101–109.

Medina, J. (2012), *The epistemology of resistance: gender and racial oppression, epistemic injustice, and the social imagination* (Oxford: Oxford University Press).

Meskell, L. (2002), 'Negative heritage and past mastering in archaeology', *Anthropological Quarterly* 75(3): 557–574.

Nic Craith, M. (2008), 'Intangible cultural heritages: the challenges for Europe', *Anthropological Journal of European Cultures* 17(1): 54–73.

Northern Mine Research Society (n.d.), Colliers of the British Isles. Available at: www.nmrs.org.uk/mines-map/coal-mining-in-the-british-isles/collieries-of-the-british-isles/ (accessed 10 January 2019).

Platt, G. (2010), *Grimethorpe colliery band plays Gresford (The Miners Hymn)*. Available at: www.youtube.com/watch?v=w6nS8aqA0Hc (accessed 10 January 2019).

Pocock, D. (2013), *The story of Durham* (Stroud: History).

Scott, C. (2009), 'Contemporary expressions of coal mining heritage in the Durham Coalfield: the creation of new identities', *Folk Life: Journal of Ethnological Studies* 47: 66–75.

Stephenson, C. and D. Wray (2005), 'Emotional regeneration through community action in post-industrial mining communities: the New Herrington miners' banner partnership', *Capital & Class* 29(3): 175–199.

Sykes, J. (1835), *An account of the dreadful explosion in Wallsend Colliery, on the 18th June 1835: to which is added a list of explosions, inundations &c. which have occurred in the coal mines of Northumberland and Durham, more complete than any hitherto published* (Newcastle upon Tyne: Printed for J. Sykes).

Taylor, D. (2016), 'Saving the "live"? Re-performance and intangible cultural heritage', *Études Anglaises* 69(2): 149–161.

Temple, D. (2011), *The big meeting. A history of the Durham Miners' Gala* (Washington, Tyne and Wear: TUPS).

Tunbridge, J. and G. J. Ashworth (1996), *Dissonant heritage. The management of the past as a resource in conflict* (New York: Wiley).

Wozhere, D. (2017), Durham Photographic Society website. Available at: www.durhamps.co.uk/?s=Cathedral+Exhibition+2017 (accessed 25 August 2018).

Wray, D. (2011), 'Images, icons and artefacts. Maintaining an industrial culture in a post-industrial environment', in L. Smith, P. A. Shackel and G. Campbell (eds), *Heritage of labour and the working class* (London: Routledge), 106–118.

Wray, D. (2009), The place of imagery in the transmission of culture: the banners of the Durham Coalfield, *International Labor and Working-Class History* 76(1): 147–163.

# 9 Sound structure as political structure in the European folk festival orchestra *La Banda Europa*

*Simon McKerrell*

European folk musics are diverse and have been strongly tied to national and regional politics for at least 200 years. However, attempts to construct pan-European musical identities rest upon the notion of bringing forward new, original compositions based upon these numerous musical identities and often occur in the context of large-scale festival commissions. Drawing on ethnomusicological theories of sound structure and social structure, this chapter examines the ways in which concepts of the 'new' and pan-European belonging surface in a festival folk-orchestra designed specifically to express it, whilst simultaneously drawing upon the sonic affordances of long established, traditional musical heritage from across Europe. The chapter focusses upon the various performances of *La Banda Europa*, which was an ensemble formed in 2007/8 specifically to perform complex, new folk–orchestral compositions, drawing on some of the most well-established European folk musics, including the Scottish bagpipes, Swedish *nyckelharpa*, French hurdy gurdy, Austrian accordion, Galician *gaita* and Armenian *duduk* traditions.

Representations of belonging and identity are grounded in the textural and timbral characteristics of the instruments, whilst the newness, and consequent contemporary notions of Europeanness, are performed in and through melodic and harmonic elements of this contemporary 'orchestra' through collocation of images and sound.

As a case study of one explicitly European musical festival project that I have been involved in since its inception *La Banda Europa* can help us in, thinking through the relationship(s) between musical and political structures and how these are mediated and performed in sound. *La Banda Europa* essentially is an orchestra of European folk musicians drawn from across the EU and beyond, stretching out into the Caucasus and resting upon the composition of Jim Sutherland who first brought this festival concept to life in the early 2000s. The chapter considers from a participatory perspective how *La Banda Europa*, as a folk orchestra conceived for European festivals, constructed a sense of European belonging without simultaneously conflating it with any essentialising notion of 'European music'.

One of the central concerns of ethnomusicology has been the relations between sound structure and social structure. Before the plurality (and complexity) of globalisation and human relations really began to eat away at the universalising ideals of the mid-twentieth century academy, earlier generations of ethnomusicologists in the 1950s through to around the 1990s spent a considerable period of time and effort thinking through the possible homologous or metaphorical relations between sound structure and social or political structures. In the very highly cited paper of that name, 'Sound Structure and Social Structure' published in 1984 by Steven Feld (inspired by the famous 'Song structure and social structure' by Alan Lomax (1962), Feld claims, based on his ethnographic research with the Kaluli people of South America that 'sound structures are observably and undeniably socially structured' (1984: 385). My concern in this chapter is to examine that relationship between musical intangible cultural heritage (ICH) and Europeanness through my own experiences as a musician–researcher in *La Banda Europa*. This chapter therefore explores the idea that music can and does communicate social structures but does so through a process of mediation that depends upon collocation with coexisting textual and cultural ideas, without which, music is semiotically bleached. It is in this sense, that musical structures can communicate a sense of something as complex as 'Europeanness', and it is crucial that the listener or audience reception carries with it some sort of expertise in the non-musical information surrounding the performance. In essence then, musical sound, and by extension, ICH practices, do have the communicative ability to signify complex sociopolitical structures, but this depends upon listeners' understanding of their and others' heritage and thus what can be *sonically* recognised as 'old' or 'traditional' alongside that which can be heard or understood as 'new' or 'novel'. Festivals of musical heritage in Europe are concentrated acts of identity construction that rely upon ICH which can be extremely powerful in constructing a sense of national, and as I argue in this chapter, European belonging. In this case, *La Banda Europa* signals the ICH of some of Europe's established folk traditions, yet relies heavily on the 'novelty' or 'newness' of the musical performance for the whole to overlay a contemporary, complicated and layered notion of Europeanness.

## 9.1 Brief description of *La Banda Europa*

As a musician, playing in the orchestra of *La Banda Europa* feels very much like an orchestra of European folk instruments, which it is, and it has always represented some of the most distinctive indigenous instruments of Europe. Clearly this claim is contentious; one simply needs to understand that instruments such as the bagpipe, hurdy gurdy or nyckelharpa have a long and contested organological history where claims of indigeneity are often dubious (and usually pointless). However, it remains the case that the orchestra of *La Banda Europa* was consciously contrived to include some of the key traditional musics of Europe and at different times has comprised: accordion; Scottish bagpipe; Scottish border pipes; nyckelharpas; hurdy gurdy; Armenian duduk; Galician and Asturian gaita; concertina; dulzaina; Fujara flute; Slovakian and Serbian gaide (bagpipe); button accordion; pandereta; dahul; zurna and kaval. In

130  *Simon McKerrell*

addition to these traditional instruments, there was also a fairly full complement of diatonic orchestral instruments including: cello, bass clarinet, soprano saxophone, tuba, trombone, trumpet, bass saxophone, French horn, percussion both non-pitched and pitched percussion in the shape of vibraphone and marimba. Rick Taylor, an internationally renowned brass player and arranger, was the conductor, and all of the original music was composed by the Scottish composer and percussionist Jim Sutherland who devised, composed and delivered the entire concept.

The band was originally conceived of as a festival folk orchestra in 2003 that could promenade whilst playing, perambulating in a festival context while performing: a sort of European folk promenading band. Jim Sutherland dreamt up the project in the early 2000s, and the orchestra has since performed at three major festivals across Europe including in Gateshead (2007), in Marseille (2009) and at Celtic Connections in Glasgow (2017) as well as various smaller residencies around Europe in Spain and France in the intervening years. As Jim Sutherland explains:

> In 2003 into 2004 I was in Seville, and I was working on a film called 'Festival', which is by Annie Griffin the director, and Chris Young the producer .... So I wrote a score for the film, where seventeen tracks of the score were performed by a 90-piece *semana santa* band and we brought twelve pipers from the Drambuie pipe band to work with them. The *semana santa* band worked in a pre-1920s tuning which was a quarter tone up from concert [pitch], and so it was a marriage made in heaven!
>
> And I remembering listening to this sound that we'd created, and I just thought it's kind of got something of the sound of Europe .... I just thought, Southern Europe and Northern Europe, and I thought, wow, this sounds like Europe. And I thought, wouldn't it be great to have a band that was like a European band, and that's really where the whole idea for *La Banda Europa* was born.
>
> [Jim Sutherland, fieldwork interview with author, October 2018]

Jim says about the eventual orchestra of which I was a member that 'it's really a wind band ...it's the European village band writ large' (Jim Sutherland, fieldwork interview October 2018). For him, and for many of the musicians involved, there was indeed a sense of the village about the band: over several years and various projects, musicians have come to know each other better as friends as well as professionals, and these sorts of personal relationships in the band are as much a part of the identity for members within the group as the unusual and arresting combination of instruments and sounds must be for those hearing *La Banda Europa* for the first time. Musicians are an unusual social group; despite often having very low social and economic status, they nevertheless share certain attributes with the most educated and richest members of European society. They are often extremely well-travelled, multilingual and therefore share a number of attributes with the 12.7% of Europeans from the 'highest socio-economic groups in society' who are most likely to consider themselves 'European' (Fligstein, Polyakova and Sandholtz 2012: 109f.). Moreover, music as a particularly difficult art form to interpret, offers possibly the greatest scope for constructing European identity, or a form of 'nested' or layered Europeanness. The lack of semantic specificity in musical sound has made it particularly powerful for constructing social identities, particularly those based on ethnic nationalism, and consequently the significant problems of folk music's intersection with national identities in the post-war period (see, for instance, Keegan-Phipps 2017; Lucas 2013). I argue here that the timbre and typical musical signatures of the traditional instruments used in *La Banda Europa* manage to construct a sense of European belonging rather than any notion of a 'European music', thus eliding the problems of ethno-nationalism and its collocation with national folk traditions.

The costs involved in putting on a performance of *La Banda Europa* are very significant, given that unlike most classical or art music orchestras, the players are scattered across Europe and have to come together for a minimum of a few days to rehearse and perform. Transport, accommodation and venue hire costs alone for this ensemble are high, yet the band has also performed and conducted workshops in smaller units of five or six performers at various festivals in France and elsewhere, always funded specifically from large festival budgets that have directly commissioned work from the band. In the beginning, the band was focussed upon promenading whilst performing, which for many of us used to performing seated was a significant challenge. As a musician involved from the beginning of the project, I recall the sense of novelty (and trepidation!) at being asked to wear highly stylised robes and play my bagpipes whilst walking through the streets of Falkirk, Marseille, Newcastle and Gateshead. The idea of a moving unit of performers, of this size (thirty to forty musicians) is not only unusual in everyday experience but also poses a challenge to the musicians themselves, who are used to the settled conditions of interior performance in a concert hall or smaller venue where instruments can be left secure and microphone placement and other professional aspects of performance can be worked out over a series of rehearsals for best performance.

My own role in all of the performances, beginning in Falkirk (2007) through to Gateshead (2009), Marseille (2013) and most recently Glasgow Celtic Connections Festival (2017), has been as a border piper, uilleann piper and whistle player. The scoring for my parts was like many of us, split fairly evenly between written scores with recognisable dance music structures using eight or sixteen bar repeats and with a clear and obvious melody, and in other places, employing 'through composed' sections as part of the overall timbre of the orchestra. For me personally, the discipline of playing to the score and as part of a much larger ensemble than in any normative traditional or folk practice has been technically fairly straightforward having learnt many of the Western art music disciplines of orchestral performance. In the last two decades I have performed in between twenty or thirty cross-genre collaborative performance projects involving orchestras, choirs and mixed ensembles working on pieces such as Shaun Davey's *Relief of Derry*, John Rae's *Big Feet*, Peter Maxwell Davies *Orkney Sunrise with Wedding*, Steve Forman's *Hameward Bend*, Eddie MacGuire's *Calgacus* and numerous performances at festivals across Europe and North America with classical, folk and jazz musicians. This has almost always been as a Scottish bagpiper, bringing a strong iconic folk sound to a largely orchestral art music sound and occasionally as a (Scottish) Border or (Irish) uilleann piper. On some occasions, it has involved a more experimental fusion of jazz and folk music or classical and folk musical sounds. With the exception of one or two collaborations, I have been involved in such as Fred Morrison's *Paracas* at Celtic Connections, or Nuala Kennedy's project, commissioned by the pioneering organisation Distil and supported by the then Scottish Arts Council, these musical projects have rarely sought to utilise the traditional musical heritage of the bagpipes themselves. In the case of *La Banda Europa*, the composer Jim Sutherland did spend a considerable amount of preparatory time investigating and absorbing the musical styles of each of the instruments in the folk-orchestra. This perhaps marks it out from other projects where composers have perhaps simply learned what the technical limitations and tuning of an instrument such as the bagpipes are and have then moulded its instrumental voice to suit their own intended vision of performance. Therefore, composers bring with them, either an explicit interest or disinterest in the sonic heritage of the individual tradition. The same would apply to other forms of ICH; great chefs can create interesting dishes using the high-quality ingredients of their Others, and in some cases, they will get to understand the gastronomic heritage and the ways in which particular ingredients have been traditionally used, and in others cases, they will simply use the raw ingredient for their own particular creation. This also underlines the differences here in the creative approach to composition in this project from standard Western art music orchestral composition. Jim Sutherland, essentially composed through listening to the traditional performances of each of the different instruments, using YouTube, CDs and reading around each of the different traditions. It was only after he absorbed these influences that he then went on to build on that musical heritage to compose the music for *La Banda Europa*. This compositional process differs from standard Western orchestral composition in the sense that it is an approach to composition that relies heavily upon the musical heritage of different folk traditions rather than using orchestral instruments to service the vision of the composer themselves. *La Banda Europa* was a resource, rather than simply a tool. In working this way, Jim Sutherland managed to bring forward and, in some cases, showcase the special character of the instruments in the folk-orchestra: There were fairly substantial sections that featured the Armenian duduks, the Swedish nyckelharpas and the hurdy gurdies, for instance. This is crucial for the semiotic significance of *La Banda Europa*, because if one considers musical or performative meaning to be a relational process that 'is most immediately a phenomenon of its performance' (Cook 2018:19), then this sort of showcasing of the various folk instruments from around Europe sets up a strong impression of pan-European heritage during the performance. The focus not just on one type of folk instrument but on several over the course of an hour or more in concert means that the audience is directed to take notice of the timbre, visual spectacle and special sonic characteristics of each of these instruments in the band. For the scholarship of intangible cultural heritage, the really significant point here is to consider much more strongly how multimodal performance of folk music, dance, poetry, food, craft or song structures the audience's experience providing much of the social meaning. Colour, smell, sound, taste, gesture, fonts, timbre, dynamics and so on all have semiotic affordances that contribute to the audience's understanding of what the intangible signifies and what historical traditions are being re-performed in the present.

One of the first significant performative challenges of this project was the perambulation of *La Banda Europa* both in Newcastle-Gateshead and then significantly in Marseille, which required a different mindset, where musical sounds took a backseat to the drama of the spectacle. On reflection, I now understand that this reprioritisation of musical values was difficult for me at first and was something that made me feel slightly uncomfortable. During my training and almost all of one's experience as a musician, it is the excellence of tone and accuracy of sound in performance that is prioritised above all else, this being the bedrock of one's ability to communicate with an audience. Learning to perform with a different, more public prioritisation of spectacle and drama was a challenge for many of us, all of whom had professional musical careers as performers. In this respect then, the musical heritage of the performer took second place to the performative priorities of the festival space, enforcing a shift in the values underlying performance of my own intangible cultural heritage practice but benefitting the audience and giving way to the collective will of the band's performance.

When one considers it, this subservience to the collective effort goes a lot deeper than simply prioritising the overall ensemble affect over one's individual professional musical instincts. As an orchestra, and for a group of this size (around thirty-six to forty musicians depending on the performance), the musical parts for performance have to be scored, written out professionally, in order that the whole piece works together. As anyone who has seen an orchestral score will know, this also involves the 'tacit' bars, where the instrumentalist or singer remains silent. This practice is singularly associated with European art music, or in vernacular terms, the 'classical' tradition. Musical notation is of course widespread in traditional musics and across many different intangible cultural heritage practices throughout the world including song, tunes, poetry, visual art, crafts and so on; however these written notations are almost always in the service of transmission. The key difference with *La Banda Europa* (and other cross-genre projects I have been involved in as a performer) is the idea that musical texts service the performance. Ethnomusicologists have assumed also that transmission is largely oral/aural because in fact the majority of traditional musics around the world still rely upon oral/aural transmission but often use notation as an aide memoire. Projects such as this where musical notation is the primary method of musical transmission highlight one of the key differences between ICH and more textually dependent practices. This is not to say that ICH such as music, art, food, dance and so on are not literate traditions, but that notation is almost always used in the service of practice, and transmission depends upon human face-to-face communication rather than through texts.

Indeed, the performance of such a large ensemble as *La Banda Europa* would simply not work without a score where each member has their parts written out and bars numbered showing exactly where and when to play and when to be silent. When one considers the traditional musics from around the world, there are many different schemes of musical notation (see for instance Hughes 2000; Shelemay 2010; Tokumaru and Yamaguti 1986), but they help learners to acquire their repertoire and sometimes the stylistic nuances of their art. They are almost always skeletal in form and contain very selective information often notating only the easily notable information such as pitch or approximate rhythm. This means that for musicians like me, who were brought up in a mixed environment of aural and textual transmission, much of the most important and intangible musical heritage is passed on non-verbally, mostly through listening. The variable status of musical notation underlies also the training of different genres of musicianship in jazz, folk, classical, popular, early musics etc.; to such a fundamental and aesthetic extent that it is difficult to reconcile in any sort of shared, core educational curriculum (as many of us working in music departments will readily acknowledge). This highlights one of the most fascinating aspects of intangible cultural heritage; that which is tacit, is very often most significant. As Diana Taylor has noted, '[p]roducing a record of performance, is not the same as performance' (Taylor 2016: 151). Here she is laying out the problems of the instinct towards archiving and fixity in ICH safeguarding, set against the affective immediacy of performing practices. This is exactly the same dilemma we faced in *La Banda Europa*. Almost all the musicians involved came from traditions that privilege oral transmission and varying degrees of spontaneity in performance, while the size and musical intent of the project necessitated a degree of written co-ordination and scoring of the music that downplayed the most authentic and powerful affective aspects each of us brought from our home traditions to the collective performance. However, the problems of representation, commodification and objectification remains a key one in the policy surrounding the documentation and support of ICH.

The overall 'affect' provides us with the social semiotics that allow us to 'hear' complex social structural ideas such as 'Europeanness' primarily because it relies upon the listeners broad familiarity of what can be heard as 'new' and 'old'. These two binaries are critical in the performance of musical heritage, which is always already an experience that places great value on the 'old' or the 'traditional' and similarly on the 'new'. The more expert one becomes in listening to and interpreting intangible cultural heritage performances such as bagpiping, folk dance, Portuguese fado or Turkish maqāmāt traditions, the more deeply one can read the sonic patterns and motivic content of these musics, and crucially, how far an individual is willing to depart from them.

Because the score for *La Banda Europa*'s performances were all original, newly composed music, very little of the traditional melodic material from the many and diverse musical traditions represented in the orchestra is incorporated into the musical material. This was countered to some extent by showcasing individual sections of instruments such as the four hurdy gurdies, or nyckelharpas or Galician and Asturian musicians during our festival appearances. Both to showcase the talents of the individual musicians but also to represent their cultural heritage among the amalgamated performance of the set orchestral pieces. Because of this, the most obvious signifier of cultural heritage in *La Banda Europa* became the timbre of the instruments and the visual spectacle of the instruments themselves.

The timbre of the individual instruments was the most obvious and clear distinction between this orchestra and the standard European classical orchestra with which Western audiences are familiar. When I consider the resultant sound of the orchestra and the pieces we performed, it is this timbre more than anything else that really constructs the distinct sound unlike any other orchestra I have previously heard. In pieces such as *Pillars of Hercules* and *Before the Wolf*, nyckelharpas give way to the ethereal sounds of Armenian duduks, who are bolstered by the distinctive sounds of the hurdy gurdies and bagpipes. These timbres have never been heard in this combination before, and that makes the somatic experience of hearing *La Banda Europa* something distinctive. This was recognised by Jim Gilchrist who reviewed the concert for *The Scotsman* newspaper:

> It lifted the heart to hear La Banda Europa's first gig in eight years [in Scotland], their glorious rumpus a pan-European riposte to the xenophobia currently at large … toting a bewildering range of indigenous instruments, kicked off with their Celtic Connections commission, We Are an Ocean, which emerged from primeval drones, flutings and the ineffably sad voice of the Armenian duduk to work itself into a big, brassy, cosmopolitan groove which, during the encore, became a jubilant chant of solidarity taken up by the audience.
>
> (Gilchrist 2017b)

Many Northern European people would be able to recognise the timbre and sound of the Scottish bagpipes, some also the Swedish nyckelharpa or French hurdy gurdy. Presumably fewer again would be able to recognise from its sound alone the distinctive and beautiful timbre of the Armenian duduk or the Spanish dulzaina. Each of these individual musical traditions has their own heritage and musical structures that are learnt alongside the intangible or tacit aspects of their culture. The combination of these timbres together provided a novelty or newness that for me, brings into being a third stream sense of sonic newness, which tied to the visual and contextual information of the instruments and the musicians, collocates to provide a strong reading of Europeanness. To be clear, this sense of Europeanness grounded in the timbral combination of unique indigenous European folk instruments depends somewhat upon the sonic knowledge of the Self and Other. Kockel (this volume) discusses this phenomenon in relation to ICH more broadly and its performance, resting his model upon the notion of Self and Other in private and public identities and how this constructs discrete identities.

However, importantly, detailed understanding of the cultural musical domain is not necessary for understanding timbre and newness aurally. One does not need to know how to read music notation or to know anything of the insider's musical knowledge or aesthetics to understand the sonic signification of the timbre of musical instruments, especially ones as distinctive as those in *La Banda Europa*. Timbre is however critical, because certain instruments possess more or less timbral affordances in sound. For instance, I would venture it is easier to classify a tune as French if played on hurdy gurdy than on oboe. Similarly, how many Europeans have mistaken the German-composed *Highland Cathedral* as a Scottish melody simply because of its ubiquity and association with the Scottish bagpipes (Korb and Roever, n.d.)? Timbre carries strong ethnic affordances and, in the case of this orchestra, brought them together to create a uniquely European sound.

## 9.2 Europeanness and the band

The idea of the orchestra of *La Banda Europa* was conceived of out of a sense of artistic curiosity in European folk musics but also partially with a European sense of heritage and belonging in mind but well before the spectre of Brexit, as Jim Sutherland explains:

> In 1989 I worked on a film called *Play me Something* with Tim Neat and John Berger … John considered himself a European, and this notion of being a European had a great influence on me. It was Hamish Henderson who introduced me to him. So in that period when I worked on two films with those guys … these people were very influential on me and the way to think about Europe and what I am as a person, and I think John particularly led me to want to be a European. I've always believed that people were people first, and I think the idea in *La Banda Europa* that people are people … Borders are political entities that in some way contain culture because the borders exist, however culture in my eyes, is much more amorphous, cultures spread and overlap, but there are these beacons or nodes, of cultural intensity … and the boundaries are quite blurred, there's a sort of cross-pollination. I didn't set out to make that statement, it seemed like European was a good enough thing to be; it's just a bigger container that's got lots of smaller containers within it and there's this bleed through [musically].
> [Jim Sutherland, fieldwork interview, October 2018]

However, after the 2016 referendum and subsequent Brexit discourse, thirty-six band members met again to record and perform a major concert in January

2017 at Celtic Connections Festival in Glasgow. I was also involved in this, and among the band, there was a sense of serendipitously being able to make a statement of solidarity against Brexit, albeit much of the talk centred on the potentially devastating effects and costs associated with European professional travel and work for musicians. Jim Sutherland made this generalised antipathy towards Brexit clear and collocated it with the band's performance in the national press and at the concert:

> It's not an anti-Brexit statement – although personally I am anti-Brexit, but it's looking at the underlying society, of which Brexit is a symptom, and all these things like the rise of hate and the 'othering' of people and the whole refugee crisis.
>
> [Jim Sutherland quoted in Gilchrist 2017a: n.p.]

The music of *La Banda Europa* however was not politically motivated in its genesis; it grew initially from Jim Sutherland's artistic curiosity and interest in the cultural heritage of different folk traditions from around Europe. Musically, there was no precedent; there are no folk orchestras that have been deliberately put together to reflect the entirety of Europe, despite a strong tradition of nationalist genres and folkloric ensembles in former Soviet countries (Silverman 1983; Buchanan 1995; Slobin 1996; Seeman 2012). These ensembles were both explicitly about national identity construction in the Balkans, and in former Soviet states, but have been a mainstay at folk festivals across Europe for decades, espousing and cementing an ongoing collocation between certain musical styles and instruments with nation states. The large pan-European folk festivals such as Lorient, Cambridge, Tønder or Ortigueira have always tended to set out their acts on a national basis or programming by country or ethnic origin, and consequently, perhaps counter-intuitively, pan-European folk festivals have tended to privilege national traditions and further deepen the historical construction of folk music with the national idea. The Western and Northern European national traditions have long been collocated with 'Celtic' music and thus well represented at Western European folk festivals through various forms of bagpipes, fiddles and songs in Gaelic, Asturian, Breton and other key languages strongly associated with ideas of regional or national European identity. Unlike Kaminsky, I do not see any shift away from these established national traditions at European festival programming in favour of a more 'East European bricolage— Balkan, Romani and klezmer music' (Kaminsky 2015). The audience is simply bigger and more diversely served; Scottish, Irish, Breton, Galician, Asturian, Spanish and English folk musicians are still playing and making a consistent living across Western Europe and its largest folk festivals. However, very rarely (or never) has any programmer attempted to conjoin these national musical heritages into a combined musical performance of Europeanness. There had been no attempt in folk music to construct a sense of a pan-European musical identity (for the very good reasons outlined above): This left Jim Sutherland free to begin afresh and his approach was to study the cultural heritage of each of the different instrumental traditions around Europe, and a key priority for the composition of the music was to attempt to be 'representative of all the traditions, their music style and aspects of their music traditions' (Jim Sutherland, fieldwork interview, October 2018).

The musical heritage of Europe is of course hugely diverse and plural. Many people would dispute even the commonplace national categorisations such as 'Spanish music', 'French music' or 'Scottish music' that came to prominence in the nineteenth century as essentialising and idealising categories (Gelbart 2007; Bohlman 2004; Nic Craith 2008) and continue to be used both commercially and in vernacular discussion of traditional musics in Europe. Indeed, the very idea of a 'European music' is as nonsensical as the more dangerous and subjugating older discourses about 'African music' and 'African rhythm' that did so much cultural work in constructing both a European sense of superiority and African Otherness (Agawu 1995). To me as a musician and participant, *La Banda Europa* was *not* about creating a new 'European music', but it *was* about performing a sense of European belonging; the two things are different and can easily be fallaciously conflated. In the same way that one simply cannot speak about 'African music' without displaying a deep sense of ignorance or worse, deliberately neo-colonial instincts, one similarly cannot speak of a 'European music'. In the end, the musical success of *La Banda* was in managing to supersede the ethno-nationalist semiotics of European folk musics through the use of those instruments, critically, in the service of newly composed music. This for me at least, moved the overall performances through to a point where a sort of 'nested' European sense of belonging was sonically constructed through the timbres of the instruments in *La Banda* and the multimodal, visual spectacle of the different musical traditions that are historically strongly aligned with their own nation states or regions.

The families, towns, regions and nations of today's Europe have many plural musical traditions, with individual heritages that are both ancient and sharply contemporary and changing rapidly with new immigrant populations. However, as Jim Sutherland has suggested, and as some of us felt during the various projects, one can feel a sense of shared belonging to a supra-national identity grounded in a sense of place, that binds people together in a political project. That sort of thing is complex but as I have attempted to argue, can be performed through visual (instruments, costumes) and sonic semiotics in the unique combinations of musical timbre and aural novelty. As Jayne Luscombe makes clear, the technocrats who crafted the European Union in the last seventy years assumed that culture follows or reflects the economic and the social; they had a vision based in law, trade and security where, 'integration in economic, political and legal institutions would directly lead to the construction of a sense of European identity among member states' (Luscombe 2015: 176). This has not happened; however, reflecting on the musical life of *La Banda Europa* and the broader landscape of musical Self and Otherness, one thing that has become clear to me is that complex ideas about social and political structure can be expressed in and through music. This does not require musical literacy from the audience, but it does rely upon the collocation of musical instruments with national traditions and a generalised sense of musical semiotics. When image, idea and sound are combined, then it is possible to perform a sense of complex belonging, even multi-layered sense of belonging such as Europeanness. In this way, the intangible cultural heritage of music can, and has been, mobilised to perform a sense of European belonging that transcends the individual local cultures and expresses a sense of Europeanness that draws on the sonic markers of old Europe while signalling a different, multi-voiced sense of today's Europe through new composition. This was the success of *La Banda Europa*, and I believe it poses some fascinating questions not only for ethnomusicology, heritage studies, ethnology and anthropology but also for the festival organisers and promoters in Europe and perhaps even for the technocrats of the European Union who have almost always regarded culture as an afterthought. It is clear now that most European heritage policy has focussed on the material heritage (buildings, monuments, sites), which has reflected the ideological priorities of European policymakers in whose perspective 'material and non-material heritage are still treated as following separate and distinct trajectories, with primacy given to the former' (Nic Craith and Kockel 2015), or who, as Lähdesmäki (2016) suggests, have 'placed' the intangible by collocating it with a particular site or settlement. Culture and performance can carry a great deal of semiotic luggage; perhaps even more than any static building or museum exhibit. The vitality and affect that we feel when we hear music, dance or sing together has a significant power that goes beyond the aesthetic and into the political. One wonders whether if more resources were used for showcasing and performing the full plurality of European identities around the continent on a more regular basis, certainly at festivals but also through the mass media, whether we might not in 2019 be at this critical crossroads of European division between the protectionist and inward-looking ethno-nationalism and a more cosmopolitan, elitist, supra-nationalist identity-politics? Certainly, it takes a vision and energy to bring forward attractive and novel forms of cultural practice whether rooted in past traditions or cleverly aspiring to a future vision. But it is possible, and at this moment of challenge for the European post-war settlement, it is probably one worth pursuing.

## Acknowledgement

This publication is a result of the European Union-funded Horizon 2020 research project: CoHERE (Critical Heritages: performing and representing identities in Europe). CoHERE received funding from the European Union's Horizon 2020 research and innovation programme under grant agreement No. 693289.

## References

Agawu, K. (1995), 'The invention of "African Rhythm"', *Journal of the American Musicological Society* 48(3): 380–395.

Bohlman, P. (2004), *The music of European nationalism: cultural identity and modern history* (Santa Barbara, CA: ABC-CLIO).

Buchanan, D. (1995), 'Metaphors of power, metaphors of truth: the politics of music professionalism in Bulgarian folk orchestras', *Ethnomusicology* 39(3): 381–416.

Cook, N. (2018), *Music as creative practice* (New York: Oxford University Press).

Feld, S. (1984), 'Sound structure as social structure', *Ethnomusicology* 28(3): 383–409.

Fligstein, N., A. Polyakova, and W. Sandholtz (2012), 'European integration, nationalism and European identity', *Journal of Common Market Studies* 50(s1): 106–122.

Gelbart, M. (2007), *The invention of 'folk music' and 'art music' emerging categories from Ossian to Wagner* (Cambridge: Cambridge University Press).

Gilchrist, J. 2017a. 'Interview: Jim Sutherland on reuniting La Banda Europa for Celtic Connections', *The Scotsman*, 25 January 2017. Available at: www.scotsman.com/lifestyle/culture/music/interview-jim-sutherland-on-reuniting-la-banda-europa-for-celtic-connections-1-4348289 (accessed 9 January 2019).

Gilchrist, J. (2017b), 'Music reviews: La Banda Europa | Trilok Gurtu & Evelyn Glennie', *The Scotsman*, 3 February 2017. Available at: www.scotsman.com/lifestyle/culture/music/music-reviews-la-banda-europa-trilok-gurtu-evelyn-glennie-1-4356990 (accessed 10 January 2019).

Hughes, D. (2000), 'No nonsense: the logic and power of acoustic-iconic mnemonic systems', *British Journal of Ethnomusicology* 9(2): 93–120.

Kaminsky, D. (2015), 'Introduction: the new old Europe sound', *Ethnomusicology Forum* 24(2): 143–158.

Keegan-Phipps, S. (2017), 'Identifying the English: essentialism and multiculturalism in contemporary English folk music', *Ethnomusicology Forum* 26(1): 1–23.

Korb, M, and U. Roever (n.d.), 'Highland Cathedral – Das Original'. Available at: www.highlandcathedral.de/inde.html (accessed 9 January 2019).

Lähdesmäki, T. (2016), 'Politics of tangibility, intangibility, and place in the making of a European cultural heritage in EU heritage policy', *International Journal of Heritage Studies*, 22(10): 766–780.

Lucas, C. (2013), 'The imagined folk of England: whiteness, folk music and fascism', *Critical Race and Whiteness Studies* 9(1): 1–19.

Lomax, A. (1962), 'Song structure and social structure', *Ethnology* 1(1): 425–451.

Luscombe, J. (2015), 'Promoting "European" identities at and through Pan-European events', in U. Merkel (ed), *Identity discourses and communities in international events, festivals and spectacles* (London: Palgrave Macmillan), 173–191.

Nic Craith, M. (2008), 'Intangible cultural heritages: the challenges for Europe', *Anthropological Journal of European Cultures* 17(1): 54–73.

Nic Craith, M. and U. Kockel (2015), '(Re-)building heritage: integrating tangible and intangible', in W. Logan, M. Nic Craith and U. Kockel (eds), *A companion to heritage studies* (Malden, MA: Wiley), 426–442.

Seeman, S. (2012), 'Macedonian Čalgija: A musical refashioning of national identity', *Ethnomusicology Forum* 21(3): 295–326.

Shelemay, K. (2010), 'Notation and oral tradition', in *The Garland handbook of African Music* (London: Routledge), 44–63.

Silverman, C. (1983). 'The politics of folklore in Bulgaria', *Anthropological Quarterly* 56(2): 55–61.

Slobin, M. (1996), *Retuning culture: musical changes in Central and Eastern Europe* (Durham and London: Duke University Press).

Taylor, D. (2016), 'Saving the "live"? Re-performance and intangible cultural heritage', *Études Anglaises* 69(2): 149–161.

Tokumaru, Y. and O. Yamaguti eds (1986), *The oral and the literate in music* (Tokyo: Academia Music).

# 10 Performing Scots-European heritage, 'For A' That!'

*Mairi McFadyen and Máiréad Nic Craith*

The concept of European heritage has been widely debated (Kockel 2010; Shore 2010; Nic Craith 2012; Delanty 2017) and raises many questions. Does it infer a mosaic or an amalgam of different national heritages within the continent of Europe, or is it a composite of selected prestigious symbols that have been elevated beyond the nation state to become European? The complexity of the latter scenario is captured in the motto "unity in diversity", which is frequently used to describe Europe's multilingual character. Sometimes the slogan is used more generally to capture the diversity of Europe's national heritages. In this chapter, our primary focus is on Scottish heritage and how this has contributed to, and drawn upon, Europe's intellectual heritage through the medium of Scots.

Geographically, Scotland is located on the margins of Europe. Despite its marginal position, interactions between Scotland and the Continent have been profound over the centuries and have taken many different forms. In his book *On Scottish Ground* (1998), Kenneth White makes the case that although part of the United Kingdom, Scotland has always been more European than its near neighbour, England, in terms of character and outlook. Scotland's intellectual and cultural heritage has been enriched by continental influences, just as Scotland's languages, values and ideas have taken part in continental debates and contributed to shape a European heritage throughout the ages.

Connections with Europe have been and remain diverse, reflecting the range of peoples within Scotland. The 'imagined community' of Scottish-Gaels includes Ireland and Brittany as well as the Isle of Man, Wales and Cornwall (Price 1994) and is celebrated annually at the Celtic Connections festival in Glasgow. The archipelagos of Shetland and Orkney have strong Nordic connections (Kockel 2017; Henderson 2018). This is very evident during the annual *Up-Helly-Aa* fire festivals in Shetland that end with the burning of a replica Viking ship (Clopot and McCullagh, this volume). There are strong historical links between Scotland and Poland, which continue to be celebrated today (Devine and Hesse 2011).

This chapter focuses on the Scots-speaking community and, in particular, on its use of the Scots language as a means to assert political difference in the form of a 'welcoming, inclusive civic nationalism' (McFadyen 2018). Our contribution reflects on the process of narrative building within Scotland, with its special emphasis on democracy, egalitarianism and freedom. We argue that this narrative was strongly influenced by Europe's intellectual heritage. Perhaps central to this process of narrative building is the 'Scottish myth' (McCrone 2017). Sometimes called the 'egalitarian myth', this is the belief that Scotland is a more egalitarian and democratic society than its larger southern neighbour.

Like traditions, myths connect with past realities; they draw selectively from the past (Kølvraa 2015), a process that involves selective inclusion and exclusion. In discussing the difference between history and myth, Barthes proposes (1993: 142) that 'what the world supplies to myth is an historical reality, defined, even if those goes back quite a while, but the way in which men have produced or used it; and what myth gives in return is a natural image of this reality'. Barthes nuances this further with the statement that 'myth is constituted by the loss of the historical quality of things: in it, things lose the memory that they once were made' (Barthes 1993: 142).

The myth that we critique in this chapter draws on Scotland's intellectual and ideological heritage which has roots in the notion of the 'democratic intellect' in education as well as in continental political thought. The historical veracity of this myth is perhaps less interesting than the uses to which it has been put, both politically and creatively, drawing upon both an imaginary past taken for real and an equally assumed imaginary future. Much (although not all) of this discourse has been expressed in Scots – a unique, indigenous but contested voice that has developed into a symbol of resistance, both culturally and politically, against the homogenising forces of Anglocentrism and in favour of a continental outlook.

## 10.1 Scots language and festivals

Europe is a diverse, multilingual continent (Nic Craith 2006) with twenty-four official languages as well as a range of minority and contested languages. Scots belongs to the Germanic family of Indo-European languages. These include English, Scots, German, Low German, Dutch, Swedish, Norwegian and Danish. All of these (bar Scots) have the status of language rather than dialect at the level of nation state. Indeed, Scots is sometimes regarded as corrupted English (Nic Craith 2000, 2001). This reflects the intimate relationship between language status and that of its corresponding nation state (Nic Craith 2008). It also reflects the ideology of the homogenous nation state based on common cultural traits among which language is foremost. While Dutch is internationally regarded as a distinct language, the status of Low German remains disputed. As a contested language, Scots has many counterparts in Europe. These include Alsatian, Asturian, Franco-Provencal, Karelian and Kashubian (Nic Craith 2006).

Following the union with England in 1707, Scots ceased to be the language of the state. Despite subsequent prejudice towards the language, the language has proven to be resilient, surviving in the speech of millions of ordinary Scots and in their songs, ballads and poems. This period precipitated a number of poems and songs, which are part of a long tradition of musical and literary heritage addressing the question of the national identity of Scotland, its role within the British Empire and the hostility of many towards imperialism. Towards the end of the eighteenth century, there was a flourishing of Scots poetry and song, with Robert Ferguson in Edinburgh and the 'national bard' Robert Burns in Ayrshire, who most famously brought the Scots language to the world.

In the nineteenth century, the Scottish novelist Sir Walter Scott became a world-famous writer. His Waverly novels were written in English, yet the speech of his characters was a rich broad Scots (Scott 1918 [1814]). During this century, the millions of workers who went to work in the factories in the Industrial Revolution were largely Scots and Gaelic speakers, and so Scots was very much alive in their communities and writings. Scots prose continued to appear in newspapers, often in the form of articles campaigning for social justice and for workers' rights. At the same time that Scotland was moving forward into industrial times, writers and scholars were becoming increasingly interested in the past.

In 1808, a scholar called John Jamieson published the first *Dictionary of the Scots Tongue*. In the interwar years, the Scottish literary renaissance revitalised Scottish literature where the Scots language played a vital role. In the 1950s and 1960s, interest began to revive in traditional music and song with the Folk Revival, and within that, a strand of countercultural protest song. There is, of course, a long tradition of protest song and poetry in Scotland, from Mary Brooksbank in Dundee to the 'bothy ballad' tradition protesting farm worker's conditions in the north-east.

At the beginning of the twenty-first century, Scots acquired a new status when the United Kingdom ratified the European Charter for Regional or Minority Languages (Nic Craith 2003; McDermott 2018). According to the 2011 census, the language is spoken by 1.5 million Scots. Scots is more widely available than ever before, via local radio stations and monthly podcast Scots Language Radio. Scots is also spoken in the highly successful television *Outlander* series, which features time travel through eighteenth-century Scotland. Scots is recognised as an important component of the curriculum, with new resources created for schools.

Most festivals in Scotland nowadays have a Scots strand, and these festivals give an opportunity to Scots-speakers to affirm their identity and to interact with each other in a fun context. The area most commonly associated with the Scots language is Aberdeen and the north-east of Scotland, where the Doric tongue is spoken and performed annually at the Doric two-week festival in autumn. In this part of Scotland, local Poles regularly perform Scots traditional songs within the Polish–Scots Song and Story Group. Poland has a more than five-centuries-old relationship with Scotland, and the Polish language community here has produced a guide to the Scots language, designed for those who may visit or work in the area: *A Scots-Polish Lexicon / Leksykon szkocko-polski* by Kasia Michalska (2014). Here the community heritage practice of singing together in a contested language expresses uniqueness at a local level, while also promoting social cohesion within a European ideal of 'unity in diversity' (see Kockel 2010: 125ff.). This performance of Polish–Scottish identity is a projection both inwards and outwards of belonging and identity that is both shared and unique (see identity model in chapter 1 and in Kockel, this volume).

Scots is performed and celebrated at local and national literary festivals such as the Borders Books Festival, the Edinburgh International Book Festival or the Wigtown Book Festival, which run a Scots poetry competition every year. TRACS (Traditional Arts and Culture Scotland) has a policy to celebrate both Scots and Gaelic and supports several festivals with a prominent Scots strand; these include the Scottish International Storytelling Festival, the summer TradFest, the Winter Festivals (which includes Burns Night) and the Carrying Stream Festival.

There are numerous other grassroots and community-led organisations dedicated to promoting education in and transmission of cultural practices in Scots. The TMSA (Traditional Music and Song Association) supports a network of smaller festivals, for example, at Kirriemuir, Blair Atholl or Cullerlie, that are dedicated to traditional song in regional dialects of Scots. This network has its roots in the earlier Folk Revival movement, which featured unaccompanied traditional song in the variety of Scots dialects. There are also local folk festivals that showcase Scots song, such as Innerleithen in the Borders area or Perthshire Amber in Dunkeld.

## 10.2 'The egalitarian myth'

An egalitarian ideology has long been associated with Scotland. It has a long cultural history, with roots as far back as the Declaration of Arbroath (1320), written in Latin, which has been described by Neal Ascherson (2002: 18) as 'Europe's earliest nationalist manifesto'. (In 2016, the declaration was placed on UNESCO's (n.d.) Memory of the World register.) This declaration rejected the position of Edward I of England as overlord of Scotland and argued that a King owed his power to his peers rather than to God. The declaration of freedom derives from an old idea that also underpins the Presbyterian '*lad o' pairts*', which refers to the potential of any individual to rise from humble beginnings into good fortune (largely thanks to the distinct education system). This idea also lies behind the historical belief that the Scottish working class has an instinct for radical, if not revolutionary, international socialism, and the contemporary belief in Scotland as a more welcoming, inclusive nation than its southern neighbour. The myth is reflected in Robert Burns' song '*A Man's A Man For A' That*', which was performed at the opening of the Scottish Parliament in 1999.

This myth operates in different ways and at different levels. 'Myth' here does not refer to something which is manifestly false. Like traditions, myths connect with past realities; they draw selectively from the past, a process that involves selective exclusion and inclusion. The ambiguity of the myth helps to account for its persistence. It is perhaps most commonly expressed in the ubiquitous phrase: '*We're Aa Jock Tamson's Bairns*' (Anon 1848: 29). This is interpreted in a metaphorical sense as a statement of egalitarian sentiments confirming equality: that no-one is fundamentally any better than anyone else or perhaps that we are all heirs to the same fortune and misfortune that might befall in the course of a life. The phrase is used in common speech and in cultural life generally in Scotland. The origin of the phrase is uncertain; the earliest reference is in the *Dictionary of the Scots Language* in 1847, which describes the phrase as 'an expression of mutual good fellowship very frequently heard in Scotland' (Anon 1848: 29).

## 10.3 The Enlightenment and democratic intellectual heritage

We have already linked the decline of Scots to the Union of Parliaments with England in 1707. At that point, Scotland gave up its political and economic independence; however, Scotland retained its right to follow its own policy in culture, religion, law and education. The eighteenth century was a period of intellectual enrichment in Scotland, commonly known as the Enlightenment. A core feature of this period was the concept of a democratic intellect that affirmed the ability of every individual to arrive at their own conclusion. Broadie (2001: 1) defines a key characteristic of this period as: 'the demand that we think for ourselves, and not allow ourselves to develop the intellectual device of assenting to something simply because someone with authority has sanctioned it'. Moreover, the expression of that demand in the public domain would be without fear of penalty or punishment.

That is essentially similar to the Kantian definition of the Enlightenment. One of the most influential philosophers in eighteenth-century Europe, Immanuel Kant examined reason and the nature of reality. He argued that in order to be truly enlightened, every individual must have the wisdom to use his or her own intellect. Kant argued:

> Enlightenment is man's emergence from his self-incurred immaturity. Immaturity is the inability to use one's own understanding without the guidance of another. This immaturity is self-incurred if its cause is not lack of understanding, but lack of resolution and courage to use it without the guidance of another. The motto of enlightenment is therefore: *Sapere aude*! [Dare to be wise!] Have courage to use your own understanding!
> 
> [Kant 1991: 1]

This promotion of the ordinary individual as intellectual was supported by a semi-continental style of education in Scotland, which was very distinct from practice in England. This continental dimension of Scotland's intellectuals is taken up by Kenneth White, who traces Scotland's ancient connections with continental intellectuality through the figure of the 'wandering Scots' who were known to be the most avid seekers of knowledge. Beginning with the Celtic monks, he references the twelfth-century philosopher Duns Scotus, Renaissance Scots in France, the Republican-minded George Buchanan, the

Scots College in Paris, David Hume in the eighteenth century, Robert Louis Stevenson in the nineteenth and Patrick Geddes into the twentieth. Given his own Scottish–French background, it is hardly surprising that White draws particular attention to the French–Scottish intellectual heritage, noting that 'it was in Scotland, as a page at Mary Stuart's court, that Ronsard learnt the rudiments of lyrical writing. And it was in France that Buchanan plunged into the opening field of the New Knowledge, writing the best Latin poems of the age in Paris and in Bordeaux, and in the bygoing teaching Montaigne' (White 1998: 122–123).

The continental character of Scottish education was profiled by George Elder Davie in his book, *The Democratic Intellect* (1961). Drawing on Scotland's Presbyterian inheritance, he argues that metaphysical Scotland, in contrast to utilitarian England, always favoured the generalist, philosophical approach. 'The barrier between North and South was proverbially located in the contrast between rationality and the rule of thumb, between principle and precedent, and the English with their tolerant good-humour could refer to the complex sister-nation as "metaphysical Scotland"' (Davie 1961: xix). Students were expected to inquire into the connections between subjects, their intellectual and ethical grounding and relationships, as well as their functional application to the community. They were guided by a philosophy of common sense that was both social and epistemological. From this generalist grounding, expert skills could be pursued, safe in the knowledge that specialising students were so well educated in the philosophical perspective, they would always refer their specific area of expertise back to its relationship and significance within the generalist context.

This resonates with the Humboldtian idea of the university. In the early decades of nineteenth-century Germany, an ideological change in Prussian universities placed new emphasis on the role of academics as researchers as well as teachers. This shift had theoretical implications and generated a 'spiritual and philosophical rejuvenation' (Watson 2010: 228), which also had implications for students at these universities. Humboldt argued that the 'primary purpose of a university is "to cultivate learning in the deepest and broadest sense of the word," not for some practical or utilitarian end, but for its own sake as a "preparatory material of spiritual and moral education"' (Watson 2010: 233).

It is this intellectual insistence, writes Davie, that makes for democracy in the Scottish tradition. Class, colour and religion are irrelevant in a philosophically based education. The application of knowledge was not thought to be a separate issue and the high point of Scotland's worldwide contribution in engineering, industry, science and architecture coincided with the pinnacle of the country's philosophical and literary influence in the Enlightenment. Davie's later work, *The Crisis of the Democratic Intellect* (1986), charts a narrative of decline where continental traditions are held in tension with the more pragmatic influences from England in the context of Empire.

## 10.4 Burns' celebrations and the French Revolution

Much of this egalitarian ideal has been expressed in Scots – a linguistic heritage that was considerably enriched by Robbie Burns, sometimes known as Scotland's national bard (McIntyre 2009). Having been born into poverty himself, Burns was quick to propagate the egalitarian ideas of the French Revolution through Scots, a theme that is regularly remembered at the annual worldwide celebration of Burns' supper on or near the anniversary of Burns' birthday (25 January 1759). The bard was born in Ayr, a town on the west coast that had a long tradition of trading with European ports from the Mediterranean to the Baltic.

Burns developed political leanings towards issues of equality and freedom that were key ideals of the French Revolution. Crawford (2009: 368) notes Burns' reference to one of his own songs as being 'not only about the historical Scottish struggle for "Liberty & Independence" but also "associated with the glowing ideas of some other struggles of the same nature, not quite so ancient"'. Unusually for the period, Burns extended these ideals of liberty and equality to women as well as men. At the time of the French Revolution, Burns composed verses on contemporary political concerns. There were allusions in some of his poetry to Thomas Erskine, who was Tom Paine's lawyer (Crawford 2009). Paine had actively engaged with the French Revolution and is especially known for his *Rights of Man* (1791), which subsequently sold nearly a million copies. Although highly controversial, Paine survived these years of political turmoil and was a participant in the committee that drafted the constitution for the French Republic, but he subsequently fell into disfavour again. An ardent revolutionary, Burns sympathised utterly with this European intellectual heritage and expressed these ideals in his own Scots verses.

For many people today, the poet and the annual celebration of this Burns' festival is strongly associated with these republican ideals and resonates with the Scottish egalitarian narrative. Aamer Anwar, a human rights lawyer writes: 'Burns was a poet of the common man who championed universal suffrage and the abolition of slavery long before it became fashionable. Inspired by the American and French Revolutions with their ideas of liberty, equality and fraternity, Burns stood against the corruption of the gentry, nobility and royalty' (Anwar 2009: 34).

One of Burn's more famous Scots' poem is entitled '*A Man's A Man For a' That*' (Burns 1993) and celebrates the idea of democracy and the equality of all human beings. The poem argues that, regardless of personal wealth or poverty, every individual is entitled to the same respect. The novelist Andrew O'Hagan calls it 'a secular hymn to the dignity of the common man that outstrips any holy writ or any national anthem'. O' Hagan regards the poem as: 'a song for every colour, every class and every creed, the notion of brotherhood and equality as the greatest testament to humanity's essential compassion, a goal that everyone can share' (O'Hagan 2009: 46).

This egalitarian ideal has strong resonance among all Scots, whether born in Scotland or recently arrived. 'New Scots' is the term commonly used in Scotland to describe migrants and refugees – a phrase designed to suggest inclusivity as an expression of the same egalitarian myth. New Scots have celebrated the Burns tradition by organising an alternative 'Burns' Supper' as part of Glasgow's Celtic Connections festival. BEMIS (Black and Ethnic Minorities in Scotland) aims to promote inclusion and democratic citizenship. Their annual Burns' supper is a grand-scale multicultural *Ceilidh* (or gathering) honouring Robert Burns' transcendent beliefs in human equality, kinship and conviviality and reinforces Scotland's image of itself as a democratic, egalitarian society that gives voice to the subaltern.

## 10.5 MacDiarmid and socialism

More than a century after his lifetime, Burns' poetry in Scots was edited by Hugh MacDiarmid (1949), who was culturally significant in Scotland as a socialist poet. Harvie (1999: 113–114) notes that MacDiarmid was 'influenced by right-wing thinkers. He must have read Maurras and Barrés while in France at the end of World War I and been attracted towards their gospel of French provincialism. He also seems to have accepted the Italian Futurists' characterisation of Mussolini as a kind of indigenous Lenin'. However MacDiarmid never actually engaged with Scottish Fascists.

Having joined the Royal Army Medical Corps at the beginning of the First World War, MacDiarmid served in Salonica, Greece and France before returning to Scotland. 'Galvanised by the knowledge he gained in the Great War to wage his own war for Scotland, MacDiarmid adapted the generalist tools of the Scottish democratic intellect to stimulate a modern Scottish Renaissance and write the Scottish Republic' (Lyall 2006: 25). A strong believer in socialism, MacDiarmid was politically as well as culturally active. MacDiarmid's worldview followed Marx in his Hegelian rejection of empiricism as the reduction of reality to facts. Instead, he believed that 'the importance of such facts was always contingent on their overall context and on the fact of change' (Harvie 1999: 112). Like Marx's, MacDiarmid's worldview was synthetic.

In 1920s Scotland, a modernist literary and cultural movement heralded a political drive towards renewed political as well as cultural self-determination. In his attempts to encourage cultural confidence, MacDiarmid thought it necessary to free Scotland from the yoke of Anglicisation that had effectively quashed any new and original expressions of national character for hundreds of years. MacDiarmid believed that a Scottish worldview could not be adequately expressed in English. To achieve this new self-confidence, he consciously adopted the use of the Old Scots Tongue, or *Lallans*, as the new form came to be known, which was a synthetic idiom borrowing from many different varieties of the Scots language, spoken at different times in different parts of the country, instead of English for much of his poetry. Some of his best work is written in Scots, including the famous *A drunk man looks at the thistle*, an epic critique of

Scottish culture expressing MacDiarmid's animosity towards a Scottish culture which was becoming Anglicised and intellectually barren.

From MacDiarmid's perspective, there was an inherent diversity in the creative expression of Scots and all its rich dialectical variations which could be used as an expression of resistance to homogenisation and Anglicisation. Effectively, McDiarmid was inviting Scottish writers to find a new and distinctive Scottish voice which led to a 'literary renaissance' that was rooted in a pluralistic cultural and linguistic experience in Scotland. It included writing in Gaelic, standard English as well as Scots. This period inspired writers such as Lewis Grassic Gibbon, Neil Gunn, William Soutar, Edwin Muir, James Bridie, Ewan MacColl, Joe Corrie, Ena Naomi Mitchison, Catherine Carswell, Willa Muir, Nan Shepherd and others to recover a vast neglected heritage of literary and creative practice from Scotland's past. Rather than identifying a unique Scottish experience, these writers were addressing universal conditions through diverse Scottish realities. This inherent diversity in the creative expression of Scots and all its rich dialectical variations can be read here very much as resistance to homogenisation and an invitation to artists to find a new and distinctive Scottish voice. While they may not align themselves with MacDiarmid's extreme cultural politics of the early century, more modern writers like James Robertson, Tom Leonard, James Kelman and Irvine Welsh still continue in the tradition of cultural reclamation and the determined use of localised Scots languages.

## 10.6 Henderson, Gramsci and the People's Festival

Scotland's concept of egalitarianism is one that respects all people, whether rich or poor, native or migrant, participating in high or low culture. It challenges the notion of an established, bourgeois culture and promotes ideas not dissimilar to Antonio Gramsci, the Sardinian Marxist, best known for his theory of cultural hegemony. This proposes that the bourgeoisie maintain their order and values over others by the promotion of their own practices as the norm. Force is not necessary to maintain this order. Instead through their dominance of cultural institutions, upper-classes reproduce and maintain the *status quo*. Boothman (2008: 2003) interprets Gramsci's concept of hegemony as 'consent backed by coercion'. This model of power relations can be traced back to Machiavelli's centaur, who is half-animal and half-man, and must learn to know both natures if he is to survive (Machiavelli 1950).

Gramsci's thinking was highly influential on the Scottish folk collector Hamish Henderson (1919–2002) who dominated the folk scene in Scotland in the second half of the twentieth century. Henderson travelled the country recording ordinary people singing and telling stories, including those from the Travelling communities. He was part of the very folk process he sought to understand, bringing the phrase 'the carrying stream' into cultural consciousness and writing songs like *Freedom Come All Ye*, which was adopted by the Peace Movement and the CND's anti-Polaris campaign. For Gramsci as for

Henderson, folk culture presented an alternative, a subaltern view of society and history, alternative to the official, or establishment version of the rulers. 'Folklore can be understood only as a reflection of the conditions of cultural life of the people, although certain conceptions specific to folklore remain even after these conditions have been (or seem to be) modified or have given way to bizarre combinations' (Gramsci 2000: 360–361).

During 1948–1951, Henderson translated Gramsci's Prison Letters (*Lettere dal Carcere*) into English (Gramsci 1998). Henderson saw many cultural parallels between Gramsci's native Sardinia and Scotland. His translation of Gramsci is peppered with Scots words, with expressions such as 'wee' or 'daft' used many times, and an Italian Jacobin described as having 'bees in his bonnet'. Henderson was particularly drawn to Gramsci's conception of folklore. Gibson (2010: 243) argues that Gramsci's writings 'can be seen to account for a large part of the foundations of Henderson's conception of folk-culture, and to represent crucial assertions that were to be reified through his long investment in Scottish folksong revivalism'.

In the early 1950s, Henderson became actively involved in an arts festival in Edinburgh known as the Edinburgh People's Festival, which ran from 1951 to 1954. The festival was originally inspired by the 1945 Labour Government as a celebration of the arts 'for the people, by the people'. Henderson regarded the revival of folk song more generally, and this festival in particular, as an opportunity to democratise folk traditions and bring them to the masses. He regretted the apparent divide between modern popular culture and the popular culture of folklore.

The first People's Festival *Ceilidh* – which some say was an early forerunner of the Edinburgh Festival Fringe – took place in the Oddfellows Hall on 31 August 1951, the same year as the School of Scottish Studies was founded at the University of Edinburgh. Henderson played a significant role in the organisation of the People's Festival *Ceilidh*, which he saw as a catalyst for the development of the folk song revival in Scotland, describing it as 'Gramsci in action'. He explained how the idea for the festival related to Gramsci:

> Attracting people who felt excluded by the International Festival, keeping the prices low and including children – it was Gramsci in action! One of the things that attracted me to Gramsci was his great interest in popular culture. He was a Sardinian, and the Sardinian folk song is rich and bountiful and vigorous to the nth degree. When he was in prison he wrote to his mother and sisters asking for details of their folk festivals. Gramsci in action was the People's Festival.
>
> [cited in Davidson 2010: 258]

The festival provided artists and singers that had previously been recorded by Henderson in his position as researcher at the University of Edinburgh with an opportunity to perform to a wider audience. While the festival was subsequently embroiled in political controversy, the egalitarian message had been received, and that festival is regarded as the forerunner to the Edinburgh Festival Fringe that now runs in parallel to the Edinburgh International Festival of high culture every summer and has vastly outgrown the latter in terms of audience numbers and performances.

## 10.7 *Freedom Come All Ye* at the Commonwealth Games

Henderson's egalitarianism came to the fore with the Commonwealth Games in Glasgow in 2014, when his song *Freedom Come All Ye* was performed at the opening ceremonies by South African Soprano Pumiza Matshikiza. The title is a nod towards the genre of songs known as 'Come all ye's', the kind of song that begins with a call to listen – 'Come all ye (sons of liberty/ good people/ tramps and hawkers etc.)' and listen to my song. Scots have used traditional song as a means for expressing and constructing political views and musical practice to challenge the larger structures of power. Song is an incredibly potent and affective form of embodied musical practice. The semantic power of words expands the awareness of possibilities ranging over past, present and future, while the sounds of voice and melody and their intonation focus the awareness in the present through a visceral, embodied experience. The power of political song provides a sort of relational empowerment where those who sing and those who listen bond with one another in the performance of shared values and aspirations (McFadyen 2018).

On the national and international stage, the emotional impact of the performance of *Freedom come all ye* at the Commonwealth Games shows how songs can communicate to the world. The Scots song – which calls for freedom, equality and an end to war and speaks for social justice, inclusion and understanding throughout the world – refers to Nyanga, one of the oldest black townships in Cape Town. This is where Pumeza Matshikiza lived as a child. Taking inspiration from this, her reinvention of the song mixes Scottish and South African instrumentation. The performance of this song was especially poignant in Glasgow, a city that has a special relationship with the struggle against apartheid South Africa, embodied in Nelson Mandela, who, while still a political prisoner, was bestowed the Freedom of the City in 1981 (Bort 2013).

This song is so rich in imagery and symbolism that it is impossible to give a full explanation of it here. Neal Ascherson (2002: 168) has described it as 'socialist battle-song'. The main theme is anti-imperialism coupled with the recognition of the part that Scots have played in the conquest and subjugation of other peoples within the British Empire. Although Scottish people were 'so long misled and abused, [Scotland] is still strong enough to tear off the alien uniform which it has been persuaded to think its own, and to regain its true, noble and universal nature' (Ascherson 2002: 168). The song anticipates the day when all peoples are truly free and can meet in peace and friendship.

## 10.8 Hogmanay Celebrations 2019

As New Year 2019 was rung in, there was a special Hogmanay celebration in Edinburgh. As well as 'Auld Lang Syne', a traditional Scots song performed around the world on this festive occasion, the fireworks celebrated Scotland's cultural, historical and social connections with Europe. At a time when the Westminster government was intent on leaving the European Union, Edinburgh's iconic fireworks were accompanied by a soundtrack created by the German techno-marching band *Meute*. Six of Scotland's leading writers composed love letters to Europe. These letters were projected onto six buildings in the Scottish capital between 1 and 25 January. The idea for these letters was developed in partnership with Edinburgh's International Book Festival and Edinburgh as UNESCO City of Literature. The letter written by author and radio presenter Louise Welsh, displayed at the Tech Cube in Summerhall, featured words from Scots and other European languages and was designed as an expression of shared European origins and cultures.

These letters could be interpreted as a form of resistance to moves by the parliament in London to withdraw the United Kingdom from the EU against the democratically expressed wishes of the majority of the Scottish people. Although a small majority overall in the United Kingdom (51.9%) voted in in favour of leaving the EU in the 2016 referendum, that perspective was not reflected in Scotland, where over 62% of those eligible to vote preferred to remain within the EU (BBC 2016). Given Scotland's continental empathy, this result was hardly surprising and should be set against the referendum for Scottish independence in 2014 (Kockel 2015), during which EU citizens were told that a vote for independence would jeopardise Scotland's membership of the EU!

How we listen to and perform our linguistic heritage contributes not only to our own sense of belonging and authenticity but also to how we project this on to others. Given Scotland's cultural and political heritage, there has been no less a sense that the traditional arts community had a responsibility to contribute to the national debate, irrespective of political leanings or differences of opinion. However, in a climate of rising political tension, public arts organisations and networks involving traditional arts were careful to avoid taking an explicit position in the independence debate. Contributions had to come from individuals and independent groups. One of us, Mairi, was an active campaigner at this time, taking a lead in catalysing the campaign group TradYES, part of the wider non-party creative cultural campaign National Collective (McFadyen 2013, 2018).

One Scots song that rose to prominence during that campaign reinforced the egalitarian narrative that we have discussed in this chapter. Written in the Borders (Southern) dialect of Scots, Matt Seattle and David Finnie's *Theme for the early days of a better nation* (2014) rejoiced in the diversity of people in Scotland, whether native or migrant (McKerrell and West 2018). The title was inspired by the famous words of author and artist Alasdair Gray, quoting Canadian poet Dennis Leigh: 'Work as if you live in the early days of a better nation'. The lyric used two images from Scotland's natural heritage, drawing on a strand of rurality that has a long pedigree in Scotland. Composer Matt Seattle explained: 'The wandering geese represent those who are welcomed as new Scots, and the shimmering salmon represent the struggle of all those who swim against the current, as in the Peebles motto *contra nando incrementum*, which means "against the stream they multiply"' (Seattle 2014). This song became a campaign favourite, later recorded by singer Lori Watson and the orchestra McFall's Chamber as part of the Distil project.

## 10.9 Conclusion

Heritage is a dynamic concept (Kockel and Nic Craith 2007). As Europe evolves, so does its heritage. Language is a crucial element of the heritage expressing local and transnational belonging at one and the same time. It enables people to find their place in society. In using Scots, people in Scotland are connected with others throughout Europe who speak a contested languages. In speaking Scots, people are re-affirming an element of European heritage that was almost lost and are challenging the forces of homogenisation that are gathering momentum at the beginning of the twenty-first century.

This chapter has been set in the context of a particular political and cultural moment in late modern Scotland and its transitioning relationship with the United Kingdom, and the United Kingdom's transitioning relationship with the EU. It traces Scotland's emphasis on the equality of individuals and the links between that ideology and ideas in Europe. It has focused on the promulgation of this myth through the Scots language and the many festivals associated with it. There is no suggestion, however, that empathy with egalitarianism is the sole prerogative of speakers of Scots, and we are aware that there are multiple 'Scotlands' and multiple ideologies within it. Our interest in Scots has been inspired by its increasing visibility in the public sphere at a time of transition and the perception that its rise could be seen as a form of resistance to the Westminster parliament. Our primary focus has been on the affinity between Scotland and Europe – and that empathy seems set to continue. Neal Ascherson (2002: 304) noted that Scotland has a sense of European identity 'as a small North Sea nation which needs to encounter the world directly rather than through the priorities of Great Britain'. As this chapter has indicated, the relationship with Europe is centuries old and the notion of resistance well rehearsed!

## Acknowledgement

This publication is a result of the European Union-funded Horizon 2020 research project: CoHERE (Critical Heritages: performing and representing identities in Europe). CoHERE received funding from the European Union's Horizon 2020 research and innovation programme under grant agreement No. 693289.

## References

Anon. (1848), 'John Tamson's man', in *The Scottish journal of topography, antiquities, traditions* 1(2): 29–30.
Anwar, A. (2009), untitled contribution in T. Malley and R. Gillespie (eds), *As others see us: personal views on the life and works of Robert Burns*, (Edinburgh: Luath).

Ascherson, N. (2002), *Stone voices: the search for Scotland* (London: Granta).
Barthes, R. (1993), *Mythologies*, selected and translated by A. Lavers (London: Vintage).
BBC (2016), *EU referendum: Scotland backs remain as UK votes leave*. Available at: www.bbc.co.uk/news/uk-scotland-scotland-politics-36599102 (accessed 11 January 2019).
Boothman, D. (2008), 'The sources for Gramsci's concept of hegemony', *Rethinking Marxism* 20(2): 201–215.
Bort, E. (2013), *'Free Mandela! Free Mandela!' Hamish Henderson, Nelson Mandela, and the fight against Apartheid in South Africa*. Hamish Henderson Memorial Lecture 2013 – Edinburgh People's Festival. Available at: www.edinburghpeoplesfestival.org (accessed 10 January 2018).
Broadie, A. (2001), *The Scottish Enlightenment: the historical age of the historical nation* (Edinburgh: Birlinn).
Burns, R. (1993), *The complete poetical works of Robert Burn*, edited by James A. Macay (Ayrshire: Alloway Publishing).
Crawford, R. (2009), *The bard. Robert Burns a biography,* (London: Pimlico).
Davidson, N. (2010), 'Gramsci's reception in Scotland', *Scottish Labour History* 45: 37–58.
Davie, G. (1986), *The crisis of the democratic intellect: the problem of generalism and specialisation in twentieth-century Scotland* (Edinburgh: Polygon).
Davie, G. (1961), *The democratic intellect* (Edinburgh: Edinburgh University Press).
Delanty, G. (2017), *The European heritage: a critical re-interpretation* (London: Routledge).
Devine, T. and D. Hesse (2011), *Scotland and Poland: historical encounters 1500–2010* (Edinburgh: Birlinn).
Gibson, C. (2010), '"Gramsci in action": Antonio Gramsci and Hamish Henderson's folk revivalism', in E. Bort (ed.), *Borne on the carrying stream: the legacy of Hamish Henderson* (Edinburgh: Grace Notes), 239–258.
Gramsci, A. (2000), *The Antonio Gramsci reader: selected writings 1916–1935*, edited by D. Forgacs and E. Hobsbawm (New York: New York University Press).
Gramsci, A. (1998), *Gramsci's prison letters: lettere dal carcere,* introduced and translated by H. Henderson (London: Zwab, in association with *The Edinburgh Review*).
Harvie, C. (1999), *Travelling Scot: essays on the history, politics and future of the Scots* (Glendaruel: Argyll).
Henderson, G. (2018), *The Norse influence on Celtic Scotland* (Classic Reprint) (London: Forgotten Books).
Kant, I. (1991), *An answer to the question: 'what is Enlightenment?',* translated by H. B. Nisbet (London: Penguin).
Kockel, U. (2017), 'On becoming indigenous: Building, dwelling and thinking future heritages of a Nordic Scotland', in H. Hieta, A., M. Mäki, K. Siivonen and T. Virtanen (eds), *Rajaamatta: Etnologisia keskusteluja Hanneleena* (Turku: Kirjapaino Juvenes), 367–389.
Kockel, U. (2015), '"Aye'll be back": the quest for Scotland's Independence', *Anthropology Today* 31(1): 1–2.
Kockel, U. (2010), *Borderline cases: the ethnic frontiers of European integration* (Liverpool: Liverpool University Press).
Kockel, U. and Nic Craith, M. (2007) *Cultural heritages as reflexive traditions* (New York: Palgrave).
Kølvraa, C. (2015), 'European fantasies: on the EU's political myths and the affective potential of utopian imaginaries for European identity', *JCMS: Journal of Common Market Studies*, 54(1): 169–184.
Lyall, S. (2006), *Hugh MacDiarmid's poetry and politics of place: imagining a Scottish Republic* (Edinburgh: Edinburgh University Press).
MacDiarmid, H. ed. (1949), *Robert Burns poems* (London: Grey Walls).

Machiavelli, N. (1950), *The prince and the discourses*, translated by L. Ricci and revised by E. Vincent (New York: Modern Library).

McCrone, D. (2017), *The new sociology of Scotland* (London: Sage).

McDermott, P. (2018), 'From ridicule to legitimacy? "Contested languages" and devolved language planning', *Current Issues in Language Planning* (online first), DOI: 10.1080/14664208.2018.1468961.

McFadyen, M. (2018), 'Referendum reflections: traditional music and the performance of politics in the campaign for Scottish independence', in S. McKerrell and G. West (eds), *Understanding Scotland musically: folk, tradition, policy* (London: Routledge), 60–77.

McFadyen, M. (2013), National collective launches #TradYES. Available at: http://nationalcollective.com/2013/07/10/national-collective-launches-tradyes/ (accessed 30 March 2017).

McIntyre, Ian (2009) *Robert Burns: a life* (London: Constable).

McKerrell, S. and G. West (2018), *Understanding Scotland musically: folk, tradition and policy* (London: Routledge).

Michalska, K. (2014), *A Scots-Polish lexicon: Leksykon Szkocko-Polski* (Glasgow: Savage).

Nic Craith, M. (2012) Europe's (un)common heritage(s), *Traditiones* 42(2): 11–28.

Nic Craith, M. (2008), 'Intangible cultural heritages: the challenges for Europe', *Anthropological Journal of European Cultures* 17(1): 54–73.

Nic Craith, M. (2006), *Europe and the politics of language: citizens, migrants, outsiders* (New York: Palgrave).

Nic Craith, M. (2003), 'Facilitating or generating linguistic diversity: the European charter for regional or minority languages', in S. Wolff and G. Hogan-Brun (eds), *Minority languages in Europe: frameworks, status, prospects* (London: Palgrave Macmillan), 59–72.

Nic Craith, M. (2001) 'Politicised linguistic consciousness: the case of Ulster-Scots', *Nations and Nationalism* 7(1): 21–37.

Nic Craith, M. (2000), 'Contested identities and the quest for legitimacy', *Journal of Multilingual and Multicultural Development* 21(5): 399–413.

O'Hagan, A. (2009), Untitled contribution in T. Malley and R. Gillespie (eds), *As others see us: personal views on the life and works of Robert Burns*, edited by Tricia Malley and Ross Gillespie (Edinburgh: Luath), 46–47.

Paine, T. (1791), *Rights of man. Being an answer to Mr Burke's attack on the French Revolution* (London: J.S. Jordan).

Price, G. (1994), *The Celtic connection*. (Lanham, MD: Rowman & Littlefield).

Scott, W. (2018 [1814]), *Waverley, or 'tis sixty years since*, 2 Volumes (London: Penguin).

Seattle, M. (2014), Facebook page – *Theme for the early days of a better nation*. Available at: www.facebook.com/ThemeForTheEarlyDays/ (accessed 25 October 2018).

Shore, C. (2010) *Building Europe: the cultural politics of European integration* (London: Routledge).

UNESCO (n.d.), *Memory of the world register*. Available at: www.unesco.org/new/en/communication-and-information/memory-of-the-world/register/ (accessed 12 January 2019).

Watson, P. (2010), *The German genius: Europe's third Renaissance, the scientific revolution and the twentieth century* (New York: Simon and Schuster).

White, K. (1998), *On Scottish ground: selected essays* (Edinburgh: Polygon).

# 11 European Capitals of Culture

## Discourses of Europeanness in Valletta, Plovdiv and Galway

*Cristina Clopot and Katerina Strani*

'What is Europe? It's not just a series of banknotes', an interviewee remarked when asked about European heritage. Our study of European Capitals of Culture (ECoC), one of the main European heritage programmes, proceeds in the same spirit, informed by the complex and disputed discussions of what Europe is (see, for example, Sassatelli 2002) and how, within such shifting grounds, European heritage might be interpreted (see, for instance, Delanty 2017; Niklasson 2017). Described by some as large-scale bottom-up cultural programming (Immler and Sakkers 2014), the ECoC programme has seen several cities across Europe compete for the title of European Capital of Culture for more than three decades now. Our research has focussed on three cities, Valletta as ECoC 2018, Plovdiv as ECoC 2019 and Galway as ECoC 2020. We are conducting a discourse analysis of the submitted bids as the key documents related to each city's participation in the programme; we are then investigating four common themes that emerge from this analysis: Europe, heritage, diversity and future.

The cities are not chosen at random; all the capitals selected represent edges of Europe and therefore have the potential to illustrate particular challenges based on their geographic and ideological positions. Valletta was chosen as it is the last stand post in the Mediterranean, with a closely connected history (and language) to the African continent. Plovdiv in Bulgaria represents a new EU member (Bulgaria joined the European Union in 2007) at the southeast edge of Europe. Galway in Ireland brings a temporal balance by representing an 'older' EU member (it joined in 1973) as well as another geographical edge on the west side of the continent. The case of Galway was also chosen because it reflects the revised guidelines for the application process, as discussed below (Immler and Sakkers 2014). Including both newer and older EU members in our analysis can also be justified by the strategic selection of the cities each year, which places on par older and newer EU members to support a concrete process of cultural 'Europeanisation' (Lähdesmäki 2014: 482). In investigating the common themes of Europe, heritage, diversity and future, our study aims to answer the following questions:

- How is European heritage (Delanty 2017; Lähdesmäki 2016a,b) presented in the ECoC bids, and how do these cities address the local, European relationship?
- What are the implications of these discourses of Europeanness (Wodak 2007) for current policy?

## 11.1 Setting the scene

The idea of the ECoC project was shaped by Melina Mercouri, at the time the Greek Minister for Culture, who anticipated the idea at the centre of recent European Union (EU) rhetoric now: 'unity in diversity' (EC 2018). Moreover, Mercouri's vision was shaped by the idea that to strengthen the Union we need a focus beyond economic integration (Immler and Sakkers 2014). Culture was not on the agenda of EU actions at the forefront, but as Calligaro (2014: 61) has noted, it was introduced with an aim of 'fostering popular support for European integration and strengthening its legitimacy'. Against this backdrop, the ECoC action, managed by the European Commission (hereafter EC), aims, among others, to 'safeguard and promote the diversity of cultures in Europe and to highlight the common features they share as well as to increase citizens' sense of belonging to a common cultural area' (EC 2014a; original emphasis).

Placing culture, rather than heritage, at centre-stage, the action is presented as an arts and culture initiative. The EC schedules two or more countries per year which are eligible to bid for the title, for four or more years in advance. As we discuss below, this outlines the fragility of the procedure, as cities can undergo major shifts in their political, economic and social life during that period. The nomination has an associated prize of €1.5 million which is awarded at the end of the year-long celebration, if conditions are met. As most ECoC cases have already shown, the budgets for the programme significantly outweigh that figure, and cities such as Glasgow and Liverpool have attracted significant public and private investment following their nomination (see, for instance, Immler and Sakkers 2014; Lähdesmäki 2014). With the programme evolving over time, the EC has commissioned periodic evaluation reports (see, for instance, Palmer 2004; Garcia and Cox 2013) which have constantly outlined the weak 'European dimension' in the bids. Garcia and Cox (2013: 15) further found 'a common disparity between stated objectives (at the bid stage, in mission statements) and their eventual programme implementation'. These shortcomings aimed to be addressed through a set of revised application guidelines for the period 2020 to 2033. As the guide for candidate cities (EC 2014a: 3) notes:

> This is a *European* award with standard criteria and objectives defined at EU level. Successful cities combine their local objectives with this European (and often international) aspect.

In this context, our analysis of two bids prepared based on the older guidelines and one prepared based on the revised guidelines is pertinent and necessary.

First, though, a brief consideration of key sources and research on ECoC programmes and EU policies is needed.

## 11.2 Heritage, identity and diversity

Whereas discussions of European identities are complex and multifarious (see, for instance, Delanty 2017; Sassatelli 2002; Lähdesmäki 2016b), in this study we are particularly interested in notions of Europeanness and European identification that are 'context-dependent' (Reisigl and Wodak 2001: 89) and serve the purpose of winning the ECoC bid – identification for promotional purposes. We are ultimately investigating how these notions might be indicative of shaping the contours of ECoC as one of the main European heritage programmes.

Given its protracted history, substantive research exists on the ECoC programme and its various cities. A common theme that was addressed in previous studies is that of 'European identity-building' (Sassatelli 2002; Palmer 2004; Immler and Sakkers 2014). Sassatelli (2002: 436) argues that Europe 'is becoming more and more like an icon, if not a totem, whose ambiguous content seems to reinforce the possibilities of identification with it'. In this almost chimerical view of Europe, cultural aspects are constantly renegotiated, and the pendulum swings between unity under European cultural heritage and the celebration of cultures (cf. Shore 2006).

Equally challenging and vague is the notion of 'European heritage' (Niklasson 2017; Delanty 2017) that the ECoC programmes aim to promote. The idea of a common, shared heritage is proposed in several actions of the EU (Niklasson 2017), such as the European Heritage Label or the European Year of Cultural Heritage celebrated at the time of writing; however, that does not make its definition or contents more approachable. Delanty (2017) has recently argued that European heritage needs to be considered in terms of connections outside Europe that have shaped the past. In spite of the vagueness of European heritage, Calligaro (2014: 67) observes that 'to play its function of catalyst of European identity, [European heritage] was expected to give substance to this identity' and sometimes defined in terms of shared values. However, branding something as European heritage also has political implications, as the debate over the continent's Christian heritage has shown, for instance. Still, the contours of European heritage are not made more explicit, but instead the concept is used as a 'self-explanatory shorthand's [sic] to address everything from horse breeding practices to endangered Roma heritage' (Niklasson 2017: 139). To follow Lähdesmäki's conclusion, European heritage can be conceived in a similar manner to the general concept of heritage (Kirshenblatt-Gimblett 1995) 'as a metacultural practice: its meanings and uses are produced through multilevel cultural, social, societal, political and spatial relationships and operations' (Lähdesmäki 2016a: 543). The cases considered in this study reflect on this theme and discuss different interpretations of European heritage as seen from the perspective of the candidate cities, both as self-identification and as self-promotion.

'Diversity' is another contested theme and a term commonly used within EU policy and rhetoric, one that has generated significant attention over time. Reflected in the EU's controversial adage 'unity in diversity', the diversity that is proposed is mainly conceived as national and subnational diversity (Shore 2006). It is reflected primarily in notions of nationality and language, or in vague and generic references to 'cultural diversity'. For example, Article I of the *Framework Convention on the Value of Cultural Heritage for Society* of the Council of Europe (2005) highlights the importance of 'the role of cultural heritage in the construction of a peaceful and democratic society, and in the processes of sustainable development and the promotion of cultural diversity'. It becomes clear that 'Diversity *is* the EU brand' (Rasmussen 2009: 9, added emphasis). And yet this diversity is superficial, vague and incomplete. It refers merely to the contact between languages and cultures and 'has rather failed to address issues of identity, values and inclusion' (Delli 2017: 118), let alone race, gender, sexuality, disability or any other protected characteristics. Shore's (2006: 18–19) vehement criticism of the construction of European identity and of documents that refer to European cultural heritage highlights the fact that these documents 'make virtually no mention of the contribution of writers, artists, scholars, and cultural practitioners of non-European descent' and that their contribution to the European project is ignored.[1] Overall, the slogan of 'unity in diversity' appears to be merely a 'bureaucratic formula fraught with ambiguities' (Shore 2006: 10), or 'either empty rhetoric or as hiding a centralising hegemonic project' (Sassateli 2008: 231), where 'diversity has been acceptable only in so far as it does not jeopardise unity' (Delli 2017: 118). Despite all this, this flawed and simplistic concept of diversity remains influential today. As Wodak (2018) has recently observed, the presentation of diversity is mainly positive, highlighting the wealth of European states rather than the negative aspects.

In addition to reinforcing the idea of belonging to a shared space, land and community, many analyses of past ECoC have emphasised its support for regeneration and revitalisation processes (Immler and Sakkers 2014; Garcia and Cox 2013, etc). In this light, the theme of 'future' is connected with these projected transformations of the city. Most ECoCs of the past have included projects related to physical transformation (e.g. Lähdesmäki 2014; Garcia and Cox 2013). As Garcia and Cox (2013: 65) observed in their report, 'this notion of transformation has become prevalent', and an increased emphasis is placed on the legacy of the project and long-term effects. This is captured in our study under the theme of future, whereby we include both the prevalent objective of generating 'culture-led urban regeneration' (Sassateli 2008: 236), and also visions of an imagined future for the city and the proposed impacts of the programme. The theme of the future was deemed more suitable rather than that of legacy commonly discussed in EC (2014b); Palmer (2004) and others, for its semantic complexity and wider application.

Discussing these themes is essential to reflect on the cities' Europeanness presented through this mega-festival, 'aimed at strengthening their belonging to the European cultural and social sphere' (Lähdesmäki 2014: 483).

## 11.3 Data and method

Our study uses the ECoC bid books of Valletta, Plovdiv and Galway as the data for the analysis. It also draws on ECoC guidelines/policies (EC 2014b) as the background and main reference to this data, in particular when it looks at the above themes intertextually.

To investigate the European Heritage themes and discourses of Europeanness that are used by Valletta, Plovdiv and Galway in the ECoC bids, we are using discourse analysis, and in particular elements of the Discourse Historical Approach (DHA). Carter, Freeman and Lawn (2015: 2) have argued that Europe has long been imagined 'as an object – an entity of one sort or another, but an object nonetheless'. Such monolithic views of Europe ignore its constructed (politically, economically, but also socially, culturally and discursively) and therefore dynamic nature. In our study of how cities construct and promote their Europeanness for the ECoC bid, we are using discourse analytical methods to capture not only the specific strategies used but also the changes in their representation of their Europeanness, depending on which theme(s) they decide to focus on. We will be focusing on the analysis of texts and will not be using a multimodal approach including visual semiotics, for instance.

Due to space and time constraints, the above both 'semantic and latent relevant themes' (Braun and Clarke 2006) of 'Europe', 'heritage', 'diversity' and 'future' were selected after a preliminary analysis. We identify and analyse these themes as *topoi* of Europeanness used in the candidate cities' bid books. *Topoi* (the plural of *topos*, from the Greek, meaning 'place') constitute argumentation frames (Reisigl and Wodak 2001: 55; Wodak 2018: 78 and elsewhere) and may be categorized into *topoi* of history or knowledge, for example (Reisigl and Wodak 2001: 80). These *topoi* implicitly map onto the ECoC guidelines, policies and websites.

In this study, we understand 'discourses' broadly – not as narratives specifically, but as (re)presentations of collective memory expressed and realised through texts (see Fairclough 1992; but also Wodak 2018; 2011 and her previous works). Fairclough (1992, 2003, 2015) has rightly emphasised that it is impossible to capture the entirety of a discourse, because discourses go beyond a text to include the (social, political, cultural, economic) context. But discourses are also ways of representing lifeworlds (Habermas 1987) and subjectivities, and discourses are constructed and produced for specific purposes. Lähdesmäki (2014) frames her analysis in social constructionism. We adopt a similar and perhaps stronger approach, in line with German sociologist Niklas Luhmann, who argued that meaning (*Sinn*) is nothing more than a selection made by a social system.[2]

Scholars who have investigated narratives and discourses of Europeanness and European heritage have used narrative analysis (Lähdesmäki 2017; Kølvraa 2015 on mythical narratives), Critical Discourse Analysis (Krzyżanowski 2010; Mole 2007), the Discourse Historical Approach (Wodak 2018; Reisigl and Wodak 2015) or the Discourse Mythological Approach (Kelsey 2015; Lähdesmäki

2018). Narrative analysis is not suited to our aims of identifying themes as *topoi* of Europeanness, because these *topoi* are constructed on the basis of linguistic strategies aiming at promoting the cities in question to win the ECoC bid. These are different from strategies of identity building or identity construction but instead refer to identity reinvention and branding for a specific purpose.

The Discourse Historical Approach (DHA) constitutes a Discourse Analytical method developed by Ruth Wodak (see, for example, Reisigl and Wodak 2001), who has written extensively on the discursive construction of European identities (for example, Wodak 2018). Glynos et al. (2009) offer a good overview and explication of Wodak's transdisciplinary method. They explain that DHA belongs to the same family as CDA, but instead of focussing on structures of power and inequality, DHA focuses on the interdependence of discourse and sociopolitical change (Wodak 2018), which means that it often needs to be combined with fieldwork and ethnography (Glynos et al. 2009: 20). In our case, the analysis of texts is combined with fieldwork in Valletta and Galway in May and June 2018, while Plovdiv's analysis is supported by secondary material. More importantly, in examining discourse and sociopolitical change, DHA focusses on the 'memory of practices' (Reisigl and Wodak 2001). In this way, history and memory are brought to the fore 'as a relevant context that needs to be taken into account' (Glynos et al. 2009: 19).

There is a noticeable lack of useful accounts of how to conduct and write up a discourse analysis (except, for instance, Goodman 2017). Glynos et al. (2009) offer a comprehensive overview of the main approaches and techniques to the study of discourse, namely: discursive devices, rhetorical strategies, interactional resources, rhetorical resources and subject positions (how speakers construct themselves and others in discourse). We will be referring to these general discourse analytic devices, together with intertextuality. However we will be using Wodak's DHA model, as presented in Reisigl and Wodak (2001, 2015) and Wodak (2018). According to this model, DHA analysis consists of two levels: a) entry-level analysis, which focusses on the thematic dimension of the texts being analysed and maps out their contents; and b) in-depth analysis, which is informed by the research questions and involves the identification of the genre, analysis of macro-structure of the respective text, strategies of identity construction and of argumentation schemes and analysis of other means of linguistic realisation (Wodak 2018). The in-depth analysis will involve the categorisation into relevant content-related *topoi*, as mentioned above, and the results of the analysis 'will be interpreted taking into account the knowledge of the relevant context' (Wodak 2018: 8)

## 11.4 The case studies

Before discussing the discourses of the Valletta (Malta), Galway (Ireland) and Plovdiv (Bulgaria) bids, in line with Wodak's (2018) approach to DHA, we are providing some contextual information and points of collective memory that contributed to framing the discourse of the bids.

162  *Cristina Clopot and Katerina Strani*

The first case study, Valletta, the capital of the small state of Malta and a World Heritage site, is a fortified city founded by the Knights of St John in the 1500s (see Figure 11.1). The history and landscape of the city is marked by waves of colonialism that have left behind a patchwork of built and intangible heritage that the ECoC bid has drawn on. As several observers have noted (for instance, Mitchell's 2002a, 2002b, 2018 studies are worth mentioning), Malta's accession to the EU posited problems at the societal level. The modern ways associated with Europeanisation were perceived as going against traditional ways of life, leading to 'a profound ambivalence' (Mitchell 2002b: 44).

To create the bid and implement the project, a dedicated structure was created, Valletta 2018 (V18 as it is commonly referred to). The Nationalist

*Figure 11.1* Valletta 2018 programmes stand (Photo: Cristina Clopot, 2018)

Party was in power when the Maltese received their nomination news in 2011 and started preparing the 2018 bid. Following elections in 2017, Labour leader, Joseph Muscat was sworn in as Prime Minister. The political change led to a change in the top management of the foundation, including the Executive Director, Programme Coordinator and Visual Arts Curator. To complicate matters further, an incident that drew the attention of international media was the death of local journalist and government critic, Daphne Caruana Galizia, a moment that Mitchell (2018: 62) notes 'led to a major crisis of conscience in Malta'. Following this, the V18 Foundation's chief became the target of national and then international calls for his resignation.[3] The development of the programme and its perception were marked by these controversies at the heart of a programme focused on re-branding the image of its capital city.

Galway's case has raised similar controversy, although the setting is different, both in terms of the history it draws on as well as the particularity of the application for the title, following the enhanced guidelines (see Figure 11.2). Set on the west coast of Ireland, the city is one of the major outposts of the Gaeltacht (the Irish-speaking region of Ireland). Similar to Valletta, Galway has a thriving tourism industry. In size, Galway is the middle city in terms of inhabitants, with about 80,000 people living in the city. As the bid highlights: 'The people of Galway are known for their fierce independence, forged by resistance to

*Figure 11.2* Galway city centre (Photo: Cristina Clopot, 2018)

centuries of oppression and the harshness of our way of life on the western edge of Europe' (Galway2020 2016: 3). The statement hints at the fact that, similar to Valletta, Galway's history is marked by colonialism and struggles such as the nineteenth-century famine. The bid document further mentions that the geographical position, on the edge, also affords Galway a position as a bridge between Europe and America. The controversy in Galway's case relates to the difficulties encountered by the Galway 2020 Foundation in fulfilling their mission and preparing the 2020 programme, which included the resignation of the creative director, the CEO of the foundation as well as the public withdrawal of one of their main partners and board member, the Druid Theatre[4] (see, for instance, Siggins 2018).

The last case study included here, that of Plovdiv, brings another dimension to the study by extending the analysis to the eastern borders of the EU. Plovdiv is an ancient city, the second largest city in Bulgaria, with about 300,000 inhabitants (Plovdiv2019 2014). Petrova and Hristov (2016: 1) note the city's protracted history as 'one of the oldest living urban areas in Europe' was marked by Thracian, Byzantine, Roman and Ottoman heritages among others. Similar to the other two case studies, the city's history relates to colonialism. More recently, the city's past was marked by the communist period. Plovdiv's designation was met with enthusiasm, similar to the other cities discussed here, as an occasion to address a problematic present, where culture and heritage are not as valued today: 'We are proud of the European culture that built Plovdiv over the millennia, but now culture seems dispensable to many citizens and Europe feels far away' (Plovdiv2019 2014: 4). Taking a similar view to other post-socialist cities that have received the designation (e.g., Pécs, Maribor, Pilsen (Plzeň), Wrocław), Plovdiv's involvement seems to be influenced by the common realisation that the East and West division of Europe still marks relationships today (see also Turşie 2015). In this respect, ECoC would present an opportunity to place the city firmly on the European map and 'broaden the notion on Europe and European cultural identity by narrating the socialist history, heritage and experience as part of Europeanness' (Lähdesmäki 2014: 491). This amicable contrast between the socialist past and the European future as complementing each other makes Plovdiv's bid stand out from the others.

## 11.5 Analysis

A first reading of the text has identified a series of rhetorical devices that outline common patterns of discourse in the ECoC bids, which are connected with the themes discussed above: synecdoche, repetition, the use of pronouns or adverbs.

### 11.5.1 Europeanness: tensions between topoi of history and geography

With regard to the European dimension, all bids are using a trope of Europeanness that is allegedly rooted in their history. This 'topos of history' is problematic, as in each case aspects of national or local history are purposefully framed as European, ignoring any tensions that may have existed (or still exist). The most common rhetorical device used to mitigate the local/national – European tension is that of making use of a synecdoche, a strategy, which constitutes using part of a concept to refer to its entirety. Galway's bid for instance notes: 'We identify in ourselves a microcosm of the current existential challenges to Europe and our core values as Europeans' (Galway2020 2016: 3). Plovdiv's bid also highlights this idea that the local represents the European in a smaller scale:

> In the process of transforming the objectives into project concepts we have focussed on themes that are important for Plovdiv but also relate to the bigger picture of issues being discussed and tackled in other parts of Europe.
> [Plovdiv2019 2014: 34]

To substantiate the problematic[5] 'European dimension', cities have made recourse to similar legitimation strategies by reflecting on the pertinence of the themes on a wider scale: 'Migration, language and landscape are elemental themes in the make-up of Galway, as they are in European and world cultures' (Galway2020 2016: 4). In line with the reviewed guidelines for the bidding process, the references to Europe and the European dimension, although not necessarily less problematic, are better emphasised in Galway's bid. A repetition that stands out in the Galway bid is that of 'European partners'. This trope of collaboration is also one of the most popular strategies to emphasise the Europeanness of the programme in Valletta and Plovdiv (Palmer 2004).

Despite the *topos* of history and tropes of collaboration and Europeanness, it is interesting to note that all three candidate cities position themselves outside the perceived European geographical space.

> Malta's marked history of close ties with Europe is inspirational for today's artistic collaboration.
> [Valletta2018 2012: 32]

> It is readily acknowledged that Europe has made enormous economic and social investment in Ireland. It is not therefore surprising that we are now reaching out to Europe, as never before.
> [Galway2020 2016: 3]

In a similar manner, an interviewee in Malta described the festivals and events included as: 'They feel more like we're exporting Malta to Europe rather than we're importing Europe to Malta, or we're celebrating our Europeanness'.

The '*topos* of geographical position' and specifically on the margin of Europe (East, West, South) also unites the three case studies, each of the candidate cities reflecting on their placement on the map of Europe in legitimisation strategies: 'Valletta, though placed on the edge of Europe, will put itself firmly at the centre of European cultural activity' (Valletta2018 2012: 39). Similarly Plovdiv is 'a city on the "edge" of Europe' (Plovdiv2019 2014: 32). Most of the arguments turn the geographical position on the edges into a positive aspect, opening connections to surrounding non-European neighbours, 'at the centre of a web of international cultures' (Galway2020 2016: 3) reminiscent of Delanty's view of European identity and European heritage shaped by inter-connections. The use of interactional markers such as first person pronouns are indicative in this sense also, with the pronouns used to mark locality rather than Europeanness, the city. For instance, the Plovdiv bid mentions: 'We have a huge European cultural heritage – Plovdiv is older than Athens and Rome' (Plovdiv2019 2014: 4).

Whereas Galway is the oldest member of the three studied, questions of European identities are not better addressed than in the case of the others. For example, the bid proposes that the ECoC title will encourage the first generation of Irish people to feel deeply European: 'without compromising our pride in wearing the Maroon or the Green jersey' (Galway2020 2016: 5).

### 11.5.2 *(Topoi of) Heritage, unity and history*

All three bids make recourse to notions of both tangible and intangible heritage, relating to both local and European heritage, although the local/national heritage takes precedence. This could be categorised as a distinct *topos* of heritage itself.

Galway, for instance, reflects on ECoC as an occasion 'to joyfully celebrate *our* unique cultural heritage' (Galway2020 2016: 30, added emphasis). The main elements that are brought to the fore are natural heritage (labelled as landscape) and language. Although migration features as one of the main themes of the bid, the reference to *migrant heritage* is mainly included under the umbrella of multilingualism. The local heritage elements the bid draws on are varied, including religious heritage, storytelling, folklore, dancing and literary heritage.

Within this *topos* of heritage, where Europeanness is built by reflecting on common themes, the sub-*topos* of unity is evoked rather than making recourse to the *topos* of history. Several of the projects promoted include similar locations from Europe, such as the Monument project (for example, Galway2020 2016: 14) which aims to reflect built heritage on several European islands. Although the reference to 'shared heritage' is repeated several times, its contents remain vague at the bid stage, with the only instances of actualisation presented through European music, European fairy-tales and the Gilgamesh epic (Galway2020 2016: 42).

Although Galway would be expected to draw more on European heritage, it is Plovdiv that makes more explicit recourse to European heritage, created through a metacultural operation, mainly through the *topos* of history: 'Plovdiv contributed to the model of the European city in the past' (Plovdiv2019 2014: 6). Shared heritage with particular countries and areas of Europe is also reflected through the inclusion of projects related to Thracians and the Etruscans, the Cyrillic alphabet, the Bauhaus movement and Homer's legacy.

Moreover, hinting at the contentious socialist legacy, Plovdiv aims 'to open up a discussion on the European level about problematic architectural heritage in the contemporary context' (Plovdiv2019 2014: 46). Local heritage is also present, of course, mainly through built heritage but also through a series of intangible elements such as the 'Chitalishta community centres' of the past, music and crafts.

A notable commonality for the case studies, not always reflected in the discourse of the bids, is the understanding of heritage as belonging to the past, an outmoded commodity to be used for the purposes of tourism. For instance, the Plovdiv programme 'aims at reviving the cultural heritage and connecting it to the contemporary context' (Plovdiv2019 2014: 63). Similarly, Valletta's bid book presents contradictions to the vision presented in the final programme. Various local crafts, built environment and shared heritage items (mainly Mediterranean – for example seafaring traditions) are reflected in the bid book:

> Our heritage, seen in street life, festivals, museums, cultural events and buildings and in the Maltese language, is a springboard for learning and appreciation, enabling deeper awareness of our unique social and cultural environment.
>
> [Valletta2018 2012: 18]

However, the final programme, available online, as well as the discussions with different Maltese interviewees reflected a different view: 'We are very much past oriented so obviously heritage is a very important aspect in our identity, in who we are and what we have, but we found it sometimes a bit challenging to sort of ensure that we are also a bit forward-looking' (V18 representative 2018). In a similar vein, one of the Galway interviewees reflected on the need to use the future tense in writing the bids.

### 11.5.3 Diversity and the topos of unity

The *topos* of unity represents a further common theme, either as a *topos* in its own right, or as a sub-*topos* of heritage, realising in discourse the controversial adage of the EU 'unity in diversity' discussed in section 3 above. In Plovdiv's case, the topos of unity is conveyed through the repetition of the adverb 'together', sometimes ambiguously: '"Plovdiv Together" wants to unite what is now divided in the city' (Plovdiv2019 2014: 7). The concept, while mainly referring to the city and its inhabitants, aims for a dual understanding, bringing the European dimension to the fore: 'This is supposed to be Europe? The diverse, multi-ethnic, multi-cultural, "together" Europe that Plovdiv claims to be part of?' (Plovdiv2019 2016: 4). The Plovdiv bid makes use of such rhetorical questions to address problematic interactions and tensions between ethnic groups (e.g., the ghettoisation of Roma) as well as lack of dialogue. Moreover, the Plovdiv bid also uses persuasive elements such as emphatic adverbs (e.g., 'will undoubtedly add a high level of expertise' (Plovdiv2019 2016: 14), 'they demonstrate the absolute necessity of finding the true meaning of the word "together"' (Plovdiv2019 2016: 8)).

In most of the instances, diversity is perceived mainly in a positive light, through the *topos* of unity:

> We *firmly* believe that the similarities within us, be it in the different groups in Plovdiv or the different cultures in Europe, are more and stronger than the differences.
>
> [Plovdiv2019 2014: 4, added emphasis]

> The ECOC creates a secure space in which to celebrate and exchange our cultural diversity.
>
> [Galway2020 2016: 3]

Yet, unlike Wodak's (2018) recent study emphasising the positive view of diversity, negative patterns emerge in the texts of the bids also.

> The Balkans share a common space and history but between the countries there are many unresolved problems. We often forget that there is more to unite than to divide us.
>
> [Plovdiv2019 2014: 44]

> Malta is a place of diverse cross-cultural exchanges, whether for trade, tourism or even as a refuge. However not all of these encounters are necessarily comfortable ones.
>
> [Valletta2018 2012: 24]

The antithesis is used to position Galway in a better position than the rest of Europe, echoing in particular the crisis generated by the refugee situation: 'While Europe struggles against a wave of closing borders, hearts and minds, Galway is seeking to challenge ambivalence towards difference and diversity' (Galway2020 2016: 15). Overall, the image of diversity constructed discursively is mainly that of ethnic, cultural and linguistic diversity. Each of the three bids presents their own 'others'. In the case of Valletta these are not clearly outlined, presented under the general label of immigrants, although a mention of a detention centre suggests connection to refugees, a topical theme for current Maltese society. Galway does not highlight specific groups either but notes that immigrants form 24% of its population. Plovdiv's emphasis is mainly placed on the Roma as well as historic minorities: Jews, Greeks, Armenians and Turks.

### 11.5.4 Future: topos of change

The theme of the future also permeates the bids, although markedly so in the case of Plovdiv and Galway. Arguably, the main *topos* presented in connection to this theme is that of change: 'Our vision for Galway 2020 is that it will be a catalyst for a future of inclusivity, participation and cultural sustainability' (Galway2020 2016:4). Plovdiv's view of the future outlines the ambitious objectives included in the programme, with culture-led regeneration centre-stage: 'Our approach to the future, with the project ECoC as a stepping stone, is to apply culture as a strategy to support even seemingly culture-unrelated issues' (Plovdiv2019 2014: 24). The rhetoric construction of the future is not clearly articulated in any of the bids analysed. The basic ethos resonates that of previous ECoCs of driving social, cultural and economic transformation. For instance Valletta2018's (2012: 4) bid includes a statement such as: 'It is inspired by its call to imagine a future which is better than its present'. Moreover, all bids share the view that the implementation of the programme will lead to a renewed interest and participation in cultural activities. They furthermore emphasise the objectives related to empowering creative industries within their cities and upscaling cultural provision.

## 11.6 Conclusion

We began our chapter with a statement, that Europe is represented by more than banknotes and economic shared spaces. The ECoC mega-festival, with its complex programming over a year of events and festival, presents a productive case study to reflect on what Europeanness might mean and how it is implemented bottom-up (Lähdesmäki 2016b). The three case studies selected present similar challenges and offer food for thought for European policies of integration as well as the current cultural agenda. As our discursive analysis has shown, although ECoC aims to promote shared European heritage, cities find the notion as vague as the academic discourse has found it, and devise particular strategies to approach it by drawing on shared histories or shared (constructed) themes of relevance for several countries.

In similar vein with previous studies (Lähdesmäki 2016b; Shore 2006; Sassatelli 2002; Strani, Klein and Hill 2017 and others), our analysis has highlighted the difficulties in actualising in discourse the European dimension. The geographical and historical positioning of these cities reflects the complexities of the ECoC programme, as well as its possible shortcomings in fostering a sense of shared identity. In these bids, Europe is most commonly elsewhere, a non-defined space to interact with rather than substantively belong to. The local and the national (heritage) thus take central stage, and all three cities emphasise the opportunity to propel themselves upwards in the hierarchy of European cities.

## Acknowledgement

This publication is a result of the European Union-funded Horizon 2020 research project: CoHERE (Critical Heritages: performing and representing identities in Europe). CoHERE received funding from the European Union's Horizon 2020 research and innovation programme under grant agreement No. 693289.

## Notes

1 For a discussion of 'whiteness' and 'diversity' in a European context, see Strani, Klein and Hill (2017).
2 For a concise overview of Luhmann's social systems theory and his concept of *Sinn* in particular, see Strani (2010).
3 Among these there was a petition signed by 100 creative industries professionals and artists, open letters from PEN international and an open letter signed by MEPs. (see, for instance, Pen International 2018; Anonymous 2018).
4 The Druid Theatre is an important player in the local cultural scene as one of the main Irish-speaking theatre companies in the city.
5 Indeed, a more critical view is stated in interviews. One of the interviewees in Galway, a member of the bidding team, reflected: 'It's a really tough ask; you can't sell the people of the city on this idea of celebrating a European dimension'.

## References

Anonymous (25 April 2018), 'More than 100 local artists call for Jason Micallef to quit Valletta 2018', *Times of Malta*. Available at: www.timesofmalta.com/articles/view/20180425/local/more-than-100-local-artists-call-for-jason-micallef-to-quit-valletta.677395 (accessed 5 December 2018).

Braun, V. and V. Clarke (2006), 'Using thematic analysis in psychology', *Qualitative Research in Psychology* 3(2), 77–101.

Calligaro, O. (2014), 'From "European cultural heritage" to 'cultural diversity'? The changing core values of European cultural policy. *Politique européenne* 45, 60–85.

Carter, C., R. Freeman and M. Lawn (2015), 'Introduction: governing Europe's spaces: European Union re-imagined', in C. Carter and M. Lawn (eds) *Governing Europe's spaces* (Manchester: Manchester University Press), 1–24.

Council of Europe (2005), *Framework convention on the value of cultural heritage for society*. Available at: www.coe.int/en/web/conventions/full-list/-/conventions/treaty/199 (accessed 10 December 2018).

Delanty, G. (2017), *The European heritage: a critical re-interpretation*, 1st ed. (London: Routledge).

Delli, V. (2017), 'European values and virtues in discourse: Political sphere or public space?', in J. House and T. Kaniklidou (eds), *Europe in discourse: identity, diversity, borders* (Athens: Hellenic American University), 117–129.

EC (2018), 'European Capitals of Culture'. Available at: https://ec.europa.eu/programmes/creative-europe/sites/creative-europe/files/ecoc-fact-sheet.pdf (accessed 15 December 2018).

EC (2014a), Decision No 445/2014/EU of the European Parliament and of the Council of 16 April 2014 establishing a Union action for the European Capitals of Culture for the years 2020 to 2033 and repealing Decision No 1622/2006/EC. Available at: https://eur-lex.europa.eu/legal-content/EN/TXT/?uri=CELEX%3A32014D0445 (accessed 15 December 2018).

EC (2014b), 'European Capitals of Culture 2020 to 2033 – a guide for cities preparing to bid'. Available at: https://ec.europa.eu/programmes/creative-europe/sites/creative-europe/files/capitals-culture-candidates-guide_en.pdf (accessed 15 December 2018).

Fairclough, N. (2015), *Language and power*, 3rd edn. (London: Longman).

Fairclough, N. (2003), *Analysing discourse: textual analysis for social research* (London: Routledge).

Fairclough, N. (1992), *Discourse and social change* (Cambridge: Polity Press).

Galway2020 (2016), 'Making waves: Galway application for European Capital of Culture 2020'. Available at: http://galway2020.ie/en/about/galway-2020-bid-book/ (accessed 12 December 2018).

Garcia, B. and B. Cox (2013), 'European Capitals of Culture: success strategies and long-term effects: study'. Available at: www.europarl.europa.eu/RegData/etudes/etudes/join/2013/513985/IPOL-CULT_ET(2013)513985_EN.pdf (accessed 10 December 2018).

Glynos, J., D. Howarth, A. Norval and E. Speed (2009), *Discourse analysis: varieties and methods*, Discussion Paper, ESRC National Centre for Research Methods NCRM/014.

Goodman, S. (2017), 'How to conduct a psychological discourse analysis', *Critical Approaches to Discourse Analysis Across Disciplines* 9(2): 142–153.

Habermas, J. (1987), *The theory of communicative action* (Boston, MA: Beacon).

Immler, N. and H. Sakkers (2014), '(Re)Programming Europe: European Capitals of Culture: rethinking the role of culture', *Journal of European Studies* 44(1): 3–29.

Kelsey, D. (2015), 'Journalism, storytelling and ideology: a discourse-mythological approach', in D. Kelsey (ed.) *Media, myth and terrorism* (London: Palgrave Macmillan), 23–50.

Kirshenblatt-Gimblett, B. (1995), 'Theorizing heritage', *Ethnomusicology* 39(3), 367–380.

Kølvraa, C. (2015), 'European fantasies: On the EU's political myths and the affective potential of utopian imaginaries for European identity', *JCMS: Journal of Common Market Studies* 54(1): 169–184.

Krzyżanowski, M. (2010), *The discursive construction of European identities: a multi-level approach to discourse and identity in the transforming European Union* (Frankfurt am Main: Peter Lang).

Lähdesmäki, T. (2018), 'Founding myths of European Union Europe and the workings of power in the European Union heritage and history initiatives', *European Journal of Cultural Studies* 00(0): 1–18.

Lähdesmäki, T. (2017), 'Narrativity and intertextuality in the making of a shared European memory', *Journal of Contemporary European Studies* 25(1): 57–72.

Lähdesmäki, T. (2016a), 'Scholarly discussion as engineering the meanings of a European cultural heritage', *European Journal of Cultural Studies* 19(6): 529–546.

Lähdesmäki, T. (2016b) 'Politics of tangibility, intangibility, and place in the making of a European cultural heritage in EU heritage policy', *International Journal of Heritage Studies* 22(10): 766–780.

Lähdesmäki, T. (2014), 'European Capital of Culture designation as an initiator of urban transformation in the post-socialist countries', *European Planning Studies* 22(3): 481–497.

Mitchell, J. (2018), 'Anthropology of Europe redux: déjà vu in the south', *Anthropological Journal of European Cultures* 27(1): 58–63.

Mitchell, J. (2002a), *Ambivalent Europeans: ritual, memory and the public sphere in Malta* (London: Routledge).

Mitchell, J. (2002b), 'Corruption and clientelism in a "systemless system": The Europeanization of Maltese political culture', *South European Society & Politics* 7(1): 43–62.

Mole, R. (2007), *Discursive constructions of identity in European politics: language and globalization* (London: Palgrave Macmillan).

Niklasson, E. (2017), 'The Janus-face of European heritage: Revisiting the rhetoric of Europe-making in EU cultural politic', Journal of Social Archaeology 17(2): 138–162.

Palmer, R. (2004), *European Cities and Capitals of Culture – city reports*, Part 1 (Brussels: Palmer/Rae).

Pen International (2018), 'Open Letter – 6 month anniversary of the assassination of Daphne Caruana Galizia', Sunday 15 April. Available at: https://pen-international.org/news/6-month-anniversary-assassination-daphne-caruana-galizia (accessed 10 November 2018).

Petrova, P. and D. Hristov (2016), 'Collaborative management and planning of urban heritage tourism: public sector perspective', *International Journal of Tourism Research* 18(1): 1–9.
Plovdiv2019 (2014), 'Plovdiv 2019 application form'. Available at: plovdiv2019.eu/en/documents (accessed 10 December 2018).
Rasmussen, S. (2009), *Discourse analysis of EU public diplomacy messages and practices*. Discussion Papers in Diplomacy (Den Haag: Netherlands Institute of International Relations 'Clingendael').
Reisigl M. and R. Wodak (2015), 'The discourse-historical approach (DHA)', in R. Wodak and M. Meyer (eds), *Methods of critical discourse studies*, 3rd ed. (London: Sage), 23–61.
Reisigl, M. and R. Wodak (2001), *Discourse and discrimination: rhetorics of racism and anti-Semitism* (London: Routledge).
Sassatelli, M. (2002), 'Imagined Europe: the shaping of a European cultural identity through EU cultural policy', *European Journal of Social Theory* 5(4): 435–451.
Shore, C. (2006), '"In uno plures" (?) EU cultural policy and the governance of Europe', *Cultural Analysis* 5: 7–26.
Siggins, L. (3 October 2018), 'Druid Theatre withdraws major production from Galway 2020', *Irish Times*. Available at: www.irishtimes.com/culture/stage/druid-theatre-withdraws-major-production-from-galway-2020-1.3649506 (accessed 10 December 2018).
Strani, K., G. Klein and E. Hill (2017), 'Diversity in a European context: the challenge of creating a shared critical vocabulary', in J. House and T. Kaniklidou (eds), *Europe in discourse: identity, diversity, borders* (Athens: Hellenic American University), 170–182.
Strani, K. (2010), 'Communicative rationality and the challenge of systems theory', in C. B. Grant (ed.), *Beyond universal pragmatics: studies in the philosophy of communication* (Oxford: Peter Lang), 123–148.
Turşie, C. (2015), 'The unwanted past and urban regeneration of Communist heritage cities. Case study: European Capitals of Culture (ECoC) Riga 2014, Pilsen 2015 and Wroclaw 2016', *Journal of Education Culture and Society* 2015(2): 122–138.
Valletta2018 (2012), 'Imagine 18: final application for the title of European Capital of Culture 2018 in Malta'. Available at: valletta2018.org/the-bid-book-story/ (accessed 10 December 2018).
Wodak, R. (2018), 'Discourse and European integration', MIM Working Paper Series 18: 1 (Malmö: Malmö Institute for Studies of Migration, Diversity and Welfare).
Wodak, R. (2011), 'Critical Discourse Analysis: Challenge, Overview and Perspectives', in: G. Andersen and K. Aijmer (eds), *Pragmatics of Society* (Berlin: Mouton de Gruyter) 627–650.
Wodak, R. (2007), 'Doing Europe': the Discursive Construction of European Identities', in: R. C. M. Mole (ed), *Discursive Constructions of Identity in European Politics* (Basingstoke: Palgrave Macmillan) 70-94.

# 12 Negotiating contested heritages through theatre and storytelling

*Kerstin Pfeiffer and Magdalena Weiglhofer*

Theatre and storytelling are two cultural practices that can be found in almost every society, and many of their traditional forms, from *Hezhen Yimakan* storytelling in China to puppetry in Slovakia, are officially recognised forms of intangible cultural heritage (ICH), that is as practices which store and transmit customs, skills, traditions and thus knowledge from generation to generation (Logan, Kockel and Nic Craith 2015). Festive events often provide fora for these living heritage practices. The Elche Mystery Play in Spain (also known as *Misteri d'Elx* or *La Festa*), for example, is a chanted drama of medieval origins and is performed by local volunteers in the Basilica Santa Maria and the streets of Elche on 14 and 15 August every year. As a celebration of the death, assumption and crowning of the Virgin Mary, it is one of the last vestiges of the once rich tradition of religious drama in Europe but is mainly understood today as a symbol of Elche's identity and of Valencian cultural heritage. It was inscribed in the Representative List of the Intangible Cultural Heritage of Humanity in 2008 (UNESCO 2018). Storytelling as a cultural practice is similarly celebrated in festivals throughout Europe, including the Alden Biesen International Storytelling Festival in Belgium or the Wales International Storytelling Festival, in which classic storytelling sessions are combined with music, poetry, theatre and circus performances, as well as workshops, movie screenings or puppet shows.

Yet both storytelling and theatre occur, of course, in many other forms and contexts. The *commedia del'arte* of sixteenth-century Italy, the musical *Cats* and scripted scenes from the life of Saint Columba at the UK City of Culture festivities in Derry/Londonderry can all be understood as theatre. Storytelling covers everything from amateurs passing on myths or fairy tales in a private setting to performers telling traditional or cultural stories in public – sometimes combined with music and/or dance – or individuals (both professional and lay actors) relating memories of (their) lived experience in a theatrical environment.

As part of heritage festivals, theatre and storytelling can provide people with a sense of history, community, generations and with a sensitivity to spoken language and its importance to ICH (Nic Craith 2008). As cultural practices in themselves they are a means of exploring narratives of self, of place and of community. Thus, they offer tools for empowerment and inclusion because they can illuminate the collision of simultaneous truths and allow their participants (including audiences) to engage with their own experiences and those of others in a facilitated space (Kuftinec 2009; Snyder-Young 2013; Nicholson 2014; Thompson 2009). Both have therefore been used for peace building and reconciliation in places where cultures coexist or collide.

In this chapter, we examine the social and cultural work that theatrical performance and storytelling can do to negotiate contested cultural heritages and memory in two specific geographical contexts: Northern Ireland, where deep-rooted divisions between Catholics and Protestants remain a fact of life, and the border region between Bavaria and Bohemia, where the historical conflict between Germans and Czechs continues to have an impact on their relationship to this day. Focussing on two specific projects, we seek to illustrate the potential inherent in theatre and storytelling for challenging preconceived or deeply ingrained notions of both personal and collective identity which can prevent or hinder exchange and reconciliation. Our first case study focusses on Theatre of Witness (ToW), a performance project which brought together Northern Irish people from different cultural, socioeconomic and geographical backgrounds and encouraged the telling of personal memories from experiences during the Northern Irish conflict and its aftermath so that they could be performed as autobiographical narratives on stage. The second case study centres on the *Čojč Theaternetzwerk Böhmen Bayern*, a German-Czech theatre network that regularly brings together German-speaking and Czech-speaking young people aged between 14 and 26 years in theatre workshops of one to three weeks.[1] The workshops are usually led by a German–Czech tandem of facilitators and ideally involve equal numbers of Czech and German speakers. In the past decade, they have often focussed on historical topics such as the expulsion of Germans from the *Sudetenland* after World War II, which challenge the participants to engage with questions of cultural identity in the border region.

The guiding assumption behind both initiatives is that interpersonal interaction can lead to genuine relationships across societal divides and therefore constitute a steppingstone for breaking down cultural barriers. They are examples of applied theatre, an 'ecology of practices' (Hughes and Nicholson 2016: 3), which considers its key purpose to be socially or politically transformative (Neelands 2007; Nicholson 2014) and therefore engages directly in social praxis, whether it be in a closed group of a drug rehabilitation scheme, in a performance about oral history in an ethnically mixed inner-city community, as museum theatre or as a performance at a heritage site such as the re-enactment of the Battle of Bannockburn in 2014. Like most applied theatre initiatives, both Theatre of Witness and *Čojč* use participatory practices in order to build performances from small segments of theatre, which are reflective of the participants' experiences, without a preconceived script. In *Čojč* workshops, the participants create improvisations based on stimuli which are then developed into scenes and sequences for performance. While they naturally gravitate towards certain roles in the creative process, ideally the work becomes the property of the whole group and everybody helps to develop it. Theatre of Witness used the process of telling life stories, first, in private one-on-one interviews with the artistic director and, second, within the group of project participants to structure and construct the participants' life narratives and to create a script that could be performed to a wide audience across Northern Ireland and the bordering counties of the Republic of Ireland. While written by the artistic director, the script was exclusively produced from the words of the story holders and the participants had total control over the final version of it. The storytellers then learned their own script and created and rehearsed a performance to go with it.

Collaborative creation and communication are interdependent. Therefore, facilitating meaningful communication between the participants is one of the main aims of both ToW and Čojč theatre workshops. Or as Kasimír, an experienced Čojč workshop facilitator, remarked: 'We teach the kids to communicate and our medium is theatre' (Interview, 30/08/2017).[2] This is often not as straightforward as it may seem. In the bilingual (if not multilingual) Čojč rehearsal room, the participants must work out how to communicate in linguistically mixed groups in order to create and improvise a scene. Theatre of Witness placed careful and non-judgemental listening to one another's stories at the centre of its attention. The goal was to create a space for storytelling that focussed on openness and learning.

Our aim in discussing two case studies is, firstly, to highlight the importance and expectations attached to social encounters and exchange, and secondly, to analyse the role that engagement with the past can play within this process. In doing so, we seek to illustrate that both Theatre of Witness and Čojč workshops with a historical topic focus bring the past into the present with the express intention of shaping a different future. They are dynamic tools for intervening in both self and culture that foreground the individual as a lens through which to see realities which demand reflection if the present is to change into a better future. In other words, they are each a 'backwards and forwards looking act' (Park-Fuller 2000: 28).

## 12.1 Meeting the alienated 'Other'

The Theatre of Witness project (Figure 12.1) was funded by European Union money allocated to 'peace building' in Northern Ireland,[3] as its self-defined aim was to 'foster stability, reconciliation and peaceful human interaction in the post-conflict society of Northern Ireland' (Derry Playhouse Theatre 2008). The overall initiative lasted two years, from January 2009 until December 2010 but was subdivided into two individual projects.[4] Each year, a group of six people from different backgrounds, of diverse ages and from varied geographical areas performed their own stories around a dozen times across Northern Ireland and border counties of the Irish Republic. The first project included six men and one woman; the second involved exclusively women.[5] The project was

*Figure 12.1* Theatre of Witness participants performing *I Once Knew A Girl...* (Photo: Magdalena Weiglhofer)

accompanied from start to finish by one of the authors in her role as a scientific production associate while writing her doctoral thesis (Weiglhofer 2014a).

Considering that people in (post-)conflict societies do have (sometimes well-thought through) reasons not to talk about their past, it is understandable that they would be apprehensive about speaking out within a group of people who are each conscious that they have a whole different set of experiences, viewpoints and upbringing. Dan Baron-Cohen has spoken in this respect of a *barricade culture* (Pilkington 1994), in which internal and external voices were typically sealed by the principle, "Whatever you say, say nothing" (Baron-Cohen 1999: 178). At the same time, sometimes the mere possibility of sharing a room with individuals who are or were in the past linked to a group or organisation that had inflicted harm or represented antagonistic world views to one's own seems difficult or not feasible altogether. In order to illustrate some of the impacts and challenges of sharing stories of contested heritage within a heterogeneous group, we will focus on what happened within one specific triad of people who got to hear each other's accounts.

Erin, Maeve and Laura participated in the second of the two projects. The artistic director had provided every participant with basic information on the other members of the group, and as a consequence, Erin, who had served in the Irish Republican Army (IRA)[6] for a short time, was concerned to meet especially one person who she anticipated would be hostile towards her:

> My biggest concern was Maeve because I would have been active [in the IRA] at the time that her husband was killed [by the IRA]. I had heard rumours that she was a tough one, she was black and white and … no bullshit … and I was sort of thinking, 'I walk here and this woman is gonna put me down and I'm gonna end up crying and … I have to just stand there and take it and … whatever she has to say, I have to stand there and take it.' […] And then I was the first to tell my story and I was super conscious that she was sitting beside me.
> 
> [Interview, 09/12/2010]

Erin's statement draws a picture of the encounter that clearly reflects the fears connected to it. It also suggests that she must not have been clear about how the narration sessions would be facilitated, since she was convinced that she had to 'just stand there and take' whatever Maeve said. While the philosophy of ToW indeed supported implicit respect for each other's story, whatever it might entail, it also maintained the rule not to challenge each other.

However, Erin was highly conscious that she had been described to the others in terms of *one* element in her story – namely that of having been a member of a paramilitary organisation. Walking into a group of strangers and being the first one to tell of this contested element, without knowing much of the listeners' backgrounds, demonstrates courage on her part. In fact, when speaking to other members of this group, they confirm that meeting Erin was something that caused apprehension and second thoughts on whether or not to take part in the project at all.

Laura, for instance, grew up in a tight-knit Protestant working-class area that did not leave much space for world views other than its own. She remembers her reaction upon receiving the information that there would be 'a woman that had been in the Provisional IRA':

> That was daunting because I had never really stepped out of my comfort zone. I was reared in a Protestant area, went to a Protestant school. It was not just meeting a Catholic, not just a Republican, but an activist. And I did struggle a bit with that. But I said to myself, 'You have to go and meet this person, meet her as a person'. I didn't have a problem with meeting the others. Just with Erin. What was gonna be said and what would come out. You just didn't know.
> 
> [Interview, 20/12/2010]

Meeting Erin as 'a person', not associating her with the (for her) dehumanising image of an IRA activist, presented the challenge that Laura was to take on if participating in the mutual storytelling. At the same time, this thinking process is not unproblematic as it demonstrates thinking with double standards. As a matter of fact, Erin simultaneously is both a person *and* an activist; placing one before the other denies the reality of each. Accepting Erin as person must include the acceptance of her past self since it significantly influences her present personality. However, Laura did not seem prepared to go that far. Yet, she understood that if she wanted to 'get [her] community's view out there', as she had made clear earlier, she also would need to listen to uneasy stories that, in fact, *did* make her 'very angry', as she admitted later. Laura herself had been in an incident where she – heavily pregnant – only narrowly escaped a bomb explosion that had been planted by female IRA combatants. Conversely, however, through the relatively long process of story sharing, Laura came to understand and to admire Erin's courage to tell her story. Finally, she decided that Erin must have gotten 'wrapped up in it'. In the same interview, Laura described how she reached that view:

> Yes, there was things heart rending and … you know… because I think of what happened to me, because it was IRA women that put the bomb in the café I was in. It could have so easily been me. And … But I thought she [Erin] was very, very honest and very, very brave. And that I admire. It's one of those things. She got wrapped up in it. […]. There were wee things … you were talking and you were trying to talk honestly, you didn't want to hurt or offend any of the rest. But I think we … as a group all accepted what each other said. You mightn't have liked it, but you accepted it 'cause [of] the person [who] was saying it.
> 
> [Interview, 19/12/2011]

While Laura's upbringing and present surroundings as well as personal experiences would form her opinion about republican activism, she acknowledges a personal achievement when she says:

> It's made a change in me. It's made me come out of my area and go to meet people that I never … dreamed I would meet, never *wanted* to meet. And now … I've been down, I've stayed in Erin's house!
> 
> [Interview, 19/12/2011]

By taking on the opportunity to exchange stories with people of 'other persuasions', as Laura calls it, she found that she was able to acknowledge how Erin could have become 'wrapped up' in the conflict, how she had developed her views. However, this acknowledgement seems only possible by diminishing Erin's agency in becoming involved. She reconnects and compares Erin's story with her own, which allows her to understand (while not necessarily approving of) the reasons for certain decisions and subsequent actions. Choosing to look at and make efforts to understand the individual rather than the affiliated organisation has resulted in finding connections with an alienated other.

In order to get a holistic picture of the interpersonal impact, it is interesting, at this point, to have a look at Maeve, the third in the triad presented here and the woman at the centre of Erin's worries. This is how Maeve remembered their first meeting:

> I had been told at the beginning that there was an ex-IRA woman among the cast. That didn't bother me because I had been working with ex-paramilitaries for about fifteen years. [...] But it was prominent in my mind to meet with this ex-IRA woman. And it was very strange the way it happened. It turned out that I was anxious to meet her, but I wasn't frightened to meet her. But she was frightened to meet me because she didn't know what kind of reaction that I would have to her. She was more nervous meeting me than I was meeting her. Ten years ago it mightn't have been so easy.
> [Interview, 11/12/2010]

Maeve's attitude demonstrated above is likely to have been the reason for the way she ultimately reacted to Erin's story, as related by Erin:

> After I [Erin] got it all out, she [Maeve] just gave me a big massive hug. [...] And that acceptance was incredible! And maybe I hadn't given her a chance. I just sort of thought, 'Her husband was killed by the IRA. Why would she even want to sit in a room with me?' And at one stage she probably would have never sat in a room with me.
> [Interview, 09/12/2010]

The apprehension of Erin, as well as the illustrated response of the supposedly antagonistic counterparts, highlights quite clearly the level of personal development that a majority of those involved already had achieved *before* joining the project. Their agreement to participate in this cross-community project underlines the change of mind and attitude of the individuals who had not been disinclined to use violence to achieve their goals in the past. The listeners, some of whom had been strongly affected by violence, were willing to remain non-judgemental *despite* possible connections to their own stories that could and did cause intense emotions. In both ToW projects, tears were not only a constant reminder of how vulnerable people chose to make themselves by sharing honest thoughts and feelings but also of how much the opportunity to be heard seemed to be longed for and appreciated.

Telling a life story within a group of people from heterogeneous cultural identity backgrounds can lead to acknowledging that others have suffered, too, which may (and did in this case) result in the creation of empathy for (former) opponents.[7] As some (e.g., Senehi 2002; Bar-On and Kassem 2004) have determined, storytelling can be 'critical for bringing people together on a personal level' (Senehi 2002: 56) when stories provide clues of personal circumstances and therefore may pave the way for understanding of how certain standpoints were reached. By transmitting knowledge from generation to generation but to a different audience, such as a former opponent, storytelling as ICH contributes to negotiating contested heritages.

Our second case study illustrates that bilingual applied youth theatre workshops can similarly provide a forum for exploring how contemporary identities can be negotiated and shaped in the face of a past that is characterised by conflict. In what follows, we draw on interviews with network members and on participant observation to explore, firstly, the importance that network members attach to social encounters between Czech and German young people for fostering cohesion. Secondly, we seek to illustrate how looking back to the shared history and heritage of Germans and Czechs is considered by network members to play a crucial role for finding one's place within the social and cultural world of the border region.

## 12.2 Meeting the historical 'Other'

German–Czech relations today are characterised by a relatively high degree of cross-border co-operation in a variety of fields from trade to infrastructure and education (Germany Trade & Invest 2018; Čzerná 2009). Yet for much of the nineteenth and twentieth centuries, the two countries formed a 'community of conflict' (Křen cited in Houžvička 2015: 14) because of the tensions between Czech- and German-speaking inhabitants in the border regions, as well as the atrocities committed by the Nazi regime and the subsequent expulsion of ethnic Germans from Bohemia following World War II. Moreover, from 1945 to 1989/90, the two countries were further separated ideologically by the Iron Curtain. The historical conflict between Czechs and Germans, and especially the post-war mass migration out of Bohemia of the German-speaking minority, continue to influence social relations between the two countries to this day to a certain extent even if, on a political level, steps have been taken to acknowledge responsibility on both sides for causing suffering (Houžvička 2015; see also Kockel in this volume).

In the past decade, the *Čojč Theaternetzwerk* has regularly tackled these difficult aspects of borderland history and culture through projects like *Das verschwundene Dorf – Místo na dně* (The vanished village, 2011), *Začarovany – Zauberland* (Magic land, 2016) or *Schwanenmostek – Labutíbrückl: Grenzlandkultur 1938 revisited* (2018). All of these projects have proven popular with participants and are considered by network members to make a particularly pertinent contribution to fostering social cohesion between Czechs and Germans – the declared aim of the network.[8]

In Western Bohemia, it is difficult *not* to notice the cultural and linguistic remnants of the entangled past of German- and Czech-speakers under the Austro-Hungarian Empire. Kasimír observed:

> If you want to understand the culture here in Western Bohemia, you have to know German. German has deep roots here. […] In Moravia, I feel more like a foreigner than when I go to a pub in Lower Bavaria – even though they speak the same language [in Moravia].
>
> [Interview, 30/08/2017]

This sense of a shared past is mentioned repeatedly when network members speak about their motivation for getting involved with Čojč, and it is frequently coupled with a keen awareness of the cultural and social damage caused by decades of separation. Tanja, a project participant, admitted that she knew very little about life on the other side of the border until she joined Čojč despite growing up very close to the border and that such a lack of knowledge allowed prejudice to flourish. Thus, she admits that before she met young Czech people, who have now become firm friends, she 'just had this image … I don't know… of poor, smoking prostitutes' (Interview, 28/08/2017). The positive impact of encounters and shared experiences for redefining social relations between Germans and Czechs is something that many Čojč network members and participants commented on. Some, like Tibor, even expressed a sense of responsibility for (re-)building cross-border relations:

> We are neighbours, and it is important to get to know the Germans. Then relations can improve […]. There was a strong historical link between [us] and Germany. But now because of the Second World War, because of Stalin, because of Hitler … so … it is a pity.
> [Interview, 28/08/2017]

For Jan, an assistant workshop facilitator, this sense of responsibility is not only grounded in the shared history and geographical proximity of the two countries but in the understanding that his generation (i.e., that born after the fall of the Iron Curtain) is less encumbered than previous ones by the traumatic experiences and conflicts of the past:

> I always think it is down to us to normalise the relations because the generation before us didn't get the chance, and the generation before them, so that of my grandparents, had the atrocities and the invasion in '38 on the Czech side as well as the … well … the events after '45 on the German side. Perhaps it is our duty to rebuild the contacts, and *this* I see in a larger context – that people make contacts and start friendships. Maybe it is easy to separate people, but it is perhaps harder to separate friends or lovers even.
> [Interview, 25/08/2017]

Interestingly, the 'duty to rebuild the contacts' seems to be linked, for him, to an implicit fear that the shadows of the past still have some power to return, even though the Czech Republic and Germany are now both members of the EU. Others do not necessarily echo this fear. For Kasimír, for example, the opening of the borders heralded an entirely new dawn. In the early 2000s, he says, project-related cross-border travel and exchange 'seemed so European to me and like we are really building a new Europe […] It was such an intercultural and amazing experience'. For him, Čojč projects are not only made possible by European integration, they also contribute to 'building a new Europe' by encouraging social interaction. For him and many other network members, shining a light on the shadows of the past by giving new life to stories of places and people is an important element in the network's approach to fostering and normalising cross-border exchange.

The latest theatre project in July 2018 may serve as an example of how the Čojč network seeks to make the past relevant for the present and the future in a bilingual applied theatre project. *Schwanenmostek-Labutíbrückl: Grenzlandkultur 1938 revisited* was a week-long theatre workshop, which brought together thirteen German- and Czech-speaking young people in Waldmünchen (Germany) to work on producing theatrical material focussing on the lost village of Schwanenbrückl – or Mostek in Czech (Figure 12.2). Only a stone-throw away from the border between Germany and the Czech Republic, Schwanenbrückl was home to Germans and Czechs, Jews and Christians before 1939. Today, all that remains of it are the overgrown ruins of houses as the village was abandoned with the migration of its German-speaking population. The aim of the project was to take the participants and the audience on a journey back in time to 1938 in order to give them an insight into life in the village (Čojč 2018). There was no script to facilitate this time travel. In the course of the week, the participants built a performance from scenes and images they created in response to different stimuli, which could be visual (e.g., a photograph), aural (e.g., music), textual (e.g., a diary) or abstract (e.g., a word or a theme).[9]

A key starting point for *Schwanenmostek* was the book *Auf Nachricht warten* by Regina Gottschalk, a distant descendent of a Jewish family living in Schwanenbrückl in the late 1930s. Based on personal letters and historical

*Figure 12.2* Performance planning for *SchwanenMostek* (Photo: Martina Buchna)

documents, Gottschalk illustrates the family's reaction to the annexation of the *Sudetenland*, their fears, hopes and dreams. In the course of the week, the project participants read excerpts from the book and from diaries as part of their research; they attended a reading with Bernard Setzwein, author of *Der böhmische Samurai*, a historical novel, and visited Schloss Ronsberg, where the novel is set. In addition, they spent time in a synagogue in Kdyne and explored the forest, which now grows over the ruins of Schwanenbrückl. These engagements with stories, memories and the topography of Schwanenbrückl and the surrounding area were transposed into images, sequences and scenes.

The public performance of *Schwanenmostek-Labutíbrückl: Grenzlandkultur 1938 revisited* was site-specific and interactive: it took the participants and their 80-strong audience from a conversation between villagers in the local pub just outside Schwanenbrückl to the site of the half-forgotten village where the spectators witnessed scenes of school life, participated in Sabbath celebrations and watched a family photo being taken, for example. The performative reanimation of Schwanenbrückl relocates the village, its people and their stories in time and space yet the strength of the historical narrative that *SchwanenMostek* presents does not rest in claims to truthfully recounting what happened in the village in 1938. Even where historical events such as a fire in a local barn, which was the talk of the village in 1938, provide the material and *dramatis personae*, the resulting scene is never a re-telling but a re-imagination because the project's exploration of spaces, objects and ideas focussed on sparking a personal connection and on the participants' creativity rather than on historical accuracy.

Čojč facilitators frequently stress the 'very creative atmosphere' in Čojč projects which gives the participants the feeling that 'everything is possible' (Kasimír, Interview 30/08/2017) – a clear indication that they believe in the transformative potential of applied theatre (Nicholson 2014; Thompson 2009; Snyder-Young 2013). In the case of *Schwanenmostek*, the creative process encourages the participants to interrogate the boundaries between the factual and the fictional and promotes, provokes and challenges their understanding. For example, how should we refer to the migration of the German-speaking minority out of Schwanenbrückl after 1945? German uses the word *Vertreibung* (expulsion). In Czech, it is usually referred to as *odzu* (transfer). Discussions over terminology in the rehearsal room can thus highlight larger contexts and raise questions about authority in relation to the performative construction of history. As Martin, a workshop leader with considerable experience in facilitating history projects, explained:

> I made the experience that [the participants] have been socialised differently into historical culture, especially as far as the twentieth century is concerned. [...] I wouldn't expect a project to have a particular influence in terms of transmitting factual knowledge ... but it can show up the different perspectives, and that's something that a play can also do really well.
>
> [Interview, 20/11/2017]

For Martin and Kasimír the exposure to different discourses about history and memory, the creative process and theatre's ability to present multiple perspectives all guard against what Baz Kershaw has criticized as the 'performance of nostalgia' which sanitises the struggles of the past (1999: 160).

As Astrid Erll (2011) observes, the telling of stories from the past often says less about the past as such than about our own, present needs for doing so. For the members of the *Čojč* theatre network, this present need can be described as a desire to extend people's understanding of their current place within their social and cultural world. As Martin explained:

> There is a saying in *Čojč* that *Čojč* creates a new *Heimat*[10], a new dynamic understanding of *Heimat* so to say, in any case a kind of rootedness, of connection, [...] of feeling at home; [*Čojč*] offers the chance to formulate a current version of this, also for the participants.
>
> [Interview, 20/11/2017]

The bilingual *Čojč* theatre projects are performative (in two senses of the word) of a new vision of *Heimat* that is based on regional cultural identity: they show or act out the hybridity of the border region, for example, by using the hybrid language *Čojč* alongside Czech and German on stage, and in doing so, they affect the real world in that they can contribute to a (re-)definition of what and where *Heimat* is – and who is part of it. Through the performance, the village and its people become part of the lived experience of the participants and spectators who inhabit Schwanenbrückl in the theatrical moment. By interweaving the historical and the imaginary, the performance requires *all* to engage with the constructed side of our relation to the past as much as with the individual, embodied and lived.

## 12.3 Conclusion

The Theatre of Witness and *Čojč* projects each provide a space to 'reimagine community and reanimate ethical relationships' (Kuftinec 2009: 1) in contexts where cultural heritage(s) are contested. Based on the idea that interpersonal interaction builds bridges across societal divides, both projects facilitate encounters that enable participants to access view points and narratives that they might not have heard easily otherwise. Yet the participants do not simply share a space: they engage creatively with their own personal stories and those of others through theatrical techniques that are adapted to the specific requirements of the project context. This can challenge the preconceived notions of personal and collective identity and opens up ways of understanding a formerly alienated or historical other. The examples of Laura and Erin illustrate the personal transformations that looking back to one's own life story and sharing it may bring about. *Čojč* history projects like *Schwanenmostek* re-enliven the shared cultural heritage of the border region as well as the struggles of the past for new audiences. Participants and spectators alike gain access to a plurality of perspectives, which – through the act of performance – become part of their own lived experience. Looking back thus becomes an important element in interrogating and establishing the contours of a borderland identity. In other words, the creative and theatrical techniques used in both projects enable participants (and audiences) to negotiate, cross-reference and borrow, and thus to construct and rehearse, future identities among the narratives of others, past and present. Theatre and storytelling thus open up the past in the present as a resource for a contemporary formulation of a future vision that offers points for identification, which reach beyond contested heritages.

## Acknowledgement

Research for section 12.2 of this chapter was conducted as part of the European Union-funded Horizon 2020 research project: CoHERE (Critical Heritages: performing and representing identities in Europe). CoHERE received funding from the European Union's Horizon 2020 research and innovation programme under grant agreement No. 693289.

## Notes

1 The word *Čojč* is a blend of the Czech word for the Czech language, *česky*, and the Czech spelling for the word *deutsch* (German): *dojč*. It is also used to refer to the hybrid language that the *Čojč Theaternetzwerk* uses in the rehearsal room as well as in performance.
2 In order to maintain the anonymity of our interlocutors, we use pseudonyms throughout.
3 The Good Friday Agreement set off a proliferation of peace-building initiatives at community and institutionalized level, with the Special EU Programmes Body (SEUPB) being the biggest supplier of funds for this purpose.
4 Due to the project's success, it was subsequently extended for another two years (2011–2012).
5 Both performances included a seventh character onstage that, in 2009, was intended as a (mainly) quiet embodiment of all those who cannot or do not want to speak out and, in 2010, as a representative of the performing women's youth.
6 The Irish Republican Army was a paramilitary movement in Northern Ireland in the twentieth and twenty-first centuries dedicated to Irish republicanism, that is, the belief that all of Ireland should be an independent republic. It was also characterised by the belief that political violence was necessary to achieve that goal.
7 For a more rounded discussion of impacts, see Weiglhofer (2014b, 2015). Research for section 12.2 of this chapter was conducted as part of the European Union-funded
8 The network motto is: *Mit divladem theater hýbat grenzen hranicemi bewegen* (Moving borders through theatre). *Grenzen* is a multi-facetted term in German, as it can refer to political borders, personal limits or barriers of different kinds. It is deliberately ambiguous here.
9 The project received funding from the 'Europeans for Peace' programme by the Stiftung 'Erinnerung–Verantwortung und Zukunft' (EVZ) and the European Regional Development Fund in recognition of its aim to foster reconciliation and exchange. For further information about the pedagogical approach taken in this project, see Reinert & Kopůncová (2018).
10 We are leaving this notoriously troublesome, affect-laden German concept, which can encompass places, spaces and people untranslated here as the quotation provides a reasonable gloss.

## References

Bar-On, D. and F. Kassem (2004), 'Storytelling as a way to work through intractable conflicts: The German-Jewish experience and its relevance to the Palestinian-Israeli Context', *Journal of Social Issues* 60(2): 289–306.
Baron Cohen, D. (1999),'Listening to the silences. defining the language and the place of a new Ireland', in S. Brewster,V. Crossman, F. Becket and D. Alderson (eds), *Ireland in proximity: history, gender, space* (London: Routledge), 173–188.
Cojc (2018), *Cojé všem für alle!* Available at: http://cojc.eu/cs/ (accessed 4 August 2018).
Čzerná, K. (2009),'German-Czech relationships and identity in a cross-border region,' in J. Carl and P. Stevenson (eds), *Language, discourse and identity in central Europe: The German language in a multilingual space* (Basingstoke: Palgrave Macmillan), 96–121.
Derry Playhouse Theatre (2008), *Funding application form (Part B) peace III to special EU programmes body* (Derry/Londonderry: Derry Playhouse Theatre).
Erll, A. (2011), *Memory in culture* (Basingstoke: Palgrave Macmillan).
Germany Trade & Invest (2018), *Wirtschaftsdaten kompakt: Tschechische Republik*. Available at: www.gtai.de/GTAI/Content/DE/Trade/Fachdaten/MKT/2016/11/mkt201611222060_159030_wirtschaftsdaten-kompakt---tschechien.pdf?v=3 (accessed 7 November 2018).
Houžvička, V. (2015), *Czechs and Germans 1848–2004: The Sudeten question and the transformation of central Europe* (Prague: Karolinum).
Hughes, J. and H. Nicholson (2016), 'Applied theatre: ecology of practice', in J. Hughes and H. Nicholson (eds), *Critical perspectives on applied theatre* (Cambridge: Cambridge University Press), 1–12.
Kershaw, B. (1999), *The radical in performance: between Brecht and Baudrillard* (London: Routledge).
Kuftinec, S. A. (2009), *Theatre, facilitation, and nation-formation in the Balkans and the Middle East* (Basingstoke: Palgrave Macmillan).
Logan, W., U. Kockel and M. Nic Craith (2015), 'The new heritage studies: origins and evolutions, problems and prospects', in W. Logan, U. Kockel and M. Nic Craith (eds), *A companion to heritage studies* (Chichester: Wiley-Blackwell), 1–26.
Neelands, J. (2007), 'Taming the political: the struggle over recognition in the politics of applied theatre', *RiDE: The Journal of Applied Theatre and Performance* 12(3): 305–317.
Nic Craith, M. (2008),'Intangible cultural heritages: the challenges for Europe', *Anthropological Journal of European Cultures* 17(1): 54–73.
Nicholson, H. (2014), *Applied drama: the gift of theatre*, 2nd ed. (Basingstoke: Palgrave Macmillan).
Park-Fuller, L. (2000), Performing absence: the staged personal narrative as testimony, *Text and Performance Quarterly* 20(1): 20–42.
Pfeiffer, K. "Borderland Stories: Engaging with the Past in German-Czech Bilingual Theatre', CoHERE Conference "Who is Europe?", POLIN Museum, Warsaw, 22-23 November 2018.
Pilkington, L. (1994),'Dan Baron Cohen: resistance to liberation with Derry frontline culture and education', *TDR* 38(4): 17–47.
Reinert, M. and R. Kopůncová (2018), *Methoden zweisprachiger lokalhistorischer Jugendbegegnungsprojekte am Beispiel des Projekts Schwanenmostek – Labutíbrückl: Grenzlandkultur 1938 revisited*. Available at: http://cojc.eu/images/veda/2018-09-19-cojc-schwanenmostek-publikace/2018-09-19-cojc-schwanenmostek-publikace-01.pdf (accessed 28 November 2018).

Senehi, J. (2002), 'Constructive storytelling: a peace process', *Peace and Conflict Studies* 9(2): 41–63.

Snyder-Young, D. (2013), *Theatre of good intentions: challenges and hopes for theatre and social change* (London: Palgrave Macmillan).

Thompson, J. (2009), *Performance affects. applied theatre and the end of effect* (Basingstoke: Palgrave Macmillan).

UNESCO (2018), *Mystery play of Elche*. Available at: https://ich.unesco.org/en/RL/mystery-play-of-elche-00018 (accessed 28 November 2018).

Weiglhofer, M. (2015), '"Who am I without My Story?": Uncertainties of Identity (Presentation) in Performed Autobiographical Storytelling', *Storytelling, Self, Society* 11(2): 263–279.

Weiglhofer M. (2014a), *Presencing past for the future? The function of performed storytelling in Northern Irish post-conflict peacebuilding*, unpublished PhD thesis (University of Ulster).

Weiglhofer, M. (2014b), 'The function of narrative in public space: witnessing performed storytelling in Northern Ireland, *Journal of Arts and Communities* 6(1): 29–44.

# 13 Commemorating vanished 'homelands'

Displaced Germans and their *Heimat Europa*

Ullrich Kockel

The twentieth century has been described (e.g., Piskorski 2015) as a century of displacement. While globally the comparative scale of involuntary population movement may not have differed significantly from earlier centuries, its perception has changed radically, leading in the early twenty-first century to the dramatic resurgence of xenophobic populism across Europe and beyond (see Kaya 2017; De Cesari and Kaya 2019). Throughout the 'refugee crisis' of the 2010s, the German government's moderate policy towards new migrants was widely criticised. The ideological foundation for that policy was, arguably, the country's experience of integrating millions of ethnic German expellees and refugees from Central and Eastern Europe in the aftermath of the Second World War.

Annual heritage events celebrating the regions of former German settlement have been a regular feature of the German festival calendar since the institution of the annual *Tag der Heimat* ('Day of the Homeland')[1] as an official day of public commemoration that usually takes place in various state capitals during September. Its original impetus came from a mass demonstration in Stuttgart on 6 August 1950, where the controversial Charter of the German Homeland Expellees[2] was proclaimed. Individual regional associations have held their own festivals, such as the *Deutschlandtreffen* of the Silesians or the *Sudetendeutscher Tag* of the Sudeten Germans. While these festivals were initially quite similar in style and tone across the range of expellee organisations, and have retained similar formats, they have diverged considerably over the years in terms of political outlook, with especially the Sudeten Germans developing a strong European perspective, while other groups have remained rather more irredentist.

Drawing on ethnographic fieldwork and archival research, this chapter examines ways in which the vanished homelands of the expellees are performed, in terms of both physical spectacle and rhetoric, and in more subtle material and non-material representations of heritage. Given their explicit emphasis on a European identity, the primary focus here is on the Sudeten German associations and on the DJO-German Youth in Europe; the latter began as an umbrella organisation for expellee and refugee youth from various ethnic German regions but has since evolved into a more broadly based youth organisation (Becker 2002; Kockel 2015a; Hamel 2017). Placing the investigation in the wider context of post-war reconstruction and European integration, the analysis asks to what extent and how these organisations have indeed been exponents of a 'European spirit', as often represented by their leadership and in their own literature, and if so, whether their experience offers lessons for the formation of European heritages.

## 13.1 Historical background and political context

The settlement of German-speaking people in Central and Eastern European regions was extensive and varied (Hahn and Hahn 2010; Beer 2011). In the Baltics, returning crusaders established power bases, the largest of which evolved into the German province of East Prussia while the smaller ones created local élites that endured conquests by other powers. Having received migrants from German-speaking parts of the Holy Roman Empire since the Middle Ages, most of Silesia, formally incorporated into the Habsburg monarchy in 1526, was captured by Prussia in 1742. The boundaries of these territories remained disputed and some were subject to plebiscites after the First World War.[3] A third major area, later known as *Sudetenland* (Figure 13.1) remained within the Czech part of the Habsburg Empire until 1918, when it became part of Czechoslovakia. Further east and south, settlement was more dispersed, creating what ethnologists referred to as 'linguistic islands' (*Sprachinseln*)[4] – areas with unique patterns of interethnic cultural practices – along the Danube, in the Carpathians, the Balkans and the Russian Empire, often at the invitation of the monarch.

At the end of the Second World War, many of these settlers fled from the advancing Red Army; others were expelled by local militias or civilians. The

*Figure 13.1* Map of the Sudetenland regions within the Czech Republic (including 'linguistic islands')

total number is uncertain but likely to have been in the region of 12.75 million by 1950 (Beer 2011: 85), with most finding a new home in the British and American zones of what was then West Germany. However, integration was difficult (Lehmann 1991) as the displaced were often perceived locally not so much as fellow Germans but according to the ethnic environment from which they had come. Derogatory labels, such as *Pollacken* for expellees from Poland or *Batschacker* after a Yugoslavian region on the Danube, were used commonly; many expellees found Germany a *Kalte Heimat* ('cold homeland'; Kossert 2009).

Already in 1946, various initially informal groups emerged, quickly evolving into inter-linked organisational strands: the *Landesverbände* ('state associations'), mapping onto the states that made up post-war West Germany, represented the socioeconomic interests of expellees in their new homeland, while the *Landsmannschaften* ('compatriot societies'), based on ethno-regional origin, reflected the politico-cultural orientation towards their lost homeland. Silesians and Sudeten Germans, the largest groups with some three million each, were particularly influential in West German politics, as were the East Prussians (Kossert 2009; Franzen 2010). Relations between the *Landesverbände* and the *Landsmannschaften* were marked by personal animosities among the leadership, political power struggles and debates over the 'proper' policy (Stickler 2004; Kossert 2009).

On 5 August 1950, the day before a major rally of expellees in Stuttgart, representatives of *Landesverbände* and *Landsmannschaften* signed the Charter of the German Homeland Expellees (*Charta der deutschen Heimatvertriebenen*). This declaration, with its emphasis on the 'renunciation of revenge and retribution', unification of Europe 'without fear and force', active participation in the reconstruction of Germany and Europe and 'right to home(land)' as a fundamental human right, became a significant foundation for the subsequent work of the expellee associations and especially for the DJO (Müßigbrodt 2011: 14). However, the declaration remained controversial, its commitment to the 'renunciation of revenge and retribution' attracting particularly strong criticism (Giordano 1997; Niven 2006; Schmitz 2007).

The diverse range of expellee youth organisations proved an obstacle to securing funding from the federal government, who preferred to deal with a single body, and this led to the establishment of the DJO-*Deutsche Jugend des Ostens* ('German Youth of the East') in 1951 (Becker 2002). The *Sudetendeutsche Jugend* (SdJ; 'Sudeten German Youth') joined the DJO soon after and has played a key role in the association since. In the same year, the *Bund der vertriebenen Deutschen* (Federation of Expelled Germans) was established. *Landesverbände*, organised according to place of residence and especially important in the northern and western states, saw their role in helping the social and economic integration of expellees, whereas *Landsmannschaften*, organised by homelands and playing an important political role in Bavaria and Baden-Württemberg, saw their task more in preserving their respective cultural heritage and being concerned with politically supporting a return to the homelands rather than social integration (Becker 2002: 52f.), although there were notable differences between them.

The expellee associations were very much part of the Cold War constellation in Central Europe. Relatively few expellees had settled in the Soviet zone that became the German Democratic Republic, while for the vast majority their 'lost homelands' lay entirely on the other side of the Iron Curtain. De Gaulle had not been invited to the Potsdam conference in 1945, and consequently the French resisted implementation of the agreement reached there, which meant their zone received hardly any expellees. The establishment of the European Communities during the 1950s was in part an attempt to fortify western Europe against the threat of Communism, and this may have been one of the reasons why some of the associations subscribed to a pro-European rhetoric at least at the official level. This rhetoric is already evident in the Charter mentioned above and can be traced through pamphlets and other publications (see, e.g., Kockel 2015a).

The softening of the East–West tensions in the course of the *neue Ostpolitik* ('new politics towards the East'), pursued by the West German coalition government of Social Democrats and Liberals since the late 1960s, received a mixed reception from the associations because it entailed confirmation of the post-war borders, thus implying an end to hopes for recovery of, and return to, their 'lost homelands'. Some associations remained vehemently opposed to this new politics, while others were more ambivalent. Especially the DJO, which, being a youth organisation, was already experiencing the impact of losing its *Erlebnisgeneration* – the generation who had experienced flight and expulsion – was thrown into a deep identity crisis that found expression in controversial public stunts and the subsequent discussions in their members' magazine (Kockel 2015a), leading in 1974 to the reinvention of the organisation as *djo-Deutsche Jugend in Europa*. The fall of Communism, followed by eastward expansion of the European Union, opened up opportunities for expellees and their descendants to visit Central/Eastern European *Sehnsuchtsorte* ('places of longing') and develop new affinities to them. While opportunities had existed already during the Cold War, such as volunteering with the *Volksbund Deutsche Kriegsgräberfürsorge* (German War Graves Commission) that provided an outlet for summer activities of youth groups of the *Landsmannschaften* and for the DJO to explore their 'lost homelands', for the vast majority of expellees the viewing points near the Iron Curtain were as close as they could get. The ethnologist Karl Braun (2015), whose parents were expelled from the Sudetenland, gives an insightful account of such visits to the border while also reflecting on the identity problematic affecting young people whose ties with a 'lost homeland' are entirely through the memory narratives of their elders.

In the early 2000s, proposals to establish a 'centre against expulsions' deeply divided public opinion in Germany (Franzen 2008). This caused a peculiar quandary for the DJO, which since its 1974 reinvention has turned its focus deliberately towards the integration of refugees and expellees coming to Europe while maintaining emphasis on its origins in the German experience. Through this shifting focus, the organisation has been able to retain an *Erlebnisgeneration*, although this is now no longer ethnically German, but as geographical origins and cultural backgrounds of its members have changed so have their characteristics and political outlook (Becker 2002). At the same time, the youth organisations of the various *Landsmannschaften* have been engaged in considerable soul-searching with regard to their heritage and cultural identity.

## 13.2 Expellee associations and the European idea: *Sudetendeutsche* and the DJO

Emphasis on historically 'German' territories has been crucial for the *Landsmannschaften* although the boundaries of these territories were often historically fuzzy, making them ethnic frontiers rather than discrete territories (see Kockel 2015b). With some, their ethnic association was more Austrian than German, particularly in what since the late 1800s had come to be known as *Sudetenland*. Austro-Hungarian citizens until 1918, the inhabitants of these Czech regions, were conscious that Prague had once been the capital of the Holy Roman Empire. That loose assemblage of principalities under a common emperor never developed into a nation state in the modern sense and provides the model for some conservative visions of 'Europe', such as that of the late Otto von Habsburg, son of the last Austro-Hungarian emperor, who was a prominent voice in the European movement. Association with this 'pan-European' heritage may go some way towards explaining why the Sudeten Germans have long displayed a strong affinity with the 'European idea' (see Kølvraa 2015), emphasising the European aspects of their political aspirations – an emphasis that comparison of portrayals of their ethnicity (e.g., Nitzsch n.d.; Schmutzer 1985) suggests has become stronger over the years. Other *Landsmannschaften*, while stressing their commitment to the Charter with its accent on a 'European spirit', have been considerably less emphatic.

Given the relative size of this *Landsmannschaft*, the extent of Sudeten German input to the shaping of the DJO is perhaps not surprising. From its inception, the DJO was marked by divisions within and between the *Landsmannschaften* and their youth organisations. These divisions are evident throughout the history of the organisation even today, having surfaced with varying clarity and weight at different times. For example, the members' magazine *Der Pfeil* ('The Arrow') in the early 1950s gave considerable space to the 'European idea' and its relevance for the organisation. Ewald Pohl, the DJO's first leader, wrote about the hope that a reunited Germany would again be able to honour its duties and tasks in a free Europe in which the 'German East' would also have its place in freedom and justice (see Kockel 2015a: 320). The hope expressed here correlates with the conservative vision of Europe that was widespread at the time and which can be traced, in numerous variations, to the early twentieth century and beyond (e.g., Bugge 2002; Delanty 1995; Frevert 2003; Kaelble 2001). However, in the same magazine that extols a 'European spirit' promoting understanding and collaboration, the columnist 'Kauke' praises a group of DJO members in Hamburg for dismantling an exhibition about the post-war reconstruction of Poland because the use of Polish instead of German place names had offended the *Landsmannschaften*, especially the East Prussians (Kockel 2015a; see also Lotz 2007: 98f.).

Seeking out the experience of boundaries and frontiers was a key element of practice for the DJO in those early years (Sachers n.d.: 11). The DJO organised regular *Fahrten* (group journeys)[5] across Europe, where groups deliberately camped in border areas and ethnic frontiers, reminders of the gap between the contemporary situation and a Europe of the future (Sachers n.d.). The *Fahrten* were thus very much part of a discourse celebrating the past and future of a European 'homeland' that the DJO had a duty to help build.

The July 1952 issue of *Der Pfeil* carried a lead article signed 'D.B.' in which the role of the DJO as defenders of a European 'homeland' is emphasised. It presents a vision of a regained East once again 'German and free'. This resonates with earlier images, even preceding Nazi propaganda, of the German settlements in Eastern Europe as bulwarks against the threat emanating from the steppes of Asia, the author invoking the 'faithful Germans' as 'the vanguard of Europe' (p. 1). While the martial pathos partly reflects an older and suspect ideology, it also expressed popular fears and aspirations at the beginning of the Cold War.

In the everyday practice of the DJO during the 1950s and 1960s, major efforts were invested in *Ostkundliche Studien* – historical and cultural studies of 'the German East', with significant political emphasis. The booklets produced by authors like Hans Christ at the time would make an illuminating study for another occasion. Political activities like *Ostkunde* led many contemporaries to regard the DJO as being perilously close to the populist spirit of Nazism. The use of Germanic symbols like the *Odalsrune* reinforced this perception. The *Odalsrune*, symbolising 'home', 'heritage' and 'rootedness', had been chosen as basis of the DJO's emblem, augmented by a circle that stood for the corral of wagons of the settlers who had made their home in the East; this turned the emblem into a sun wheel signifying faith in the future; the design was completed with an arrow pointing eastward, indicating the DJO's task of re-settling the lost homeland when the time comes (Kockel 2015a: 321) – the same arrow that appears in the name of the DJO's magazine *Der Pfeil*.

At the same time, there was a different current of thought, which found expression in the 'Kiel Principles' of the DJO, issued by the 1955 *Bundesjugendtag* (General Assembly; Becker 2002: 123). These principles affirmed Herder's idea of different peoples as building blocks of humanity, and Europe, consequently, as a union of free peoples in peaceful coexistence. This current of thought underpinned the DJO's involvement in European folklore festivals and related activities, such as the establishment of EFCO, the European Folk Culture Organisation. Dance troupes associated with the DJO, such as the *Klingende Windrose* in North Rhine–Westphalia, have also performed 'traditions of the German East' at other types of popular festivals, including the *Landesgartenschauen* (state garden festivals), where their appearances have been framed as expressions of a European spirit.

On the eve of the *neue Ostpolitik*, the controversial DJO leader Ossi Böse marked the 1965 'Year of Human Rights' with a speech in which he presented his vision of a world in which universal human rights provided the foundations for a 'Europe of free peoples and ethnic groups' in which borders would merely have ethnographic or administrative meaning (Kockel 2015a). This vision was also expressed in a DJO declaration on human rights that emphasised the creation of a better world in collaboration with, not against, neighbouring peoples. Reading between the lines, one can also detect an interpretation that might turn this rights discourse against those same neighbours by, for example, pitching the historical injustice of expulsion against the right to a home(land). However, in his address during the organisation's twentieth anniversary celebrations in 1971, DJO leader Henning Müßigbrodt reiterated that there was no desire for a political order that Germany's neighbours in the East would not also welcome and support (Kockel 2015a). In the same year, discussions about the DJO's name led to a competition in which *Deutsche Jugend für Europa* (German Youth for Europe) came out as favourite (Becker 2002: 196). This debate resumed at the annual gathering in 1974, following a report on a meeting between representatives of the DJO and the federal government where the DJO's position concerning the *neue Ostpolitik* had been discussed. The DJO board recommended acceptance of the new political reality and only narrowly survived a vote of no confidence. By the end of that gathering, a new name for the organisation – *djo-Deutsche Jugend in Europa* – had been agreed that signalled the modernisation of the DJO without relinquishing its history and fundamental goals; the *Odalsrune* with the arrow of the settlers was replaced by a compass (Becker 2002: 197). However, this transformation was not universally implemented; the *Landesverband* Baden-Württemberg, for example, retained an emblem reminiscent of the *Odalsrune* until recently, and some of the *Landsmannschaft*-aligned member organisations – notably the Silesians and East Prussians – disassociated themselves from the DJO whom they saw as no longer representing their interest in regaining their 'lost homelands', while the remaining ones tended to concentrate on cultural heritage preservation (Becker 2002: 208). The DJO's transformation into an ordinary youth organisation with strong international connections particularly to Central and Eastern Europe was followed in those countries with critical interest (e.g., Kołacki 1988).

Under the umbrella of the DJO's *Ostkunde*, the *Sudetendeutsche Jugend* produced over the years a range of materials related to Sudeten German heritage, including booklets for use in schools and youth groups that contextualised and discussed the issue of a Sudeten identity. An early version from the 1960s highlights the interethnic character of Sudeten German cultural heritage and the diversity of identities, while at the same time postulating a 'duty to the whole' arising from a historically evolved ethnic consciousness (Nitsch n.d.: 19). A later version contains a short essay, offering a historico-political location and goal projection for this ethnic group, that speaks of an *Ineinandergreifen* ('interlocking'; Reichert 1985: 95) of German and Czech movements (see Pfeiffer and Weiglhofer in this volume) as signposts towards new ways of creating Europe that facilitate a revival of Sudeten German traditions in the Sudeten regions (Reichert 1985: 96). An extension of this is the emphasis by the *Sudetendeutsche Landsmannschaft* on the European credentials of the ethnic group that it represents. An early political spokesperson claimed by this group was Count Richard von Coudenhove-Kalergi, son of an Austro-Hungarian diplomat and member of the Bohemian nobility. His 1923 manifesto *Paneuropa* postulated a unified European polity and laid the foundation for the International Paneuropean Union, which describes itself as the oldest European unification movement. Coudenhove-Kalergi was the Union's key personality, and its president until his death in 1972, when he was succeeded by Otto von Habsburg. The Union has four basic principles: liberal conservatism, Christianity, social responsibility and pro-Europeanism, which it shares with the founders of the Social Market Economy model that underpinned Germany's post-war recovery.

## 13.3 Commemorating displacement

Beginning with the rally in Stuttgart on 6 August 1950, there have been regular events to commemorate the expulsion and celebrate the culture and history of the 'homeland' of the various *Landsmannschaften*. A federal *Tag der Heimat* (Homeland Day), held annually on the first Sunday of September in Berlin, is the central commemoration event involving all groups. This is followed by regional events in the state capitals. The *Tag der Heimat* events regularly feature high-ranking politicians and government representatives, giving the events an official character. 'Europe' has appeared occasionally in the motto of the *Tag der Heimat* in Berlin, for example, as a place of freedom in 1978 (*Freies Deutschland, Freies Europa*), a location of belonging in 1984 (*Heimat, Vaterland, Europa*) or European unification as the outcome of overcoming perceived injustices in 2018 (*Unrechtsdenken beseitigen – Europa zusammenführen*).

Since 2015 there is a federal Remembrance Day for the Victims of Flight and Expulsion. Motivated by concerns that the memory of displacement might lose its societal relevance as the *Erlebnisgeneration* is passing away, the proponents wanted to ensure intergenerational transmission of this 'heritage' (Deutscher Bundestag 2010). The original plan of designating 5 August, the date of the 1950 Charter, seen by the proponents as a 'milestone' on the path towards European integration and a 'foundational document' of post-war Germany, caused some controversy, and as a compromise, the day is now held on 20 June in conjunction with World Refugee Day, introduced by the UN in 2001.

The *Landsmannschaften* have continued to hold their own events, with participants more than seventy years after the end of the war still numbering tens of thousands. The events follow a similar format, usually over two or three days. Key elements are: a folklore evening; an ethnic 'village' where culinary heritage is presented along with traditional crafts, music and dance; meetings of local and district associations; a High Mass celebrated by senior clergy; and a main rally addressed by senior political figures. Federal gatherings usually also involve a conference and workshop programme. Of the three largest *Landsmannschaften*, the

*Ostpreußen* (East Prussians) hold federal gatherings every three years in varying locations. The biennial gathering of the *Schlesier* (Silesians) since the late 1970s alternates between Nuremberg and Hanover. Unlike the *Ostpreußen*, whose mottos have made no reference to Europe, the *Schlesier* have given it profile on three occasions, linking Europe with freedom in 1981 ('*Schlesien, Deutschland, Europa – in Freiheit*'), the future in 2001 ('*Schlesien im Europa der Zukunft*') and their 'homeland' in 2005 ('*Heimat Schlesien in Europa*'). The *Sudetendeutsche Tag*, which takes place annually on Pentecost weekend, differs from this quite markedly. By its seventieth anniversary in 2019, 'Europe' will have featured explicitly in 20% of its mottos, indicating the salience of the theme in internal discourse and external self-projection of the association: Beginning in 1958 ('*Heimat – Deutschland – Europa*'), 'Europe' appeared twice in the 1980s, 2000s and 2010s, and even three times in the 1970s – the decade of the *neue Ostpolitik* – and the 1990s, following the collapse of Communism.

### 13.4 Celebrating European heritage(s)?

The *Sudetendeutsche Tag* 2018 did not have 'Europe' in its actual motto, which emphasised culture and 'homeland' as foundations of peace ('*Kultur und Heimat – Fundamente des Friedens*'). Held during 18–20 May 2018, it took up about half of the Augsburg Exhibition Complex, with its 8,200-seater *Schwabenhalle* as a venue for the Pontifical Mass and main rally, two large halls filled with stalls and designated areas for the various local and regional associations, a smaller hall serving as meeting place and cinema, and the conference centre. The central yard framed by these buildings was used for outdoor activities.

The programme began in the city centre with a press conference, followed by a German–Czech symposium that did thematise Europe: '*Unsere Heimat – Kulturerbe Europas*' (Our Homeland – Europe's Cultural Heritage). It focussed on what was described as a unique culture co-created by Czechs and Germans over a millennium, which the *Landsmannschaft* wished to highlight and advance in the context of the European Year of Cultural Heritage 2018 (Sudetendeutsche Landsmannschaft 2018b: 11). By linking the gathering into a broader discourse of European heritage, the *Landsmannschaft* set the tone for the weekend and a pointer for the main rally on Sunday morning. The first day concluded with the laying of a wreath followed by a festive evening involving the award of two out of seven cultural prizes sponsored jointly by the *Landsmannschaft* and the Free State of Bavaria.

On Saturday, the action moved to the Augsburg Exhibition Complex. The tickets for the weekend came in the form of badges with the logo of the *Sudetendeutscher Tag* and covered public transport for the three days. Participants arriving at the tram and bus terminal of the Exhibition Complex were greeted by a long row of black and red *Sudetenland* flags before passing along a zig-zag line of seven flags beginning with the EU, then the Czech Republic, Germany, Austria, Bavaria, the Catholic flag and finally Augsburg. Entering through the conference centre, participants were met by a Catholic newspaper stand to the left and an information hub of the *Euregio Egrensis*, which encompasses two districts of the Czech Republic along with several districts in Bavaria and the German states of Saxony and Thuringia. A series of large display boards lined the way to the exhibition halls, showing aspects of Sudeten culture and history in a 'homeland' narrative that emphasised the role of the Sudeten Germans as 'bridge builders in Europe', and was also available as a booklet (Sudetendeutsche Landsmannschaft 2018a).

The official opening ceremony was held in the *Schwabenhalle* and included the award of the *Landsmannschaft*'s most prestigious prize, the *Europäische Karls-Preis*,[6] to Cardinal Schönborn, Archbishop of Vienna. In the afternoon, a wide array of meetings, seminars, workshops and presentations, running over five hours in up to eight parallel sessions, took place in the conference centre, the smaller hall, and the *Schwabenhalle* foyer. Meanwhile, the stalls and the 'village' in the two larger halls drew some attention, but numbers there remained small, with a few, mostly elderly participants sitting on the benches marked for particular places or regions, waiting to meet others. Several ethnic food stalls offered pastries, cured meats and other delicacies, and there were performances and showcases of traditional crafts, music and dance, as well as a book fair. Saturday concluded with a folklore evening that started with a concert in the *Schwabenhalle* and finished with a folkdance fest at the 'village'.

Sunday's proceedings opened with religious services. The Catholic Pontifical Mass, with German and Czech priests, was celebrated in the *Schwabenhalle*, a much smaller Protestant service in the conference centre's Panorama Room. After the services, there were five hours of dialect readings in the conference centre. During the break after the services, the various flag bearers and *Trachtengruppen* (groups wearing traditional dress) gathered for the main rally in the *Schwabenhalle*. This began with a parade led by a group carrying the European flag. More than forty groups filed into the hall with their flags and banners, whose bearers congregated on the stage as the others took their allocated seats. The Paneuropa-Union with their distinctive version of the European flag, showing a red cross on a yellow disk inside the circle of twelve stars, brought up the rear. Against the backdrop of this forest of flags and banners, several speakers appeared, including the new Bavarian Prime Minister, Markus Söder, ex-officio patron of the *Landsmannschaft* since the Sudeten Germans were officially declared Bavaria's 'fourth tribe' (joining the Bavarians, Franconians and Swabians) in the mid-1950s. In the course of the rally, Söder received a certificate of honorary membership from the spokesperson of the *Landsmannschaft*, Bernd Posselt.[7]

In his address, Posselt called for the right to the 'homeland' to become the foundational law of the European legal order. He emphasised Sudeten German – what he described with a single compound term as a common *böhmischmährischschlesische* (Bohemian-Moravian-Silesian) – culture as closely intertwined with Czech culture. This unique intercultural fusion, he appealed to the governments of Bavaria, Germany and the Czech Republic, ought to have protection through registration on UNESCO's Representative List of the

Intangible Cultural Heritage of Humanity. The image of Czech and Sudeten culture as 'closely intertwined' contrasts sharply with the idea, dominant in the early decades of the *Landsmannschaft*, that Sudeten identity could be defined without any reference to Czech culture (Adolf Metzner, cited in Reichert 1985: 95). A greeting from Prague, delivered by leading Czech politician Jan Bartůšek, was further evidence of gradual reconciliation between Germans and Czechs; this element has become part of the proceedings since Daniel Herman, at the time the Czech minister for culture, gave a speech in German at the 2016 event during which he expressed regret over the expulsion.

Ending the speeches, the chair of the *Sudetendeutsche Jugend*, Peter Polierer, delivered a declaration of the youth organisation, entitled *Blick in die Zukunft* ('view to the future'), that clearly was a response to tension arising from the exclusion of groups from the programme. Although *Alternative für Deutschland* (AfD) was not explicitly named, this was evidently an attempt to distance the event from right-wing populism. The declaration described culture and 'homeland', paired with decency and the will to overcome nationalisms, as fundamental for the joint construction of Europe.

The rally concluded with the anthems of Bavaria, Germany and Europe. Afterwards, the assembled groups dispersed to the other halls and various events at the conference centre. The halls were buzzing, with over 130 stalls, ranging from publishers and traditional crafts projects to political parties, tourist boards, youth organisations like the DJO and religious organisations. Meeting areas had been laid out for fourteen regions and eighty-one districts. There were many examples of initiatives for German–Czech understanding and reconciliation, such as the *Kuhländer Tanzgruppe*, a folkdance troupe founded in 1974, which since 2004 has developed a partnership with the Czech *Javorník* dance troupe, together to maintain the dance tradition of their reference region. Political organisations represented ranged from Bavaria's ruling Christian Social Union (CSU) and the Catholic social network *Ackermann-Gemeinde* to the high-profile Pan-Europa Union and the less prominent *Seliger-Gemeinde*, a Sudeten German community of traditional social democrats; notably absent were far-right groups like the *Witiko-Bund*, which used to be influential in the *Landsmannschaft* and has recently issued legal challenges against the reconciliation course the *Landsmannschaft* has embarked on under Posselt's leadership. However, overt absence did not mean that their positions were not represented. The decentralised structure of the *Landsmannschaft* meant that regional associations had their own presence. In the information material available at some of their stalls, as well as in interviews with stall staff and visitors, the *Witiko-Bund*'s particular emphasis on justice and atonement was fervently expressed: focus on 'homeland' and culture is all well and good, but without justice, it is worth nothing (e.g., interview WP3-002-SL, 20/5/18). A visiting AfD-group distributed copies of a parliamentary enquiry about 'the human rights of the German-speaking inhabitants of the Bohemian lands' (Deutscher Bundestag 2018). Despite a broad emphasis on reconciliation in the displays overall, the strength of grass-roots resistance to this direction

*Commemorating vanished 'homelands'* 199

was palpable, pointing towards tensions in the identity representation of the *Landsmannschaft*.

## 13.5 Different ways of European heritages

'Europe' has been a salient figure of internal discourse and external self-projection for the *Landsmannschaft*, which, through its youth organisation, the *Sudetendeutsche Jugend* (SdJ), has shaped the DJO significantly. As early as the *Sudetendeutscher Tag* 1963 in Stuttgart, the SdJ performed a ceremony based on a poem invoking an 'old Europe' that 'has many hearts' and 'cannot die as long as you love it'.[8] Overtly pro-European, that poem nowadays finds its way into the propaganda of far-right organisations, such as the *III. Weg* (Third Way), a party describing itself as 'national-revolutionary' and striving for a 'united Europe of free peoples', outside the EU. This emphasis on a 'Europe of free peoples' echoes the 1965 speech by SdJ- and DJO-leader Ossi Böse, noted earlier. Affirmation of a common 'European heritage' (Lähdesmäki 2016) does, it seems, not necessarily imply commitment to European unification via the EU-model. But emphasis on a 'Europe of nationalities' does not necessarily imply an anti-EU stance either.

References to, and performances of, 'European' heritage(s) reviewed here can be interpreted in terms of a relational/orientational identity model (Kockel 2010: 125f; see also Kockel et al., this volume). 'Home identities' are directed 'inward', defining individuals and groups for themselves, while public identities are directed 'outward', projecting these actors to a wider public. 'Autological' (A) and 'xenological' (X) identification conveys, respectively, insights into one's Self and one's Other(s). 'Performance' (P) identities are expressive, whereas 'heritage' (H) identities are referential. Performing, for example, a commitment to European heritage(s) autologically affirms one's identity for oneself while at the same time referring to a particular heritage perceived as shared with Others. The same performance xenologically involves an audience who may not share the same heritage(s) but appreciate the significance to the actor(s), while excluding all those deemed alien to the particular heritage(s) invoked. In promoting culture and identity in terms of heritage to further inclusion and cohesion, the EU aims at the socioculturally inclusive fields AH and XP. How well do the organisations and events described here fit those policy expectations, and what – if anything – can we learn from how the vanished homelands of the expellees are performed through physical spectacle and rhetoric and in more subtle representations of heritage?

Historical analysis and contemporary ethnographic observations indicate significant shifts as well as continuities. Most obvious has been a shift in the *Landsmannschaft*'s autological identification, where emphasis has moved from AP, which excluded the Czechs as irrelevant for a Sudeten German self-image, towards AH: an 'interlocking' identity – performed now at various levels, including, for example, the cross-cultural theatre project Čojč (see Pfeiffer and Weiglhofer, this volume) – that actually needs (some) Czech involvement (XP). To what extent this has been motivated on both sides by European funding mechanisms supporting co-operation across borders cannot be examined here, but one may ponder the significance of the two stalls lining the entrance to the *Sudetendeutscher Tag* 2018 – the *Euregio Egrensis* and the Catholic newspaper: both signal connections on grounds other than nationality.

The strength of place as a source and target of identity remains undiminished and, in some respects, appears to have grown despite the passage of time, albeit with different emphasis. This has become evident in the process leading to a relaunch of the SdJ as *SdJ-Jugend für Mitteleuropa* (Youth for Central Europe) in 2015, which followed a similar move by the DJO some forty years earlier and included an emphatic distancing from nationalistic tendencies. When the SdJ-JfM talks about the *Europeade* folkdance festivals as 'a lived Europe of the nations' (Grill 2018), it projects this idea in a different light than their 1963 ceremony. Welcoming the deletion of a controversial clause from the *Landsmannschaft's* statutes that stipulated the 'reclamation of the homeland' (*Wiedergewinnung der Heimat*), the SdJ-JfM highlighted that it had already 'reclaimed' the ancestral Sudeten homeland in novel ways, through cultural activities, political education and personal contacts with their Czech neighbours, based on human rights, tolerance and mutual respect (Sudetendeutsche Jugend 2014). The focus has shifted from the material towards a spiritual reclamation of place, which necessarily involves those who live in these places now. Such recognition of ethnic diversity, combined with a strong sense of place, based in AH and dependent on a dynamic approach to XP, is quite unlike the parallel ethnies favoured by far-right groups espousing a 'Europe of the nations' rhetoric, which remains firmly within AP and relies on clear separation of Self and Other (XH). The organisation's customary 'declaration' to the *Sudetendeutscher Tag*, which its speaker delivered at the Augsburg rally, sought to reaffirm that difference in approach to ethnicity and self-determination; it struggled, as similarly intended texts inevitably do, with the limitations of terminology (see Kockel 2012a, 2012b).

The DJO, being an umbrella organisation for different groups, has admitted associations with roots in regions other than those of historical Germans settlement since 1995, arousing a debate on why an organisation originating in the experience of German expellees should become involved with foreigners (Jelitto 2011: 19). The cultural and political engagement of these new groups have not only given a major impetus to the DJO but challenged notions of 'German Youth in Europe'. Its current leader, Hetav Tek, comes from KOMCIWAN, a Kurdish youth organisation, and is also deputy chair of the federal youth organisation *Bundesjugendring*, which in the 1960s and 1970s had sought to exclude the DJO for its right-wing public image (Becker 2002). At the sixtieth anniversary celebrations of the DJO on Castle Ludwigstein in 2011, members in traditional costumes from Pommerania (formerly northeast Germany) joined with Syrian refugees in Middle Eastern folkdances.

## 13.6 Heimat Europa?

Like the DJO (Kockel 2015a: 331f.), both the *Landsmannschaft* and the SdJ have always comprised elements of a very broad spectrum of political orientations. Further research needs to address issues including the appropriation of place, beliefs and practices of belonging and patterns and processes of experiencing what some describe as a *Heimat Europa* (Kockel 2010: 173f.). What exactly did phrases like 'right to *Heimat*', which appears in the 1950 Charter, mean for actors then, and what do they mean now? How does a *Volksgruppe* (ethnic group) constitute itself beyond the loci of its longing (*Sehnsuchtsorte*)? Why were such cultural ascriptions societally relevant then, and in what ways, if at all, are they now? Navigating politically charged terminology to get to the bottom of these issues makes such inquiry exceedingly difficult in the face of a resurgent right-wing populism.

In November 2013, a workshop of the SdJ in Bad Kissingen discussed the contemporary meaning of *Volksgruppe*, asking what the label *sudetendeutsch* might signify in the third or fourth generation. One issue was the ownership of memories that make a place 'home' – whose *Heimat* is where, why and how? Individuals interviewed tend to emphasise the local rather than the regional or national (see also Nic Craith 2012); consequently, a 'homeland Europe' may be built by local interactions like the *Kuhländer/Javorník* dance collaborative, facilitating the restoration of traditions that Reichert (1985: 96) called for. 'Traditions' in place need not be limited to folk culture in the narrow sense of the term. The political tradition of the *Seliger-Gemeinde*, or the religious one of the *Ackermann-Gemeinde*, point beyond the rural bias of 'folk' imagery.

'Europe' appears in all these performances more in the convivial 'multi-cultural' version championed by the Paneuropa-Union, which resembles the loosely structured Holy Roman Empire rather than today's EU. When the *Landsmannschaft* (2015: 7) points to the special position the Bohemian Lands occupied in that supranational federation, one may wonder whether this fits more with the vision, espoused by the *Landsmannschaft* leadership, of Czech and Sudeten culture as 'closely intertwined' or with the emphasis on parallel coexistence by far-right groups, who in this context, however, see German culture as superior to the Czech. While superficially similar, the latter vision tends to be irredentist, territorial, whereas the former leans more towards a trajectorial perspective (see Kockel 2010). Developing a viable vision of Europe may require a search for tracks and traces allowing reflexive historicisation of such cultural trajectories.

## Acknowledgement

This publication is a result of the European Union-funded Horizon 2020 research project: CoHERE (Critical Heritages: performing and representing identities in Europe). CoHERE received funding from the European Union's Horizon 2020 research and innovation programme under grant agreement No. 693289.

## Notes

1 The term 'homeland' insufficiently captures the resonances of *Heimat*; for a detailed discussion, see Kockel (2010, 2012a, 2012b).
2 Common usage in Germany employs either 'expellees' or 'refugees' to designate the different experiences of Germans leaving Central and Eastern Europe after 1944; while 'expellees' remains more controversial, the distinction is not important for this chapter. Czech usage of 'migration', or of the Potsdam Agreement's term 'transfer', in this context (see Pfeiffer and Weiglhofer, this volume) remains equally controversial.
3 These frontier regions have recently engaged in interesting explorations of cultural memory, for example, through museum exhibitions (see, e.g., Kockel 2015b).
4 For an early critique of this ethnological paradigm, see Weber-Kellermann (1959).
5 *Fahrten* were a cultural practice characteristic of the German Youth Movement in the early decades of the twentieth century, with which many of the expellee youth organisations sought to align themselves.
6 The prize, named after the Bohemian king and German emperor Charles IV, is awarded for services to understanding and co-operation between the peoples and countries of Central Europe.
7 The close relationship between the *Landsmannschaft* and the Bavarian state through its main political party, the CSU, must be noted but cannot be further explored here.
8 Attributed to 'George Forestier', who enjoyed a brief spell of fame in the early 1950s, explained by later critics in terms of the contemporary attractiveness of his entirely fictional biography, construed by the real author, Karl Emerich Krämer; the deeper significance of this cannot be explored here.

## References

Becker, J. (2002), *Zuwanderung – Jugendverbandsarbeit – Integration: 'Wir woll(t)en Brücke sein!' 50 Jahre DJO-Deutsche Jugend in Europa* (Berlin: DJO).
Beer, M. (2011), *Flucht und Vertreibung der Deutschen: Voraussetzungen, Verlauf, Folgen* (München: Beck).
Braun, K. (2015), *Der Wunsiedler Friedhof und andere Grenzgeschichten* (Wien: Sonnberg).
Bugge, P. (2002), 'The nation supreme: the idea of Europe 1914–1945', in K. Wilson and J. van der Dussen (eds), *The history of the idea of Europe* (London: Routledge), 83–149.
Delanty, G. (1995), *Inventing Europe. Idea, identity, reality* (London: Palgrave Macmillan).
Deutscher Bundestag (2018), Drucksache 19/2214 vom 17.05.2018: 1–2.
Deutscher Bundestag (2010), Drucksache 17/4193 vom 15.12.2010: 2–3.
Di Cesari, C. and A. Kaya eds (2019), *European memory in populism: representations of self and other* (London: Routledge).
Franzen, E. (2010), *Der vierte Stamm Bayerns: Die Schirmherrschaft über die Sudetendeutschen 1954–1974* (Munich: Oldenbourg).
Franzen, E. (2008), 'Der Diskurs als Ziel? Anmerkungen zur deutschen Erinnerungspolitik am Beispiel der Debatte um ein "Zentrum gegen Vertreibungen" 1999–2005', in P. Haslinger, E. Franzen and M. Schulze Wessel (eds), *Diskurse über Zwangsmigrationen in Zentraleuropa: Geschichtspolitik, Fachdebatten, literarisches und lokales erinnern seit 1989* (München: Oldenbourg), 1–29.
Frevert, U. (2003), *Eurovisionen. Ansichten guter Europäer im 19. und 20. Jahrhundert* (Frankfurt am Main: Fischer).
Giordano, R. (1997), *Ostpreußen adé*. 3rd ed. (Cologne: KiWi).

Grill, R. (2018), Ein Gelebtes Europa Der Nationen. Available at: http://sdj-online.de/?p=598 (accessed 29 December 2018).

Hahn, E. and H. Hahn (2010), *Die Vertreibung im deutschen Erinnern: Legenden, Mythos, Geschichte* (Paderborn: Schöningh).

Hamel, A. (2017), 'Von der *Deutschen Jugend des Ostens* zur *Deutschen Jugend in Europa*—Selbstverständnis, Organisation und Interessenpolitik junger "(Heimat)-Vertriebener" im Spiegel gesellschaftlicher Umbrüche 1951–1974', in E. Fendl, W. Mezger, S. Paredes Zavala, M. Prosser-Schell, H.-W. Retterath and S. Scholl-Schneider (eds), *Bewegte Jugend im östlichen Europa. Volkskundliche Perspektiven auf unterschiedliche Ausprägungen der Jugendbewegung seit dem ausgehenden 19. Jahrhundert* (Münster: Waxmann), 73–100.

Jelitto, F. (2011), 'Integration—eine Erfolgsgeschichte in der djo-Deutsche Jugend in Europa?', *Pfeil* 2: 19–20.

Kaelble, H. (2001): *Europäer über Europa. Die Entstehung des europäischen Selbstverständnisses im 19. und 20. Jahrhundert* (Frankfurt am Main: Campus).

Kaya, A. (2017), 'The rise of populist extremism in Europe: lost in diversity and unity', *CoHERE Critical Archive*. Available at: http://digitalcultures.ncl.ac.uk/cohere/wordpress/wp-content/uploads/2017/01/WP-2-Kaya-Critical-Analysis-Tool-2.pdf (accessed 20 February 2019).

Kockel, U. (2015a), 'Die DEUTSCHE JUGEND DES OSTENS und die Burg Ludwigstein (1951–1975)', in S. Rappe-Weber and E. Conze (eds), *Ludwigstein – Annäherungen an die Geschichte der Burg* (Göttingen: Vandenhoeck & Ruprecht), 313–333.

Kockel, U. (2015b), 'Re-placing Europe: an ethnological perspective on frontiers and migrants', in C. Whitehead, K. Lloyd, S. Eckersley and R. Mason (eds), *Museums, place and identity in Europe* (Aldershot: Ashgate), 81–100.

Kockel, U. (2012a), 'Toward an ethnoecology of place and displacement', in U. Kockel, M. Nic Craith and J. Frykman (eds), *A companion to the anthropology of Europe* (Oxford: Blackwell), 551–571.

Kockel, U. (2012b), 'Being from and coming to: outline of an ethno-ecological framework', in L. Williams, R. Roberts and A. McIntosh (eds), *Radical human ecology: intercultural and indigenous approaches* (Aldershot: Ashgate), 57–71.

Kockel, U. (2010), *Re-visioning Europe: Frontiers, place identities and journeys in debatable lands* (Basingstoke: Palgrave).

Kołacki, J. (1988), 'Die Kultur im Programm und der Praxis der "DJO-Deutsche Jugend in Europa" 1974–1987', *Polnische Weststudien* 7(1): 77–94.

Kølvraa, C. (2015), 'European fantasies: on the EU's political myths and the affective potential of utopian imaginaries for European identity', *JCMS: Journal of Common Market Studies*, 54(1): 169–184.

Kossert, A. (2009), *Kalte Heimat: Die Geschichte der deutschen Vertriebenen nach 1945* (München: Pantheon).

Lähdesmäki, T. (2016), 'Politics of tangibility, intangibility, and place in the making of a European cultural heritage in EU heritage policy', *International Journal of Heritage Studies* 22(10): 766–780.

Lehmann, A. (1991), *Im Fremden ungewollt zuhaus. Flüchtlinge und Vertriebene in Westdeutschland 1945–1990* (München: Beck).

Lotz, C. (2007), *Die Deutung des Verlusts. Erinnerungspolitische Kontroversen im geteilten Deutschland um Flucht, Vertreibung und die Ostgebiete (1948–1972)* (Cologne: Böhlau).

Müßigbrodt, H. (2011), 'Immer mehr leisten müssen', *Pfeil* 2: 13–15.

Nic Craith, M. (2012), *Narratives of place, belonging and language: an intercultural perspective* (Basingstoke: Palgrave).

Nitsch, R. ed. (n.d.), *Sudetenland*. Ostkundliche Studie für Schulen und Jugendgruppen. (München: DJO/SdJ).
Niven, B. (ed.) (2006), *Germans as victims: remembering the past in contemporary Germany* (Basingstoke: Palgrave).
Piskorski, J. (2015), *Die Verjagten: Flucht und Vertreibung im Europa des 20. Jahrhunderts* (München: Pantheon).
Reichert, G. (1985), 'Historisch-politische Standortbestimmung und Zielprojektion für die sudetendeutsche Volksgruppe', in R. Schmutzer (ed.), *Die Sudetendeutschen: Vergangenheit und Gegenwart. Sonderheft 10 von "unser arbeitsbrief"* (Munich: SdJ/DJO), 94–96.
Sachers, B. (n.d.), *Die Deutsche Jugend des Ostens* (Bonn: Selbstverlag).
Schmitz, H. ed. (2007): *A nation of victims? Representations of German wartime suffering from 1945 to the present* (Amsterdam: Rodopi).
Schmutzer, R. ed. (1985), *Die Sudetendeutschen: Vergangenheit und Gegenwart*. (München: SDJ/DJO).
Stickler, M. (2004), *'Ostdeutsch heißt Gesamtdeutsch'. Organisation, Selbstverständnis und heimatpolitische Zielsetzungen der deutschen Vertriebenenverbände 1949–1972* (Düsseldorf: Droste).
Sudetendeutsche Jugend (2014), Änderung Der Satzung Der Sudetendeutschen Landsmannschaft. Available at: http://sdj-online.de/?cat=12 (accessed 31 December 2018).
Sudetendeutsche Landsmannschaft (2018a), *Die Sudetendeutschen: Unsere Geschichte. Unsere Kultur. Unser Leben. Heimat* (Munich: Sudetendeutsche Landsmannschaft Bundesverband).
Sudetendeutsche Landsmannschaft (2018b), *Sudetendeutscher Tag: Festführer* (Munich: Sudetendeutsche Landsmannschaft Bundesverband).
Sudetendeutsche Landsmannschaft (2015), *Grundsatzerklärung der Sudetendeutschen Landsmannschaft Bundesverband e.V.* (Munich: Sudetendeutsche Landsmannschaft Bundesverband).
Weber-Kellermann, I. (1959), 'Zur Frage der interethnischen Beziehungen in der "Sprachinselvolkskunde"', *Österreichische Zeitschrift für Volkskunde* 62: 19–47.

# 14 Afterword

Festival as heritage / heritage as festival

*Valdimar Tr. Hafstein*

Heritage festivals and festival heritage: this volume brings into focus the nexus of cultural heritage and the festival. Its key concern are practices of heritage making, and central to its chapters is the concept of intangible heritage, a concept brought into being and set to work in the world through UNESCO's 2003 Convention for the Safeguarding of the Intangible Cultural Heritage. The festival, I will argue, is central to the implementation of this convention and gives, moreover, a clue to the larger social and cultural currents to which the concept and convention belong.

A critical, comparative approach to the implementation of the Intangible Heritage Convention brings to light the dominance of certain expressive genres in the activities called safeguarding: lists, competitions, prizes, documentaries and especially the festival. It is not just that traditional festivals are heritagised, though (as the chapters in this edited volume make clear) that happens on a wide scale, and, we may add, ethnologists, folklorists, and anthropologists take an active part in that process (Leal 2016). More important still, as one part of their safeguarding, practices and expressions framed as intangible heritage are festivalised.

From Konjic woodcarving in Bosnia and Herzegovina to Chapei musical traditions in Cambodia, and from dolma making and sharing in Azerbaijan to whistled language in Turkey – to pick four recent examples from UNESCO's Representative List of the Intangible Cultural Heritage – safeguarding traditional practices as intangible heritage involves creating festivals dedicated to them. In order to safeguard its woodcarving traditions, 'the Konjic Municipality has initiated a festival titled "*Dani konjičkog rezbarstva*" (Konjic Woodcarving Days), published brochures about the element and provided support for the training of young woodcarvers', according to the Bosnian nomination form for this practice, inscribed on the Representative List in 2017 (Nomination file no. 01288).

Cambodia's successful nomination of Chapei Dang Veng to UNESCO's List of Intangible Cultural Heritage in Need of Urgent Safeguarding notes that traditionally Chapei is performed at various ceremonies and festivals. As an instrument for safeguarding this musical tradition, Cambodia proposes to invert this relationship by creating an annual Chapei festival as 'a platform to promote and celebrate' the music and to 'allow emerging artists to perform for live audiences and increase the profile of Chapei across Cambodia'. To establish the festival, the Cambodian state asks for support from UNESCO's ICH fund in the order of $43,170 (Nomination file no. 01165).

Likewise, the dolma culinary tradition is widespread throughout the Mediterranean and the Caucasus into Central Asia, and as festive food, it is associated with a variety of ceremonies, rituals, holidays, weddings and festive events. In 2017, the convention's executive committee inscribed Azerbaijani 'Dolma making and sharing tradition, a marker of cultural identity' onto the Representative List in exchange for a commitment from Azerbaijan's government to 'promote holding local and national festivals and contests among experienced dolma practitioners' and following up the First Dolma Festival held in 2016 with a second edition in 2018 with 'special focus on diversity of dolma communities' (Nomination file no. 01188).

That same year, Turkey secured international support for the urgent safeguarding of whistled language: a linguistic system developed for communication across long distances in steep and rugged mountains in Turkey's Eastern Black Sea Region. In its nomination file, Turkish authorities cite the annual bird language festival as a mechanism for its safeguarding, 'held by Bird Language Sustenance Culture and Tourism Association' since 1997 in the village of Kuşköy 'where there is strong awareness of the fact that this language should be safeguarded and maintained before it disappears'. 'The aim of the Festival, which is attended by local communities, the bearers of this cultural legacy and local and foreign tourists and is supported by both local and national government, is to keep interest in the whistled language alive at local, national and international level' (Nomination file no. 00658).

To a man with a hammer, everything looks like a nail. From craft to music and from food to language, intangible heritage brings festivals into being (Hafstein 2018). The examples could easily be multiplied by nearly a random selection from UNESCO's lists or indeed from national inventories of intangible heritage. Nor is this a recent trend: the same holds true for the very first practices and expressions inscribed. Thus the safeguarding of traditional arts and practices in the cultural space of the Jemaa el-Fna marketplace in Marrakech, Morocco, involved as a first step the creation of festivals. Indeed, the festival as a genre of display is so closely associated with intangible heritage that in Malawi new festivals are now dedicated to celebrating Vimbuza – an illness and a medical practice for its treatment – Malawi's first contribution to UNESCO's lists. By means of traditional rituals, Vimbuza healers diagnose and treat spirit-related illnesses resulting from spirit possession. The healing dance is one of its principal therapeutic rites and now the subject of safeguarding through the festival genre. No one finds this more perplexing than many of the Vimbuza healers with whom folklorist Lisa Gilman did fieldwork, who are 'especially critical of the idea of a Vimbuza festival … or other occasions where Vimbuza is performed outside of the ritual context, because these displays strip it of its significance' (Gilman 2015: 208).

To understand what is going on, it is helpful to place the heritagisation process of recent years in the context of the festivalisation process of the same period. It is an oft-commented fact that the number of festivals worldwide has grown exponentially (Laville 2014; Négrier 2015; Boissevain 1992: 1–19). Especially since the 1980s and 1990s, cultural festivals have moved beyond the arts to festivalise a miscellany of expressions, practices and identities, from pastries to pétanque, from costumes to crafts, from fishing to rituals and from ethnicity to locality, moving out from the institutionalized arts to the domain nowadays increasingly referred to as the intangible heritage (cf. Ronström 2016).

At the same time as new festivals emerge, existing festivals are marketed to tourists; indeed, festivals have always attracted the attention of travellers. As folklorist Roger D. Abrahams remarked, festivals are occasions for the festive community to show off: 'resounding times and elaborated places for excited exchange, for bringing out, passing around, for giving and receiving the most vital emblems of culture in an unashamed display of produce, of the plenitude the community may boast, precisely so that the community may boast' (Abrahams 1982: 161). Festivals are 'geared toward deliberate display' (Picard and Robinson 2006: 2), offering a 'boastful' reflection of the community to locals and visitors alike. As David Picard and Mike Robinson observe, festivals 'draw our attention as participants, tourists and scholars precisely because they provide moments of time and space to reflect upon our being in the world and questions of collective meaning and belonging' (Picard and Robinson 2006: 26).

In this light, the surge in festivals in general and the festivalisation of intangible heritage in particular may be understood in the context of reflexive modernisation (Beck, Giddens and Lash 1994) as modern technology for dealing with the consequences of modernity (Kockel and Nic Craith 2007): economic (providing financial incentive in the festival context for arts, crafts and activities that have lost their former economic basis), social (forging a sense of community in times when its dissolution is commonly decried) and political (staking claims on the allegiance of participants and showing off to neighbouring cities/towns/villages).

Like heritage itself, festivals are tasked with turning place into meaningful location and defining its uniqueness as a destination (Kirshenblatt-Gimblett 1998), for inhabitants and visitors alike. In the words of Richard Bauman: 'They are cultural forms about culture, social forms about society, in which the central meanings and values of a group are embodied, acted out, and laid open to examination and interpretation in symbolic form, both by members of that group and by the ethnographer' (Bauman 1986: 133). Thus, festivals nowadays help to stage modern societies' reflexive awareness of themselves while reforming the relationship of people to their own culture and to themselves as a social collective. When festivals come under the sign of intangible heritage, they fit like a glove on the hand of the safeguarding project. While distinct, the contemporary processes of heritagisation and festivalisation can therefore work in tandem, each assisting in and accelerating the other.

The proliferation of festivals and the proliferation of heritage since the 1980s are thus interlinked expressions of the same social, economic and cultural conditions, two overlapping results of the same forces at work (cf. Ronström 2016: 72). We could invoke in this context all the usual shorthand expressions, or buzzwords, that we throw around to describe macro-trends and forces in contemporary societies: from globalization to neo-liberalization or from the post-industrial society of services, tourism and the spectacle to governmentality, responsibilisation and identity politics. I do not think we would be wrong to invoke any of these, though admittedly we would not be very specific. But as an ethnologist, I would suggest we look again in another direction: our own.

In an article on the ethnologisation of Provence, Laurent Sébastien Fournier describes 'a slow sedimentation of ethnological knowledge that winds up influencing both how local populations look at their own culture and how they define it to those people (temporary and permanent residents) who discover it' (Fournier 2016: 2; my translation). According to Fournier, 'the 1970s marked the beginning of a new wave of ethnologisation', in which ethnologists, folklorists, anthropologists and their students 'take more and more part in administering local cultural projects, which in turn breaths new energy and meaning into the field' (Fournier 2016: 10–11; my translation).

Fournier's insight extends far beyond Provence, of course. This 'ethnologisation' of the public sphere also extends well beyond the work of people trained in ethnology, folklore or anthropology. We are witness in the past decades to an incredible success: the success of our field of knowledge (broadly defined) in shaping contemporary society's reflexive understanding of itself. It is, however, an uneven success; the perspectives, the craft and the vocabularies of ethnologists suffuse society, but often without the critical edge; reflexivity is rallied to the causes of celebration and marketing more often than it serves to strengthen critical awareness and promote change (cf. Köstlin 1997, 1999; Mugnaini 2016).

Heritagisation is an aspect of this infusion of ethnological knowledge, perspectives and concepts into the public sphere where they shape the public's understanding of and relation to expressive culture and social practices, and indeed reform those expressions and practices as part of society's reflexive modernisation. In the context of intangible heritage, such reform is referred to as safeguarding. As a genre of display characteristic of intangible heritage, the festival provides a stage for performing this reflexive modernity. Ethnologists, folklorists, anthropologists, heritage professionals and cultural administrators co-author the script and help set the stage. Indeed, by developing and communicating knowledge of heritage and festivals in Europe, this volume is a critical contribution to that script.

## References

Abrahams, R. (1982), 'The language of festivals: celebrating the economy', in V. Turner (ed.), *Celebration: studies in festivity and ritual* (Washington, DC: Smithsonian), 161–177.

Bauman, R. (1986), 'Performance and honor in 13th-century Iceland', *Journal of American Folklore* 99(392): 131–150.

Beck, U., A. Giddens and S. Lash (1994), *Reflexive modernization: politics, tradition and aesthetics in the modern social order* (Cambridge: Polity).

Boissevain, J. (1992), *Revitalizing European rituals* (London: Routledge).

Fournier, L. (2016), 'Un terrain à histoire', *Espaces Temps. Revue indisciplinaire de sciences sociales*. Available at: www.espacestemps.net/articles/un-terrain-a-histoire/ (accessed 18 March 2017).

Gilman, L. (2015), 'Demonic or cultural treasure? Local perspectives on Vimbuza, intangible cultural heritage, and UNESCO in Malawi', *Journal of Folklore Research* 52(2/3): 199–216.

Hafstein, V. (2018), *Making intangible heritage. El condor pasa and other stories from UNESCO* (Bloomington: Indiana University Press).

Kirshenblatt-Gimblett, B. (1998), *Destination culture: tourism, museums, and heritage* (Berkeley, Los Angeles, London: University of California Press).

Kockel, U. and M. Nic Craith, eds (2007), *Cultural heritages as reflexive traditions* (Hampshire: Palgrave Macmillan).

Köstlin, K. (1999), On the brink of the next century: the necessary invention of the present, *Journal of Folklore Research* 36(2/3): 289–298.

Köstlin, K. (1997), 'The passion for the whole: interpreted modernity or modernity as interpretation', *Journal of American Folklore* 110(437): 260–276.

Laville, Y. (2014), 'Festivalisation? Esquisse d'un phénomène et bilan critique', *Cahiers d'ethnomusicologie* 27: 11–25.

Leal, J. (2016), 'Festivals, group making, remaking and unmaking', *Ethnos: Journal of Anthropology* 81(4): 584–599.

Mugnaini, F. (2016), 'The haunted discipline: on the political nature of folklore and the political destiny of its study', *Narodna Umjetnost* 53(1): 15–41.

Négrier, E. (2015), 'Festivalisation: patterns and limits', in C. Newbold, J. Jordan, F. Bianchini and C. Maughan (eds), *Focus on festivals: contemporary european case studies and perspectives* (Oxford: Goodfellow), 18–27.

'Nomination file no. 00658 for inscription in 2017 on the List of Intangible Cultural Heritage in Need of Urgent Safeguarding.' United Nations Educational, Scientific and Cultural Organization. Convention for the Safeguarding of the Intangible Cultural Heritage. Intergovernmental Committee for the Safeguarding of the Intangible Cultural Heritage. Twelfth session, Jeju Island, Republic of Korea, 4 to 8 December 2017. Available at: https://ich.unesco.org/doc/download.php?versionID=43730 (accessed 10 January 2019).

'Nomination file no. 01165 for inscription in 2016 on the List of Intangible Cultural Heritage in Need of Urgent Safeguarding with International Assistance from the Intangible Cultural Heritage Fund.' United Nations Educational, Scientific and Cultural Organization. Convention for the Safeguarding of the Intangible Cultural Heritage. Intergovernmental Committee for the Safeguarding of the Intangible Cultural Heritage. Eleventh session, Addis-Ababa, Ethiopia, 28 November to 2 December 2016. Available at: https://ich.unesco.org/doc/download.php?versionID=40551 (accessed 10 January 2019).

'Nomination file no. 01188 for inscription in 2017 on the Representative List of the Intangible Cultural Heritage of Humanity.' United Nations Educational, Scientific and Cultural Organization. Convention for the Safeguarding of the Intangible Cultural Heritage. Intergovernmental Committee for the Safeguarding of the Intangible Cultural Heritage. Twelfth session, Jeju Island, Republic of Korea, 4 to 8 December 2017. Available at: https://ich.unesco.org/doc/download.php?versionID=43884 (accessed 10 January 2019).

'Nomination file no. 01288 for inscription in 2017 on the Representative List of the Intangible Cultural Heritage of Humanity.' United Nations Educational, Scientific and Cultural Organization. Convention for the Safeguarding of the Intangible Cultural Heritage. Intergovernmental Committee for the Safeguarding of the Intangible Cultural Heritage. Twelfth session, Jeju Island, Republic of Korea, 4 to 8 December 2017. Available at: https://ich.unesco.org/doc/download.php?versionID=43673 (accessed 10 January 2019).

Picard, D. and M. Robinson (2006), *Festivals, tourism and social change: remaking worlds* (Bristol: ChannelView Publications).

Ronström, O. (2016), 'Four facets of festivalisation', *Puls: Musik- och dansetnologisk tidskrift/ Journal for Ethnomusicology and Ethnochoreology* 1: 67–83.

# Index

actors 6, 83, 95–97, 99, 100, 102–107, 173, 199, 201
agency 5, 10, 23f., 26, 56f., 178
Apennines 81
audience 3, 6f., 19–21, 23, 25f., 33f., 53, 96, 98, 129, 133, 135, 137, 139, 150f., 174f., 179, 182–185, 199, 206; interaction between audience and performers 19–21; *see also* communication, spectator
authenticity 5, 7, 21, 23–25, 33, 81, 84f., 87–89, 152
Authorised Heritage Discourse 21, 24, 47, 83

Baltic States 4, 29–43
banner group 112f., 120, 124
banners 111, 113–121, 123f.
Barcelona 82
Bavaria 11, 174, 180, 190, 196–198
Belgium 8, 96f., 99, 104, 173
belonging 4f., 10, 21, 23f., 26, 29, 31f., 37, 40, 47–49, 51, 52–53, 55–59, 81, 89–91, 113, 119, 128f., 131, 136, 138f., 144, 152f., 157, 159, 167, 195, 201, 207; social 81, 89–91; *see also* identity
Berga 81
*Billy Elliott* (film) 121
Black Sea 206
Bohemia 11, 82, 174, 180, 195, 197, 198, 201, 202n6
Bosnia and Herzegovina 205
Brexit 7, 9, 11, 50, 136f.
Brittany 96, 100–104
Bulgaria 10, 156, 161, 164
Burns, Robert 142–144, 147f., 154, 155

Cappadox 5, 63–78
carnival 5, 27n2, 51, 81–82, 84–86, 88, 90–91, 100, 119

Castelnuovo al Volturno 81, 84–88, 90
Catalonia 7, 81f.
Catholic(s) 11, 174, 177, 196–198, 200
celebration 4, 29–33, 36–43, 50, 52, 54, 117, 124, 147, 150, 151, 157f., 173, 183, 194, 200, 208; *see also* Song and Dance Celebration, SDC
Central Europe 11, 191, 200
CoHERE 9, 38, 42, 185n8
*Čojč Theaternetzwerk Böhmen Bayern* 174–175, 180–184
colonialism 162, 164
commercialisation 2, 84, 88
commodification 2, 4, 56, 84–86, 88–89, 134
common European heritage 1, 12
communication 3, 19–21, 23, 26, 30, 33–37, 42f., 74, 96, 99, 102, 104, 105, 107, 122, 134, 175, 206
Communism 82, 191, 196
Communitas 48, 49, 53, 55–57
community/communities 19, 21, 29, 39–43, 47, 48, 49, 53, 55–57, 60, 69, 72, 74, 79, 80, 82, 84, 86f., 89–91, 99, 101–103, 105, 106, 110, 112–116, 119–125
Convention for the Safeguarding of the Intangible Cultural Heritage 3, 13, 59, 205
Council of Europe 12, 29, 47, 51, 58, 159
crafts 3, 31, 32, 36, 102, 133, 167, 195, 197, 198, 207
cultural identity 31, 33, 36, 68, 73, 164, 174, 179, 180, 184, 192, 206; heterogeneous 176–180; hybrid 180, 184
culture as a resource 1, 2, 5, 10, 30, 35, 39, 90, 95f., 107, 123f., 132, 161, 185
Czech Republic 7, 82, 87, 174, 180–185, 189, 192, 194, 196–201
Czechoslovakia 82, 189

## Index

dance 22, 26, 29–46, 49, 52–54, 55, 57, 82, 96, 100, 201
discourse 83, 89f., 156f., 160f., 164, 167, 169, 170–172; Discourse Historical Approach (DHA) 160f.
DJO (Deutsche Jugend des Ostens) 8, 188–201
Dolma Festival 206
Durham Miners' Gala 8, 110–127

Edinburgh Fringe Festival 150
England 8, 9, 110, 141, 142, 144, 145, 146
Enlightenment 145f., 154
Estonia 29–32, 35, 37–39, 41–46
Europe 8–11, 79–80, 82, 84, 87–88, 90–91, 107, 156–160, 164–172; European dimension 157, 164–165, 167, 169, 170; European exceptionalism 83; European heritage 1, 6, 9, 11f., 31, 74, 132, 139, 141, 153, 156–160, 166, 169, 189, 192, 196, 199; European identity 1, 3, 8f., 29, 90f., 131, 137f., 153, 158f., 166, 188; European spirit 3, 11, 189, 192f.; Europeanness 156–161, 164–166, 169
European Capital of Culture xvii, 8, 9, 10, 156–172
European Charter for Regional or Minority Languages 58, 143
European Commission 13, 38, 157
European Union 4, 12f., 29, 34, 40, 49, 55, 138f., 152, 156f., 175, 191
expellees 4, 11, 188–204

Faro Convention 13, 51, 58
Fest-noz 8, 96, 100–105
folk oratorio 9–10, 12
folklore 50–60, 63–75, 79, 83, 85
France 8, 95–106
French Revolution 144, 147f., 155

Galway 10, 156, 160f., 163–170, 172
German Youth in Europe 11, 188, 200; see also DJO
German Youth of the East 11, 190; see also DJO
Germany xvii, 146, 181f., 188–204
Giants and Dragons 8, 96f., 100, 104, 105

Henderson, Hamish 2, 136, 141, 149–151, 154
heritage 29–31, 35–37, 39, 40, 43, 47–50, 52–55, 57–59, 63–75, 112, 119–121, 124f., 156–160, 162, 164, 166–167, 169–172; boom 2, 106; community 'heritage from below' 48–50, 52, 59; contested 176, 179, 184; discontents 89–91; ethnic 48–50; European 156–158, 160, 166, 169–171; futures 2; incongruous 116, 117, 119; policy 12; shared 181, 184
heritagisation 113, 117, 124, 208
Hlinsko v Čechách 82–83, 85–88
Hogmanay 151f.
Horizon 2020 38, 42
Humbolt, Alexander von 146

identity 5–8, 21, 23, 26, 47–49, 51, 54, 56–58, 79–81, 83, 89–91, 96, 99, 105, 106, 107, 119, 120, 122, 123, 158f., 161, 164, 166f., 169–172; autological 6–7; construction 80, 89, 91; European 1, 3, 8f., 29, 90f., 131, 137f., 153, 158f., 166, 188; home 6–7; national 29, 31, 33f., 36, 44; nested 80; as processual 6; public 6–7; xenological 6–7; see also belonging
Ireland 10, 141, 156, 161, 163, 165; Northern 8, 174; see also Northern Ireland
Iron Curtain 11, 180–184
Italy 7, 73

Jews 52, 168, 182

landscape 9, 32, 36, 48, 50, 53, 55, 64, 111, 115, 118–120, 125, 138, 162, 165, 166
language 3, 10, 22ff., 32, 34–37, 58, 70, 83, 102, 137, 141–155, 156, 159, 165ff., 173, 205f.; as vehicle of ICH 3, 141–155, 173, 180, 184
Latvia 9, 29–35, 37–42, 44, 46
liminality 18–20, 24, 26, 47f., 56f.
Lithuania 29–32, 35, 38–46.
locality, social construction of 81, 84, 88, 90–91

MacDiarmid, Hugh 148f., 154
Malta 10, 161–163, 165, 168
*Masopust* (carnival) 82, 88
Masterpieces of the Oral and Intangible Heritage of Humanity 4, 30, 97
memory 1, 22, 23, 37, 72, 73, 79, 80, 85, 110–127, 142, 160, 161, 174, 184, 191, 195; Memory of the World 144; see also Theatre of Witness

Mercouri, Melina 157
migration 2, 47, 86, 119, 165f., 180, 182f.
*Mitteleuropa* 11; *see also* Central Europe
musealisation 79, 84–85, 88–89
museum 21, 88, 89, 95, 96, 99, 115, 125, 139, 167, 174

narrative 10, 11, 21, 23–25, 37, 50, 88f., 91, 114, 117, 119, 122, 142, 146f., 152, 160f., 173–175, 183–185, 197; social 85, 89
nation-branding 29, 30, 33–37, 40–44
Northern Ireland 8, 174; reconciliation 174–175
nostalgia 5, 63–78, 184

performance 48f., 51–57, 59, 96, 97, 99, 106, 124, 125; as communication 19–21, 23–26; efficacy of 20; as embodied practice 21–22, 24; ephemerality of 22; functions of 21–23; importance of location 19, 24; liminality of 19–20, 24, 26; meanings of 18–21; performative practice 29–32, 36, 43–44; research 18, 25–26; transformation 20
Plovdiv 10, 156, 160–161, 164–169, 171
Poland xviii, 141, 143, 190, 193
*Proetnica* 4, 48–50, 52, 54f., 57f.
Protestant(s) 11, 174, 177, 197
Provence 208

religion 83f., 95, 145, 146
ritual 2, 3, 7, 8, 18, 20, 24, 26, 27n2, 29, 37, 48, 50, 55–57, 79, 81f., 84–91, 95–97, 107, 123, 146, 206f.
*Rivers of Our Being* 9
Romania 4, 47–50, 54f., 58f.

Scotland 9, 13, 43, 47f., 50, 53, 135, 141–155
Scots (language) 10, 141–155
Scott, Sir Walter 143, 155
SDC *see* Song and Dance Celebration
Shetland 48, 50–57
Slovakia 82, 129, 173; *see also* Czechoslovakia

Solsona 81–82, 84, 86–88, 90
Song and Dance Celebration 4, 29–31, 33, 36–43
Spain 81, 130, 173
spectator 19, 21, 23; *see also* audience
storytelling 11; as collaborative art form 175; forms of 173; as ICH 173, 179; social encounter 174–175, 178
Sudeten German(s) 8, 11, 188–204
*Sudetenland* 174, 183, 189, 191f., 196
sustainability 2, 5, 13, 37, 41, 43, 47, 52, 57, 59, 74, 124f., 169
symbol/symbolism: 81, 83–84, 86, 90; symbolic capital 84; symbolic density/depth 81, 85, 91

theatre 11; applied 174; bilingual 174, 181, 184; as collaborative endeavour 175; forms of 173; as ICH 173; social encounter 174–175, 180–181
Theatre of Witness 175–180
tourism 2, 4, 5, 13, 35, 47, 49f., 52f., 55, 57, 65f., 74, 80–91, 95, 97, 107, 163, 167f., 206, 208
tradition(s) 2, 3, 7, 9f., 12f., 21, 23–26, 29f., 35–40, 51f., 56, 69, 72, 79, 84, 86f., 97, 99, 102, 106, 128f., 131–135, 137–139, 142, 144, 146, 150, 167, 173, 193, 195, 201, 205
Turkey 63, 64, 67, 69, 205, 206

UNESCO 3, 4, 8, 12f., 30f., 36, 47, 49, 59, 69, 79–91, 95–109, 144, 152, 173, 197, 205f.
United Kingdom 9, 58–60, 141, 143, 152f.
'unity in diversity' 4, 141, 144, 157, 159, 167
*Up-Helly-Aa* 4, 48, 50–59

Valletta 10, 156, 160–164, 166–170, 172

Weber, Max 9
World Heritage 8, 49, 69, 162

Printed in the United States
By Bookmasters